FROM THE HIP AND HEART
REBOOTING ON CRYSTAL AVENUE

LAUGHTER'S TONIC – MY MEMOIRS

ROBERT ADAMS

DEDICATED TO:

SALLY L. ADAMS—MY RECENTLY DECEASED SISTER.

RICHARD B. ADAMS—MY BROTHER WHO HELPED ME EDIT.

LINDA J. HEUREUX—THE EMBODIMENT OF LOVE AND
A SPIRITUAL LIFELINE TO ME

TABLE OF CONTENTS

Fritz Adams and Lou Carpenter, 1942.

GIVING THANKS

I WAS BORN ROBERT BRUCE ADAMS on June 16, 1949, in Pontiac, Michigan, the third son in an upper-middle class family, a kid with a purported silver spoon. This was in contrast to the poverty that entangled Navin R. Johnson in *The Jerk* (1979), played by my favorite actor/comedian, Steve Martin. He proclaims in the opening scene, "I was born a poor black child." (He was very white). His adoptive mother, a large, stereotypical southern Negro mom, assured Navin (Martin), who was struggling to understand his different skin color compared to his brothers and sisters, "Navin, I'd love you if you were the color of a baboon's ass."

That has always cracked me up. It taught me so much!

These are stories of unconditional love, intrigue and humor. They are a collection of life's magnificent lessons and the magic that I have learned. It is also a story of recovery with a reexamination of values: some reinforced, and some simply ridiculous: The lessons have come from the hip and the heart, hence the name of my memoirs.

I began this book of life's observations and inspirations to keep me smiling and lift my spirits as I was going through some very rough times. These times began some four years earlier with many events swirling in my immediate universe: a failing third marriage (Three's a charm? Nope, not here!); a faltering new business that could not find funding; a rekindled high school romance (a dead-end, one-way-only relationship); and a huge transition from being a millionaire to having too much real estate and mountains of debt. I was soon flat broke, with a negative net worth. My world was crumbling and tumbling out of control.

The flat-broke comment is not quite true as I had my social security retirement check ($1630 a month). I had professed five years earlier that I would *never* obligate our government to taking care of me, not Bob Adams! The series of events were much of my own making and some were presented to me, (like plummeting real estate values), It seemed as if I were a big-league catcher without a mitt.

I remember thinking in my twenties that I loved northern Michigan so much, if all else failed I could pump gas. Another of life's surprises hurled at me. All else had failed, and now there were no gas station jobs. The filling stations in my pristine county north of Traverse City were all self-serve and not in need of my highly focused skill set. My world had crashed; I had hit bottom.

Just like Navin R. Johnson in *The Jerk*.

The vital core of my existence was the love and respect of my two twenty-something sons, who still thought I was great, even without my earthly possessions or affluence and status that had benefitted them as well. Their respect was life saving to me, and an enormous motivator to continue on during those very dark and difficult times. As a final blow to me, my ex-wife rejected our cat, Tigger, an animal of doubtful pedigree and nearly the size of a raccoon. She didn't want the cat? But she had rescued the cat during that accumulation phase of our life together. Surprisingly, Tigger's new residency and companionship—and unconditional love— truly helped me. Yes, a damn cat. How good is that? Another lesson learned.

The Jerk, and its very sobering message, rang truer in my own life than I cared to admit.

Along my journey, I was checking out bridges and cardboard boxes as back-up shelter in case my humor, faith, new business start-ups, and some good fortune did not get me through the abyss I found myself facing. No matter what I wanted or strived for, the universe kept pushing me in different directions and my surrender finally began my march to recovery and true happiness. Unrelenting hope, deep love and appreciation for my past would serve as the building blocks to greet the new future. I am very thankful for being alive in Michigan, and in the USA.

In these memoirs, I will share the lessons and the presence of mind that pulled me through the train derailments. My mother used to refer to such life events as being "on a sinking ship." Usually she was referencing my younger sister's experiences with male relationships. The males wisely (these were Mom's words.) abandoned a sinking ship; yes, that ship was sadly my sister. Diagnosed with bipolar disorder, she struggled her whole life to seek *terra firma*. God rest her beleaguered and troubled soul. She was extremely difficult, but I loved her nonetheless, and sometimes quite less.

So, choose a sinking ship, a train wreck, or any calamity you can relate to, and you can imagine the catastrophe that was upon me. My life circumstances were quite a disaster and in turmoil. Therein are the lessons that we will explore, explain and expand upon. My new minimalist life—part circumstance, part choice—has much to embrace and today I am so thankful for all these mishaps. Yes, I'm working my way back to fiscal and mental health; I've learned they often go hand in hand, at least in my case. I'm not talking about making millions again. I'm talking about a modest existence joining my his-torical roots and gratitude for my newly acquired healthful, serene perspective.

Yes, an old dog can indeed learn new tricks! Or, as the Buddha states, "In order to gain anything, you must lose everything." Those darn Protestants, how did they miss that one?

◂ ◂ ◂ ◂ ◂

*There is nothing to writing. All you do is sit down
at a typewriter (laptop), and bleed.*
—E. Hemingway and R. Adams

The concept for the book and its structure came from reading other books (how novel is that?), and by listening and recalling pearls of wisdom in my life. I did the reading on my own, having learned to like reading from my parents simply by observing them enjoy such activities in their bedroom at night, certainly not by them making me read. So, in essence, it is a knockoff of others' ideas and formats, with my added inspiration and thoughts. I will weave a period-based timeframe in the narrative and then uncover and offer lessons that were harvested from these wonderful life experiences. Sometimes pointing them out, sometimes not.

I must mention contributors to its initial creation (besides me) and give thanks and acknowledgement to a high school English teacher, and a couple of authors from those days that inspired me to write these memoirs and fearlessly offer the lessons learned in my life! Even an older brother came to my rescue in its creation.

First was Mrs. Schwartz, an eleventh grade teacher of composition and writing. I always had trouble with sentence creation, tenses, and mechanics. What I remember was Mrs. Schwartz's insistence to just start writing and let the story unfold. She encouraged me to not be afraid to make mistakes in my writing. I think as a male I was a bit lazy and certainly challenged, but this boot in the ass by Mrs. Schwartz and her solid encouragement were greatly appreciated. I found this quote and I suspect that she had studied it, too, passing on Bradbury's advice to me, as great teachers are supposed to do:

Your intuition knows what to write, so get out of the way. — *Ray Bradbury*

Next in the serendipity of events and mentors, in the winter of 2011 I picked up a book by Andrew Weil, MD, *Spontaneous Happiness*. I didn't care for the name of the book, but through his recommendations, I began writing daily lists about being thankful, happy and joyful. Especially critical were these new daily habits and the discipline to write them down when I was feeling discouraged and emotionally raw. It actually led to my recalling, and then recording, events that happened in my life that made me laugh from the bottom of my belly. I mean really, really funny events that helped define me as a happy and thankful Bob Adams.

Humor was, and still is, at the core of my main take on life's observations. Hell, if Dr. Andrew Weil, a Harvard-trained medical doctor, could sell wild salmon and supplements and then shift into happiness and mood-altering strategies, good for him! His "why" really is all about an umbrella of wellness plans he offers to supplement the body and mind. Weil is evangelical in his pursuit of good health and places a premium on long-term quality of life strategies. I thought I could certainly join this gentleman and add sizzle with my rhetoric and develop a novel about happiness, with insights and lessons assembled from life. It became my "why."

My third major contributor was Dr. Wayne W. Dyer who wrote a book some years ago called *Wisdom of the Ages*, published in 1998. I think he too was still married then. I love the lessons (he's an interpreter and teacher, I'm an observer and student), and the brevity of his formatting was brilliant: using but four or five pages to spin observations and lessons gleaned from great writers and philosophers. (I knew of maybe half of them; and no, I have never sat with the Dalai Lama at dinner, as Dyer did.). Dyer successfully weaves lessons of faith and lasting inspiration in his chapters and this format of selecting great spiritual teachers and explaining in plain English their intent, was so helpful for the creation of my stories. Thank you Mrs. Schwartz, Dr. Weil and Dr. Dyer—you've all done very good things in your lives.

And finally my brother Dick, who began reviewing chapters and, quite gently for him, suggested changes that helped clarify and better portray my stories. He also helped create my book title, *From the Hip and Heart*. Yes, it is quite on target, so thank you, my second-oldest brother.

Hang on and here we go.

Robert B. Adams, Sr. (Summer 2013)

Sunset over Lake Michigan

CHAPTER 1

RECOVERY

MY POWDER-BLUE TUXEDO AT THE GROSSE POINTE DEBUTANTE PARTY

THIS STORY IS ONE OF IN MY TOP FIVE FAVORITES and is likely many lessons rolled into one. It is about attending my only debutante party as a teenager and learning a great lesson in recovery. Recovery is defined as the act or process of recovering, especially from sickness, shock or a setback; recuperation.

I firmly believe that we are all recovering from something, and it is this journey of coming back and starting a new day that helps us all become more resilient in our lives. It builds backbones and stomach lining. Getting knocked down and developing strategies to recover is what life is often about; and life usually delivers punches whether we want them or not. So, accept life's challenges and rub your nose in them. Feel the pain. Feel the joy. It is not a linear path that leads to success and happiness. Oh, if it only could be. Recovery in my world usually involved pain, then humor and gratitude, and it is this sequence of emotions that has characterized my life with its many opportunities for growth. My essay here depicts an early passage through "Stupidom" and my recovery response that I am thrilled to recall here.

◄ ◄ ◄ ◄ ◄

It was late spring 1966 and Donna, one of my true high school friends, asked me to join her at a Grosse Pointe, Michigan, debutante party for a childhood acquaintance. I believe it was a niece of the Ford Motor family. Donna had grown up with this soon-to-be debutante in their affluent greater-Detroit neighborhood in the 1940s and 1950s. I accepted the invitation, reasoning that it would be a new experience and Donna was fun loving and full of life. She had an infectious smile that came easily to her round and loving face. The fact that she also offered to split the twenty-dollar tuxedo rental made the date even more appealing. I had money then from my summer golf course maintenance job, and my chivalry prevailed, biting the bullet, I decided to spring for the tuxedo on my own. It was the beautiful powder-blue color of this tuxedo that was to put me in a mischief-maker role, providing the perfect platform for a lesson in recovery, at The Little Club in Grosse Pointe Farms, Michigan.

Both my father and Donna's were medical doctors and we lived in a very nice neighborhood in a northern suburb of Detroit, called Bloomfield Village. It was an amalgamation of generally newer successful, upwardly mobile families. Often these developing suburbs were defined as "new money" in comparison to the old established generation of Detroit or the Pointes. The "old money" of the Grosse Pointe area in which we were soon to be immersed seemed to offer a challenge and intimidation to my social standing. Grosse Pointe truly had the old-money homes and was a bastion of Detroit high society. It was this background, with some appreciation of the caste society that still existed, which handed me an opportunity for recovery and the growth in character that it brings.

I scoffed at such pretension with my rebellious nature; perhaps rooted in my own insecurity, or learned from my family's developing view with their iconoclastic beliefs? Mom used to sum up her view of the elite social scene that occasionally confronted our family. Simply put, Mom's position was that she and dad had the only average children in the Bloomfield area. This position was humorous from her point of view and was meant to gently mock a popular belief that so many newly elite parents in Birmingham and Bloomfield thought all their children were brilliant and deserving of the finest in private schools and fineries that money could buy.

She herself came from a privileged family in Westchester County, New York. Her father had attended University of Michigan as an undergraduate and then Columbia law school. He eventually became the chief executive of Domino Sugar, headquartered in New York City. She likely learned from her own family influences that the new upper-middle class emerging after World War II tried too hard to impress older-money families and she was bound and determined to not be party to gamesmanship on either side of this ledger. She was rock solid in her constitution, a woman of the greatest integrity and quite competitive and complex.

The day of the big debutante party arrived and I was decked out in my powder-blue tuxedo. I also rented patent leather (very shiny) shoes. These completed the ensemble, or so I thought. I had informed the proprietor of the tuxedo rental shop on Woodward Avenue in Royal Oak that I was attending such a starred event in Grosse Pointe. He highly recommended a very traditional black tuxedo with a plain cummerbund. Demonstrating an early proclivity to doing my own thing, I stated that I preferred creating a fashion statement and wanted a particular powder-blue tuxedo that I saw among the vast selection of black garments that filled the store racks. The owner of the tuxedo shop was tightly proper and reminded me of a funeral director in his mannerisms, except he had a measuring tape draped around his neck. Something a funeral director would never don unless he was, maybe, measuring a subject for a pine box in a private back room? Yes, the similarities were noted and appreciated.

The powder-blue tuxedo had jumped out at me when I searched the perimeter of the store. As I gently examined the powder-blue coat, I discovered, much to my satisfaction, that it had a brighter blue-satin piping that added a real finishing touch. It was nearly perfect. The owner conceded to my energetic disposition, and quietly flung his hands to the air, mumbling under his breath.

Rounding out my steadfast decision, I thought the tuxedo would also complement Dad's powder-blue '66 Olds Toronado that he had just leased and was allowing me to drive to the affair. The "combo" I began referring to was my tux and my Olds, giving me the complete look I was seeking for what I thought would be most appropriate for this young lady's coming-out party. I imagined looking quite suave and debonair as Donna and I drove to this eastside event. Down Woodward Avenue into the vast outer world, from our home turf in Birmingham to the Pointes, here we come.

As I pulled into The Little Club driveway the adrenalin was kicking in and I remember what Dad always told me when I was nervous, as a way to muster courage and keep my composure: Walk proud, like you own the place. Don't be cocky, but display an air of importance and stand tall. Standing tall helps gather confidence to deal with life's situations. This little tidbit is useful even today, well into my sixties.

The attendants opened car doors and escorted us to the reception line just outside the front foyer. I was very proud and happy to be with Donna. She was fun and a great friend, and we were bubbling with anticipation. We stepped through the reception line, moving closer to formally meeting and welcoming the debutante.

The young lady was gracious in her demeanor and lovingly embraced Donna while acknowledging me with a friendly smile and nice handshake with her gloved left hand. There was no early indication in her concentrated and powdered face foreshadowing what I was about to unearth at the end of the line. But, as I examined Virginia's parents next in line, I saw the brutal truth-. Unfortunately for this honored young girl, our debutante, someday in the distant future she more than likely would exhibit physical characteristics of both of her parents. This foreshadowing was not particularly kind. It is amazing how money can mask genetics. The family carried themselves quite magnificently and offered a courteous thank you to our words of congratulations.

The formality and nervousness that was part of the social interaction was soon met with my faux pas. At the end of the line, after we had paid our respects and adulations about such a lovely and noteworthy event, I was met by a dozen nicely coiffed, middle-aged waiters offering trays of champagne (not sparkling white wine, mind you). They all were wearing light blue tuxedos. In fact, their tuxes were not just similar in fashion and construction to mine; they were exactly the same, down to the bright blue satin piping. They too wore patent leather shoes.

Many in the waiter ranks showed surprised faces, I suppose wondering why a guest would wear such attire. I don't quite know who was more embarrassed, but soon I realized that I was outnumbered and smiles were apparent on several of the waiter's faces. "Poor idiot" became the defining perception among this formidable subset of characters. All I could conjure in the first three seconds was a vivid image of the tuxedo shop proprietor strongly suggesting what I should wear to such an affair. Damn, I had not yet achieved a harmonious state of self-actualization.

I was learning early in my life that regrets were not something to spend much time on, with their alluring, second-guessing mental trenches. Yes, there may have been an alternative path to my outfitting, but I didn't choose it. My young and proactive brain calculated that this was a life lesson, and almost instantly a smile came over me and I knew I could turn embarrassment into something fun.

I remarked to the majority of the waiters (especially the ones who looked squarely at me), "What cool outfits!" Then, I quickly joined their regimented line and secured a serving tray of filled champagne glasses from a one of their ranks that couldn't figure me out, or my quickly summoned actions, as he still defined me as a guest. Without skipping a beat, I began offering champagne to the very appreciative guests who were streaming into the club just behind me.

◄ ◄ ◄ ◄ ◄

Why not! It was an early lesson in recovery. I was one hell of a good waiter, with a very courteous smile, and we all had fun without upstaging the honored debutante.

CHAPTER 2
HONESTY IS THE BEST POLICY

BUYING MY FIRST HOME FROM THE COP THAT BUSTED ME IN EIGHTH GRADE

AFTER A YEAR OF JOUSTING AND POSITIONING, in the summer of 1980 Jill, my soon-to-be second wife, and I decided to tie the knot, hoping to create a life that included wonderful children. Our life together was supposed to fade into the sunset. We got about half of the equation right and produced two wonderful sons in 1984 and 1986, and for that I am forever grateful for our union. You'll read about them throughout the book and learn of their contributions to my quality of life. You'll get a glimpse at their consolidated characters that took the best attributes from each of their parents.

◄ ◄ ◄ ◄ ◄

First on the docket before the September wedding was finding a house in which to set up our "love nest." We viewed homes weekly in a more modest section of Birmingham, between Lincoln and 14 Mile Road. It was a beautiful, older section, and highly desirable. We both had been residing in apartments. Jill was in Ann Arbor off of Washtenaw in the old Hobb's mansion just east of US 23, and I in an apartment complex with very thin walls off Telegraph and Quarton Roads in Bloomfield Township.

We began looking for a home during the end of the Carter administration's last gasp of breath, just before Reagan came into office. Mortgage rates were over 22%, and 20% down payments were still required. I wasn't sure how we were going to pull off this financial miracle. I had a whopping $1,700 in my savings account. But, I'd begun to have some sales successes and there was a future commission-compensation arrangement with my boss, soon to be my partner, in the offing. He nicely offered a $5,000 advance on commissions toward a down payment for our house. That helped, but when Jill's grandma offered $6,000, we were able to amass the funds needed for the down payment. My parents left a very nice estate, but helping children out with loans for housing was not one of their messages of frugality, nor was it considered a high priority as a parental obligation. Thanks to Mr. Bob Cameron and Grandma Charlotte Dixon on this one.

Our search late one afternoon found us at a cute brick bungalow built in the decade after World War II. There was a sign on the front near-perfect lawn: For Sale by Owner–Land Contract. Both Jill and I smiled and agreed that the house was quite attractive. I went to the front door as she waited in the car. An elderly lady answered the door and said she was making dinner, but offered us an unescorted walk through the house so we could take a quick peek.

It was small, two bedrooms with one-and-a-half baths, but so well done and charming. In hindsight, it would still be near perfect for my space requirements today. At thirty, it was a very small house and many of my friends were already in four-bedroom homes. However, our upward mobility was assured with our great educational degrees and job prospects for the future. We wanted this bungalow, but soon learned that there might be some lingering clouds on the negotiating horizon, especially after I met the man of the house, Mr. Ralph Moxley. Even in his retirement, he was called Chief Moxley, and I don't mean an American Indian chief.

We learned that he was the retired police chief of Birmingham. When I knew him he was a plain-clothed detective and a lieutenant. We shook hands and exchanged pleasantries in the basement stairwell of the bungalow. He was silver haired now, with horn-rimmed spectacles; my past was resurfacing in blazing speed as I flashed back to an event in junior high that I had solidly tried to forget.

The event, you ask?

That would be stealing, i.e., borrowing, Roberta Manigold's parent's car from their driveway during a sleepover at Dave Crosby's in his Birmingham neighborhood in 1963. I was likely the main protagonist with the famous "double-dare" challenge of Chris Charlton, one of my junior high buddies. Hours after the initial theft, I finally rode in the car, amassing a grand total of fifteen minutes in the vehicle. It was exhilarating. It was, however, the setup with my famous dare that really got the chain of events going. Thankfully, no injuries or property damage occurred during the duration of the heist. This made up the "week from hell" that summer after eighth grade.

The weekend after the theft, I was babysitting my two sisters. Chris drove three miles to my neck of the woods in the stolen car to say hello. He banged on the family-room windows to roust me, seeking a solution to "our" collective problem. I scolded him that this "disaster" needed to end and it was now time to take the car back and end this stress in our lives. He concurred and quickly left my backyard, driving the vehicle back near the Manigold's home for the drop and run. I reminded him to wipe down the car with Windex and a cotton rag. Removing fingerprints was my reasoning, not goodwill. I had seen on TV how the police match fingerprints.

"Oh, yea, good idea," he responded.

I supplied the Windex bottle and rags that Mom kept in the kitchen cabinet below the huge bread drawer.

These scenes flashed again and again in my consciousness as we walked through the Moxley home. I was not focusing on anything during the house tour. Nevertheless, this new meeting with Chief Moxley went great and we were ready to commit to a purchase offer. Thank goodness he did not remember me, or the visit to my parents' house he had made over fifteen years earlier. My appearance at thirty masked my boyish appearance when he busted me. I hadn't even comprehended the next steps to securing a land contract with him as a homeowner. I just wanted to regroup and consider how to quiet this previous indiscretion that was now surfacing to haunt me.

Flashing back, I had just completed eighth grade at Derby Junior High School and about two weeks had passed since the Manigold theft had taken place. It was a Saturday in late June and I was reading the latest *Hardy Boys* adventure novel in my room. I heard our doorbell ring; Martha Moody, a nurse for dad's practice and part-time babysitter, was with us that weekend while my parents were up north with friends playing golf. The voice at the front door asked for either Dr. or Mrs. Adams. Martha indicated that they were not home. The voice then asked if Bob might be available.

Martha called upstairs and said there was a man that wanted to speak to me standing at the door. I came downstairs and cautiously opened the front door, shielding my body and exposing only my head to this unknown figure.

"I'm Bob Adams, how can I help you?" I said. I was very pleasant; a couple years of collecting money for my job as a *Detroit Free Press* carrier had helped in my front-porch manners.

"I am Lieutenant Moxley of the Birmingham Police Department. Do you have something to share with me?" The voice now had a face and body. He was a thin, middle-aged man, in a suit coat and tie. He immediately showed me a shiny metal badge attached to a leather wallet.

Oh my God. Panic came over my entire body, and for a fleeting moment I believe I almost began closing the door on this officer. I responded with a long, drawn out, "No." But I knew instantly I was caught.

He asked if he could come in so we could "talk."

I led him to the living room, which was generally off limits to us kids except on special occasions. I must have reasoned that this was, indeed, a special occasion. Yes, like my life ending.

The lieutenant's next questions came quite easily. "Do you know Dave Crosby and Chris Charlton?"

They were, of course, in my group of very best friends and were co-conspirators in the heist and instead of denying their existence I said, "I think they go to Derby and may have lockers near mine."

That was my response. I was quite impressed that I had crafted such a lucid answer.

This interrogation and the theft was bad enough, but being a tattletale was something I just couldn't deal with, or so I thought, until Moxley stated that he had been with both Dave and Chris most of the morning with their respective parents discussing the theft of the Manigold vehicle. Apparently the long and short of it was that my infamous double dare was singled out as the event that led to the crime. To my dismay, my buddies had squealed on me!

In a matter of thirty seconds, Moxley had basically disarmed me; relief actually came over me realizing that I didn't need to weave some bullshit yarn.

Over the next fifteen minutes I then revealed my account of the evening of the event and the week that followed. Lieutenant Moxley nicely informed me that he had the Windex bottle in his car (Chris left it in the goddamn stolen car—brilliant!). We scheduled a meeting for the next Monday, with one of my parents. My world was in shambles. I was caught and a criminal.

I escorted the lieutenant to the door and told him I would break the news to my parents when they returned home Sunday night.

"Good luck," he said, likely with a grin ear to ear as he hustled down the two steps of the front porch to his unmarked police car.

That Sunday night came much quicker than I had ever imagined. Even at fourteen, I had learned that dealing with an issue head-on was the developing protocol in my family. There was no bullshitting Dad; well, maybe a little. I approached him just minutes after their return and said that I needed to talk to them both about some small issue I had encountered.

They scurried around their bedroom unpacking. Dad was putting away his golf shirts and underwear from the Samsonite suitcase on the bed. He quickly placed the items in his dresser. Brevity seemed to be his utmost requirement.

"So, what's up Robert?"

"Well, Dad, I was involved a couple weeks ago in a really dumb prank with Dave Crosby and Chris Charlton. A policeman came this weekend to see you and, and…I'm in really big trouble." I held back tears.

He quickly interrupted, "What did you do?"

"Stole Roberta Manigold's parent's car."

It suddenly occurred to me that these kids were also Dad's patients.

His hands were grasping the top of the Samsonite and I remember that he went nuts for just a second and slammed the lid shut. Unfortunately, both sets of fingers were clam-shelled in the luggage. There was anguish in the air, but I needed to assess how much of this pain was his throbbing fingers and how much was what I had just told him about my trespasses. A few seconds passed; I soon learned that his anguish was mostly based on my news. I was told to get upstairs and that we would discuss this further the next morning after my papers were delivered on my *Free Press* route. Thankfully he was too tired to deal with the news and needed a good night's sleep, as did I. Distance, space and time can be so helpful in such high tension situations.

Meetings, apologies, and civic cleanups were enacted over the summer of 1963, but I somehow have blocked from memory the weeks following my disclosed criminality. I was not sent to the juvenile home in Pontiac, Michigan. I still remember the spires on top of the buildings for wayward kids. I suspect that my brothers repeatedly drove me north ten miles to show me the institution where I might end up. I still shudder to this day at the thought of being confined there.

Sixteen years later, I met with the Chief Moxley after we all had agreed on the terms for the sale of the house. I disclosed my criminal past at the age of fourteen under his watch and said I would understand if he wanted to back out of financing our purchase with their very attractive 11% land contract. Chief Moxley's major concern was that their home would go to a nice young couple.

As for the issue about my past, well, he claimed he didn't even remember the event. The fact that I mentioned it during a critical phase of our transaction, and was Dr. Adams' son and worked for Bob Cameron, that was good enough for him! He wanted to sell the damn house and I had been reformed in his eyes. He liked me. In our six years of ownership we sent many notes with our very timely monthly payments. How nice was that.

The golden rule, *Honesty is the best policy*, plays throughout this chapter and my life. It is a lesson that doesn't just happen; it takes real life challenges and tests to learn from this powerful axiom. There is a movement afoot today in which interpersonal relationships are so complex that half-truths are recommended to save the bonds of a relationship. I believe this is absolute hogwash, and building a relationship on basis of someone always trying to figure out where the other is coming from—a waste of energy and manipulation of the highest order.

Honesty is the best policy is a rule I learned through many lessons when I tried to work within shades of gray. Well, guess what, it doesn't work. Ben Franklin was a proponent of its importance in modern society, but its origin came from many lessons throughout Greek and Roman literature, such as *Aesop's Fables*. I wonder why the Bible doesn't mention it in the famous Ten Commandments?

◄ ◄ ◄ ◄ ◄

Being honest is about freedom—I love it!

CHAPTER 3

HOT LEADS

I DO NOT WANT YOU TO GO TO FT. LAUDERDALE—SPRING BREAK, 1966.

THIS WAS AN AMAZING TIME FOR ME. I was heading toward my seventeenth birthday and all-around I was joyful, except for my goddamn grades. My parents weren't harping, but my paltry GPA was beginning to scare even me. My golf game was improving, though. I had a great summer job working in maintenance at an area golf course. All and all, life was very good with a plethora of good friends represented by both genders.

I had begun to gain some confidence as a person, even if occasionally a blemish blossomed overnight, creating an insecurity of some magnitude. I proudly had a summer job where I loved honing my physical skills by working in greens maintenance at Meadowbrook Country Club in Northville, Michigan. We could play golf after work for free (we "punched out" at two thirty), a benefit we earned up and above our whopping $1.28 an hour (double time on Sundays!).

I was dating Marlene, a stunning blonde who, if truth were known, was nearly an inch-and a-half taller than me. She had Ursula Andress-like breasts, or so I imagined. I spent months studying provocative and sultry poses of Ursula in the June 1965 *Playboy*. Here she was featured in a pool under a waterfall. I was on the prowl to experience something similar to this amazing feeling that surfaced daily while viewing these pages in the magazine. This sacred time and space was my universe as I took up sanctuary in my small study room below the stairs in the basement of our house. I hung out there constantly for the privacy needs, and of course to study; at least that is how I sold this to my curious parents.

Marlene was my month-by-month girlfriend. She was breaking out into the world of boys after being a school officer and goody-two-shoes for several years in junior high and high school. Marlene was my first girlfriend that truly enjoyed kissing and mild petting. She even encouraged the removal of her bra and would be helpful in the process to boot—how nice was that! I still talk regularly to Marlene, so I do not want to cast shadows of misconduct upon our innocent dating and my fond fumbling and bumbling memories of a wonderful high school girlfriend. I would however, put her breasts in a league right up with Ursula's.

My spring trip began to take shape in the early winter of 1966 when I announced that I wanted to go back to Florida (I had gone with my cousin Mike five years earlier as a twelve-year old on a newly minted Boeing 707) and stay at Delray Beach with my recently retired grandfather and his new wife. We called his new wife Aunt Ann. My grandpa had married his secretary from the bank after Grandma died. Very soon after, actually! Grandma Adams was not a fan of misbehaving children. We had a cool relationship with little fondness for one another. She was a tough lady and I was a misbehaving child: two personality traits that mixed like oil and water.

My grandfather died a couple years after this second marriage to Ann. I recall Dad always looking after Aunt Ann out of respect for his father, I suspect. Nothing was ever quite right with Ann, but Dad let her many complaints roll off his back and just listened. I assume he learned this as a pediatrician when he had as many as fifty women in his office every day with their precious children. Efficient listening was a learned skilled and part of Dad's old-fashioned, Marcus Welby-like bedside manners. This trait did not pass on to his number-three son.

Anyway, the Florida opportunity bubbled up, taking shape very loosely in the beginning. The plan was that perhaps my parents would let me drive to Florida in their aging Oldsmobile 88 and stay with recently widowed Ann. I would have to take her out nightly to her favorite cafeteria for an early dinner. My parents would allow one friend that they approved of (actually, they would have approved of many of my buddies). I could use Dad's credit card for gasoline and would pay him back when my summer job started in June. (We paid about twenty-seven cents a gallon almost the entire trip to fill up the blue Olds Rocket 88. Yes, filled the tank for four dollars. Life was very good.)

The details were beginning to be worked out and I had posed the Florida travel opportunity to one of my best buddies, Tim Fritz. He hopped all over this and had an answer within ten minutes of consulting his mom. He wanted to go to Florida, come hell or high water. Tim and I had been constant companions since he moved in during third grade to his beautiful home one block up the hill from mine. Mrs. Fritz was a nice woman and talented artist (metal jewelry), and took all her kids to Dr. Adams.

Tim and I were together the day five years earlier in December, when he was badly injured as a result of a neighbor's driving blunder. Mrs. Blodgett lost control of her car on an icy roadway just minutes after we had gotten off the sixth-grade school bus. We were watching the aftermath of an earlier small fender-bender at a neighborhood intersection right in front of Bruce Kostere's house. I remember that day clearly because after the ambulance sped away, with its jarring high-pitched shrill rushing Tim to Beaumont Hospital, I ran home and spent hours on the telephone telling everybody the blow-by-blow details of the accident.

I was right there, side by side with Tim, when we heard the distinctive crash and crunch that tons of metal colliding on metal creates. This secondary accident created a confusion of spinning cars and the safe distance from which Tim and I had chosen to watch the aftermath of the first accident was soon breeched. To our total surprise a mass of steel with wheels was jettisoned our way. We both tried to jump out of harm's way; unfortunately Tim's left leg was briefly pinned and crushed between the front bumper of the car and the massive elm tree where we had both been standing. The damage was severe and red blood instantly soaked his pant leg as he fell to the ground in excruciating pain. I still shiver fifty years later recalling this moment. I can still hear the noise of the bumper crushing his leg.

Dad reassured me, after I placed a call to him at his office, that he would follow up on Tim's condition and would take me to the hospital to see my buddy. He immediately called me back to assure me he had talked to the attending surgeon and Tim suffered a severe fracture. Reconstructive surgery and many stitches were ensuing, but Tim would live. That had been my question for Dad.

Just before dinner, after I had been on the phone for two hours, I ventured up the hill to to Tim's house, thinking what a somber mood would be greeting me in the Fritz' household. I was nervous, but dutiful in my obligation and task of taking Tim's belongings back to his house. To my total amazement, as I entered the back hallway and kitchen, Tim's sisters were joyfully playing and laughing and Mrs. Fritz was sitting at her large kitchen table with her magnifying lens flipped up on her forehead having just soldered a piece of jewelry; I could still smell the burning flux. What greeted me was her bubbly and high-pitched voice and smile, "Hi Bob, where's Tim?"

My quick assessment was that she knew nothing about the accident.

"Oh shit," may have been my own utterance even at twelve years of age (I had older brothers that helped in my profanity development). I recall saying to Mrs. Fritz, as I placed Tim's books on the kitchen counter, that Tim had been hurt and I had assumed that the police had notified her. Taking a deep breath and gathering my courage, I calmly and quickly relayed only the facts of the mishap and informed her that he was taken to Beaumont Hospital with a leg injury. I spared her the gory details of the injury, especially the red blood.

I told her how sorry I was about Tim.

She quickly discovered after picking up the phone in an absolute panic that an extension phone must have been off the hook, as there was no dial tone. I suspected that several attempted calls had been unsuccessful in reaching her. Later we learned that Mr. Fritz had been immediately notified at his office, and thankfully was with Tim at the hospital for the several hours that had lapsed since the accident.

◄ ◄ ◄ ◄ ◄

Tim and I went through many of life's trials together and he was the perfect companion to join me in the trip of a lifetime to Delray Beach, Florida. The night before our planned departure, Dad called me into his bedroom to review some of his expectations about our vacation. Tim and I were very young to be given this responsibility to use my mom's car, with the four-barrel Rocket 88 under its hood, and be given the use of their only credit card.

Reflecting back, I was pleased that both my parents had agreed to entrust me with such confidence in our planned journey. Much of the normal parental cautions were noted and I knew that dad was being cool with his vote of confidence. I felt very adult in our dealings. We reviewed that I was acting as his stand-in by taking care of Aunt Ann and that she had a favorite cafeteria where I was to accompany her every night and be a good step-grandson.

The precautionary bombshell came at the very end of our meeting. Dad leaned forward from his chair and stated that under no circumstances were Tim and I to go to Ft. Lauderdale for our evening outings. I immediately supported his quite strong position as being infinitely wise and part of my planned behavior. To this day, I swear I had no idea about Ft. Lauderdale.

After our talk, I immediately called Tim and told him we needed to meet in our usual conference spot. The spot was a set of bushes about 150 yards between our two houses where we met often—it was the Ives' side yard. It was our little place, a sanctuary where we shared stories and bologna sandwiches with the best yellow mustard on soft, gummy white bread. I can still taste those sandwiches, especially the mustard and garlic in the bologna. True heaven!

I relayed the caution and restrictions that Dad had just presented. Tim had not heard of Ft. Lauderdale either, but we had one day left at school before our departure to check out the story: the story behind this "forbidden city" that so bothered Dr. Adams. Our quick assessment in the bushes was that it must be wonderful to cause such precautionary concerns.

Sure enough, the next day we met almost universal ridicule by our classmates about how we were so out of it, i.e. where the hell had we been? *Life* and *Look* magazines had stories and photographs galore. The true skinny was that Ft. Lauderdale was the place to be on spring break. The bottom line that really solidified our curiosity and interest was there were girls in bikinis. Hot in 1966 was the newer beginnings of braless, t-shirted females. Holy Toledo, that was all I needed. We quickly developed a plan to be there.

Sorry Dad, but thanks for the hot lead!

We had a wonderful trip. Memories could fill another book from experiences that we had on that 3,000-mile journey. Tim and I took Aunt Ann out all five nights we were with her and had her back promptly by 5:30 every night to her little condo in Delray Beach (indeed it was the Early Bird Dinner Special). Then we were off, down 1A and onto Ft. Lauderdale's many beaches by six most evenings; ogling and being pleasured watching the girls. We were home by eleven o'clock every night. Ann thought we were great and Dad was pleased to hear how well it was going, as he and Mom were in Pinehurst, North Carolina playing golf and having a ball with their friends. He had no guilt about granting me this surrogate role and was proud that he had placed his confidence in me, allowing both of us to take our respective trips.

◄ ◄ ◄ ◄ ◄

Do you think he knew all along that we would end up in Ft. Lauderdale, nearly every night? Perhaps he was beginning to throw me out of the nest and I didn't even know it!

CHAPTER 4

SILENCE IS GOLDEN

WHAT DOES "IT" WANT TO DRINK?

MARGARET "CASEY" CASEY WAS MY FIRST AND LAST hippie girlfriend, and a real love child. She was my introduction to an off-the-wall and very unique city girl. She was raised in Chicago and attended the city's Catholic schools. Casey brought up weird issues and commented on countless topics; often I had no comprehension of what she was even presenting or proposing. She was such fun and so bizarre. I think she brought out a trait in me that has been problematic: rolling my eyes to the heavens when I do not comprehend a person's point. My eyes would open very wide, then focus upward, expressing a total disbelief in a person's statement. Yes, exactly, it is truly annoying. I just now repeated the eye movements and facial expressions in the mirror to confirm I could still do it. I can and I do.

I believe Casey was either an art or philosophy major at Albion College, where we attended school together in the late 60s and early 70s. I recall just how sexy she looked with her very dark hair and stunning dark eyes; she was very attractive and wore funky dresses that Cher or Goldie Hawn from TV fame might have worn. A free spirit in every sense of the word except for sex, though heavy petting was acceptable to her, which thankfully was intertwined into our solid six-week relationship in 1969.

This "silence is golden" lesson started with a spur-of-the-moment decision to attend a party in Birmingham, Michigan, some 100 miles from our small campus at Albion. A fraternity brother named Art Kale had a date with one of Casey's friends and we decided to double and go back to our old stomping grounds. A party back in our hometown was deemed worthy of the drive and weekend commitment. We also thought that on our way back we might visit mutual friends at a party on campus in Ann Arbor.

Leaving Albion about four in the afternoon, we arrived in the suburbs of Detroit around six. I had made arrangements, by a long distance telephone call, to stop by my home and say hello to my parents and also see the family's new puppy. Missy, a Springer Spaniel, was from the breeding efforts of Dr. Fred Gasow, a local veterinarian, and his wife, Julia. We always got the runt of the litter, as we had no intention of breeding their famed offspring. The price was always right, as Dr. Adams and Dr. Gasow managed some kind of off-the-books medical barter. We just wanted a pet to love. It sure seemed to work well, as we had had a number of Gasow's spaniels over the years and our family benefited from his dedicated veterinary skills and services. I can recall that he was losing fingers as he aged, I'm sure from the effects of radiation and the thousands of gamma rays his hands absorbed while trying to steady the dogs on the x-ray table. I recall him asking me to help steady Lady, our earlier brown-and-white spaniel, on the table during one of her broken leg mishaps. Ah yes, those were the good old days when you could get in the way of x-rays either as a veterinary assistant, or view the bones in your feet at shoe stores.

We pulled in front of my parents' Overhill house and our foursome emerged from Art's car to walk up to the front door. Normally I would have proceeded up the driveway to the back of the house, entering through the garage and kitchen, but instinct told me that with a new girlfriend and unfamiliar guests, a more formal introduction to my parents in their home was indeed warranted. Coming through the back door would have been a breach of etiquette on our group's part. I rang the familiar doorbell and added a few knocks on the front door, then without missing a beat, I led my group through the front door and through the slate-tiled threshold into my parents' front hallway.

My father welcomed us first, and then my mother joined us, emerging from the kitchen. She was standing back just a bit, as she was assessing the four of us. Names were nicely exchanged and all was going well in these often-tense first meetings. The new eight-week old puppy bounded into the hallway from her safe refuge in the dining room to greet this assemblage of humans. Missy was an absolute bundle of joy. She was totally excited, wagging her tail such that it moved her entire torso in a circular pattern of euphoria.

What happened next will go down in the annals of my dating memories matching catastrophic events similar to the explosion of the Hindenburg, or the bombing of Pearl Harbor. Casey had taken off her long spring topcoat and flipped it to my mother, who at this point was still being polite. Instantly Casey sprawled out on the front hallway, kissing the new puppy's face, whiskers and paws, totally embracing the bouncing pet. She ignored my parents and proceeded to roll all over the carpet and giggle in ecstasy at this little puppy. Her skirt slipped over her head, exposing stockings, underwear, skin and other things I had never seen before.

Trying to recover, I quickly exited the front hallway and quite by accident joined my mother, who had slipped into her command center in the kitchen. Casey was still out oohing and aahing and convulsing in the hallway.

Mom looked at me as she very gently handed me Casey's coat in almost slow motion and stated in her very calm and very resolute manner, "What does 'it' want to drink?" That was good old Mom. I'm sure she had her right eyebrow tilted upward to the sky during her inquisitive exchange of these now infamous words.

I reentered the hallway and Art looked at me in total shock, began giggling nervously and tried to help take some of the focus away from this hippie sprawled out on my parents' floor. He chose to discuss the Detroit Tigers pitching line-up with Dad. Casey's antics had nothing to do with alcohol or drugs, as we hadn't even begun our partying ways, which the night would certainly bring. There was truly a spirit that possessed this young lady's inner soul. Yes indeed, that would have been my assessment of the girl's condition and psyche.

There was a tense calm that eventually prevailed as we regrouped in the family room and in double-time we finished our mixed drinks in Dad's new frosted glasses imprinted with the names of famous U.S. golf courses. The only topic I'm sure we discussed was the slow-to-develop spring thaw, which was more than fitting for this situation. We quickly noted that we were late for our intended party and had to leave. My parents expressed that it was so nice seeing us. Their non-verbal message was less than enthusiastic and very revealing.

We got in the car and closed the doors. Art broke the silence and in a soft probing voice, said, " Casey, what was that all about?"

There was a pause, and then Casey said in a diminutive voice, "Bobby, your dad is so cute."

Mom never once asked me about the girl from Chicago. I mean never, ever again!

Yes, silence is sometimes golden.

I'm smiling, as in an earlier essay I espoused the great lessons in the golden rule of always telling the truth. "Silence is golden" is the rule you use when "honesty is the best policy" is going to get you in big trouble. What I have learned is that life does have many conflicting expectations about one's conduct. The famous duality offered in the philosophy of yin and yang helps us learn that many issues have two contrasting directions, which certainly can add to the complexity of our existence. The lesson learned here is that Mom both verbally and non-verbally expressed her opinion of my new girlfriend. In the end she chose silence as the best route to avoid saying something hurtful to me. Life does have its nuances. We need to learn these to survive.

◄ ◄ ◄ ◄ ◄

"Silence is golden" is the rule to use when "honesty is the best policy" is going to get you in big trouble.

CHAPTER 5

DON'T JUDGE A BOOK BY ITS COVER

BEER BOTTLES AND REBELLIOUS TEENAGERS

THIS ESSAY HAS NO GREAT LESSON OTHER THAN IT IS JUST FUNNY. Wait, the lesson is that I would do anything to protect my young sons. No, no, wait, the real lesson that comes to me is that one's early perceptions are sometimes very wrong and when passing judgments, our biases often warp the reality of a situation. Be careful in passing judgments about certain groups based on such preconceived notions. Yes, let's stick with this lesson and develop the narrative.

The scene was our local shopping mall that housed about twelve various storefronts anchored by Farmer Jack, formerly the A&P supermarket. The small mall was located just outside the boundaries of the actual Bloomfield Village subdivision, but it served "Villagers" an almost exclusive neighborhood shopping experience, or so we thought. One of the peripheral stores in this lineup was Little Caesar's, the Detroit-based national pizza chain that promotes a Fast & Now pizza; it certainly could not boast about the taste. It was housed in the western section of the complex that made up the newer wing, forming a retail mall shaped like a C. Little Caesar's had become a hangout for teenagers and, as noted, it had cheap pizza. Often the kids congregated outside its storefront and at times there might be thirty-plus youths from area schools hanging out on afternoons during the week. They would buy a pizza occasionally and eat it out in front of the store, during acceptable weather, on tables that had been added to give the mall a friendly appearance.

In the 1950s and 1960s, kids had a choice of independent drive-ins that served as the venues for groups of teenagers to congregate. This customary meeting place changed with newly enacted loitering laws, anti-pollution devices on our cars, earlier alcohol drinking, and pre-marital sex in homes. All of these developments, along with a new generation of teenagers wanting to "do their own thing," were what catapulted the teenage crowds that hung out in front of Little Caesar's in my neighborhood. They were seedy looking in my estimation, especially with my forty-year-old businessman glasses on. I have no idea really what some social psychologist would postulate about in a PBS, or CBS special "white paper" documentary about the new faces of teenagers and their congregating habits. Kids liked hanging out together whether it was in malt shops, drive-ins, or pizza parlors; and kids were now in newer venues with the changing landscapes that fit the times, that simple. My point of view and reference had changed as an adult.

I was serving on the Bloomfield Village homeowner's association board as a volunteer trustee and the issue of these loitering teenagers was the introductory topic at every single monthly meeting. It was on the agenda because the teens were pissing off some residents in our neighborhood and they thought we could do something to effectively deal with the situation. Bottom line, we were an advisory group and had no authority to disperse the youths. The township and the village police additionally felt that the law and citizen-rights issues tied their hands. The hope was the teenagers would move on after getting bored or find some other venue that had less effect on the citizens of Bloomfield Village.

It was quite unexpected that I ended up in this advisory capacity. A neighbor had become the president of the board. He was a new member at my country club and simply asked me one afternoon in the locker room if I'd commit to this monthly meeting as a vacancy had developed. I agreed, reasoning that I had grown up in the Village in the 1950s and 1960s and through a series of jobs and career moves was fortunate to have moved back to one of my favorite sections of older homes in the mid-1980s.

Our six-member board performed this civic-minded duty and responsibility strictly on a volunteer basis. The board was established to keep standards enforced, with our main task was to review architectural and building plans to make sure that new structures complied with building codes and the character of the village. These were regulations that I never understood. Later, with practice, I discovered I needed no training, as our village manager was brilliant and an autocrat. Mr. Charlie Williams was our caretaker and manager who, when he was a very young man, joined Judson Bradway in the 1940s as an assistant. He was an amazing and unique person, and now well into his 70s.

He knew every restriction that Bradway, the 1920s developer, had envisioned. He was fastidious in detail and proclamation.

Williams ran the meetings with absolute command, his word was gospel and enforcement was our board's unanimous support of any issue where he pretended he needed our approval. One of my fellow board members, who I got to know over our tenure, was amazed how Charlie ran meetings and always suggested that he could have taught some big lessons to participants at his automotive company meetings. At the end of our term, my associate on the board became president of one of the Detroit car companies. So, our little group had some serious credentials.

Our trustee group laughed at the poor judgment that some people and their architects and builders had in trying to get some special deviance past old Charlie Williams. It would never happen under his watchful eyes. The overall atmosphere Charlie operated under was if a village homeowner wanted some ornate feature that he did not like, then they could leave and move in any direction outside of its boundaries.

"No hard feelings, whatsoever," Charlie would quip.

Our other big issue while I was on the board was the aftermath of a warranted shooting death of a young man in a nearby school parking lot by one of our village officers. A deranged young man attacked a Bloomfield Township officer and a recently hired female officer came to his assistance and shot the young man to save a fellow officer that was being repeatedly stabbed. The irony of this situation was that the village officer had recently left the Detroit police department after more than twenty years of duty, and had never had to use her weapon during her tenure in Detroit. She came to the suburbs in her new "safe haven" assignment, and in less than sixty days, she had to unload her service revolver under these most unfortunate circumstances. She needed counseling as it affected her life profoundly and our board approved a $2,000 payment for a psychiatrist in Ann Arbor in the aftermath of this tragic event.

The homeowners association was a small part of my daily existence, but it did influence my life and in hindsight I learned some lessons about committee behavior and board governance. I actually enjoyed the experience and concluded that small-population authority is really an amazing attribute and so characteristic throughout our country; local rule is one of the hallmarks that makes the USA great.

◄ ◄ ◄ ◄ ◄

In early spring, I was shopping for groceries at Farmer Jacks with my small sons on a late weekday afternoon. I had a list of items that were the core requirements that day for the family. Quite often, I would find items that I could use and would deviate from the prepared list to enhance and complete the shopping experience. I liked the store because it allowed me to take the loaded cart out of the store into the sea of vehicles that filled the parking lot. This granted the shopper access to their car with the groceries and peripherals (like children, in my case) to make loading the car much easier. It was an ordeal at times because I had two boys that would cling to the metal shopping cart, either "riding" the cart, or with the car seat straddling the upper frame and basket. It was always a bit bumpy in the parking lot, as the wheels on the carts had no real suspension. Parking lots just out and out made me nervous because vehicles were continuously backing up and little children in the lots just did not mix well with them. I always kept a watchful parental eye, much like a hawk guarding his or her nest. Being a bit uneasy would characterize my demeanor when I was in parking lots with my children.

This fateful afternoon had the Adams boys smack dab in the middle section of the vast parking lot. Dave was nestled in his riding seat and Rob was perched on the front of the cart with his new Velcro tennis shoes fixed on the lower frame and his hands firmly clutching the perimeter of the upper wire basket as we headed to the car to unload our purchases. I did my duty by buckling little Dave first in the rear-facing safety seat. I then continued around the back of the vehicle with Rob in tow and opened the rear door on the passenger side to place him in his Graco child seat, nearly a permanent fixture in my car. I had both boys in what I referred to as "lockdown mode."

I grabbed the shopping cart that had just begun slipping away under its own accord. I secured the cart that had four paper bags full of many items and two six packs of Labatt Blue beers, their longneck bottles sticking out of their cartons. I unloaded the cart and placed the bags between the boys' car seats. I put the beer on the car roof until I had the space appropriately arranged to package both groceries and children so they could be classified as secured cargo. The pesky cart again began slipping away and in a bit of frustration I grabbed it and placed it securely in a cart corral located just behind me.

Finally, I hopped in the driver's seat and announced to Rob and Dave, "Here we go boys!"

I buckled my seatbelt to complete the pre-exit routine. I started the car and efficiently backed up out of my space and headed up my row to access the outer perimeter driveway that circled the parking lot, steering my car west toward the Lahser Road exit.

I immediately noticed a large group of teenagers in front of Little Caesar's, not more than fifty feet in front of my vehicle. I would have guessed there were minimally twenty of these wayward youths gathered. What caught my eye next was quite startling as several in the group began waving their arms, revealing several tattoos. They were actually running toward my vehicle and I could hear their commotion and baffled laughter outside the closed car windows. I then heard the first "pop" and smash and thumps followed in steady succession. I saw projectiles coming out of their hands. Then more "pops." Bottles were landing on the back deck of my sedan. I thought I was under total attack. Beer bottles were now rolling off my car and smashing all around me, landing on the pavement in the parking lot. I feared for my sons and sensed that we were being attacked by these unruly youths. This was one hell of a tense situation and I needed to escape from this near riotous group of god-damned teenage hoodlums.

I was thankful that I had just gotten a new Buick that had some serious acceleration in its constitution and I sped past the hoodlums. They were now running after me with hands still waving. I could see the menaces in my rear-view mirror. My adrenaline was pumping and I was in a full-flight mentality. I quickly flashed back to the night the Tigers had won the World Series just a few short years earlier: I had a carload of family members and we avoided having our car overturned by celebrating fans as we took short cuts through Detroit to avoid motor traffic. It was a similar feeling, except this time I needed to protect my small, helpless children.

I quickly proceeded out of the lot, heading north up Lahser Road. My heart was still racing, and I wanted to put some distance between our car and the teenagers without dangerously speeding. I regained my composure, and as I was turning onto our side street half a mile up the road, Rob asked repeatedly, "Daddy, what was all that noise?"

I assured him that it was nothing to fret over and that there was a bit of a problem with those darn kids at Little Caesar's, but everything was okay. Dave was oblivious and unaware of the chain of events we had just been through. He sucked on his pacifier, unaffected by the noise. I was surprised a little, as he was facing out the rear window and saw most of the "mortar" that had been tossed onto our car.

Pulling into my back driveway I parked just shy of the fence, hopped out of the car feeling immense relief and opened the back door to retrieve my wonderful sons. I released safety buckles and quickly assessed the condition of the rear trunk hood, and surprisingly saw no damage on the deck lid. I looked into the back seat with the idea to retrieve my now seriously sought-after six packs of Labatt Blue. I wanted to have a much-needed cold, single-serving sedative plucked from the carton immediately.

The beer was nowhere to be found. They were missing?

I was dumbfounded and aghast, and then the light bulb clicked on. It dawned on me that I had left the six-packs on top of the roof in the parking lot of the Village Knoll Shopping Center. Still trying to piece the events together, I broke into uproarious laughter, grasping for the true reality of what had just transpired.

My goodness, the teenagers were simply seeing the humor in my situation and were trying to offer help in alerting me by flailing their arms with some determination to notify me of my blunder. I had totally missed what had just happened to me.

◄ ◄ ◄ ◄ ◄

Wow, was that funny and also an eye-opener in my life. Reality can strike like lightening.

Be open to it.

CHAPTER 6
FORGIVENESS

ROB'S DISLOCATED SHOULDER AT NEIGHBORHOOD HARDWARE

To err is human; to forgive, divine.
—A. Pope

HONORABLE INTENTIONS ARE STILL PARAMOUNT in all relationships and forgiveness still reigns; I open with words of wisdom in this particular vignette. These highlighted words simply represent human actions and choices. They are important lessons learned in my life, and darn good ones!

My son Rob has forgiven me for the dislocated shoulder that my actions caused when he was three years old. I asked for his forgiveness for my unintentional actions; I didn't just assume it. He just won't let me pick him up from the ground, grabbing his hand to get him up from a sitting position. That may take decades to overcome. This story has become legendary among my sons and friends, and even casual observers.

Over the years it has been seasoned and reworked by its contrast with the changing perception our society has engaged in bringing out of the closet the abuse that does occur to our nation's children. I was just trying to get my small son to get up off the hardware floor (I do hope he was pouting), so we could leave the store and get on to the barbershop to continue our Saturday morning family outing. It was part of our weekend routine: visiting the hardware store, sometimes the barbershop, and always the school playground. Simple and wonderful little adventures with my small sons.

Retelling this story is so different in my memoirs today, a much happier account than the time I saw it in print in legal briefs that occurred a few years after it took place, the workings of a contentious divorce. It became fodder for two females, a client and attorney, revealing the worst in womankind. For those readers who have experienced such legal mischief, can you just picture it? Time heals all and all is forgiven, but it has taken some growth, from my perspective.

Had I not been fortunate to have my physician father to call for consultation and offer a sensible solution, it likely would have accelerated a chain of events at our hospital emergency room with countless explanations, investigations from our endless civil-servant community, forms, and more paperwork. A total different course of events would have been the postscript in the aftermath and resolution to the dislocated shoulder that I certainly caused. Thank God for small miracles. Through it all, Rob mended (that was the goal, lest we forget), forgave me, and prospered, and lessons were learned.

I loved being a dad during this period of my life. Our outings always involved arranging Rob and Dave in a number of baby and toddler seats in the front and rear of my vehicle. Bundling the boys up and carefully placing them for safe transport in molded child car seats with the correct loops and rearward facing position (or was it forward) was always a bit of a challenge. I had little issue with the advice of the day from automotive safety experts, especially when it came to my sons. Whatever the recommendation of the day, I had the latest products and listened and followed the experts' insights and suggestions. That is quite unusual for me.

Now that I have established the case that I was a responsible dad, it is time to delve into his shoulder dislocation.

My sons and I were on our typical Saturday morning outing. I was working on some complex home improvement; this day it was a plumbing issue and I was at Neighborhood Hardware for their help. The Reynolds family ran the hardware in Birmingham and the family members all could capably handle trouble-shooting solutions for their customers. During this particular incident, I was holding my one-year-old David in my left arm. He was wearing his powder blue knitted hat with tied chinstraps and, of course, his nose was running. I was listening intently to Lee Reynolds explain how I needed to replace some O-rings in my sink faucet. A leak was caused by the hot water hardening the rubber seals. After five minutes and twenty-five cents, I had a plan in place that might allow my Dishmaster™ to stop leaking. I thought I might have the problem solved by that afternoon, or certainly by Sunday, with a worst-case scenario of a revisit to ask a Reynolds family member, "Is this what you meant?"

My son Rob was happily playing with one of his toy trucks on the store's hard linoleum floor. I was simultaneously collecting change and trying to exit the hardware store with the strategy to enter my car with both boys in proper tow. Rob was much more interested in continuing his fun with his truck than listening and responding to his dad barking commands to get up and begin the march to the Buick. I grabbed his left hand, which was attached to his arm and shoulder, and with a firm tug I helped him up off the hardware floor. Dave was still cradled in my other arm. I expected a small reaction of protest to my fatherly discipline, but what happened was disquieting to me as Rob began crying after I got him standing. I was a bit embarrassed, as the Reynolds family was witnessing this now-troubling exit from their store. Joining the gallery of observers was a handful of other customers, smiling, all likely reminiscing and thanking God they got through this stage of parenting. I clumsily had kids in both arms, along with gloves, hats, and my new rubber washers—it was time to exit for the safe environment of my car and find some needed privacy while regrouping prior to our visit to the barbershop.

We proceeded into the parking lot to my car. Rob was still crying as I opened the rear door and buckled him quickly in his larger car seat. I wondered if I had embarrassed him. Dave was safely parked on the pavement, nose still running. I moved to the other rear door and placed him in his car seat next to Rob. I was trying like hell to find the buckling receptacle for attaching his metal safety clasp. I was struggling with this alignment in the seat assembly. The folds in Dave's clothes and diaper padding were all contributing to my inability in getting him buckled and secured. Adding to the ordeal was the ever-present accumulation of months of remnant Cheerios, cookie crumbs, and sticky apple juice all decaying in the vinyl folds and crooks of the seat cushion. It was truly gross. These impediments all added to my struggle in securing my boys for our 150-yard trip down the alley to Fred's barbershop.

The barbers actually had fun watching this band of Adams warriors invade their shop every month with our supporting paraphernalia from the car. As a regular customer I had been granted the use a parking spot behind the barber's parked cars that made bringing my boys with me workable. We disembarked and came through the back door that memorable morning.

Fred's barbershop was a relic from the past. Fred was dead, and it was old-fashioned in all aspects of its décor, everything from chairs, wall hangings, magazines and pictures. Also obvious was the scent of stale cigarette smoke and its remnant tar that permeated the air and settled on the aged furnishings. The shop was built on an angle to Woodward Avenue and it was a long, thin building that housed three barbers. Paul and Bill were our main stylists and Pete was the very boring owner. Pete made me feel unsettled and I avoided him when possible.

The barbers, as part of their responsibilities, swept the floors of the day's accumulated hair clippings. It was a bit of a lackadaisical effort and I suspect they never felt comfortable with my letting the boys play on the floor in front of the rows of waiting chairs. Paul, my favorite, was a remnant from the 50s rock-and-roll era and was still a "Greaser" from his appearance. I have no idea what made his hair so slick. I never asked. He loved to whittle and carve and was very proficient at creating and decorating ducks and Christmas Santas. He was a good guy, who also loved his beer and cigarettes.

As we came in through the back door to an isolated section of waiting chairs for our routine encampment in front of the barbers, Paul quickly asked me, stepping back from his current customer, what was troubling Rob? I indicated with a slight irritation that I had disciplined Robby at Neighborhood Hardware and, "He was mad at his father." I was mumbling, expressing a series of rambling accounts of the incident. They were fielded and processed by my audience of now very attentive barbers.

I was trying to comfort Rob by hugging him and offering encouragement, but he was struggling with many tears and was also trying to be stalwart in front of the small crowd of barbers and customers in the barbershop that morning. Not making a scene was already becoming an Adams trait. My turn came quickly and I hopped up onto Paul's designated chair for my haircut. Dave had fallen asleep in his car seat carrier and Rob was slumped in the waiting chair next to Dave hiding his face, still crying with no apparent end in sight. Trying to be brave, I thought.

Paul swirled the barber's smock on me and immediately placed his hand on my shoulder and under his breath, quite concerned, said, "Bob, I'm sorry to get in your business, but Rob never cries and is always so focused in his play. Something is wrong."

I assured him that he would be all right. But frankly, I was becoming a bit unnerved at Rob's tears and continued crying, coupled now with Paul's ardent plea. This situation was becoming troublesome. Then Pete announced in his nasal tone that I better call my dad and tell him what I'd done at the hardware store in tugging Rob's arm.

That was all I could take.

"The sky is falling, the sky is falling," is what I was repeating to myself. A course of action had transpired that was totally out of my control, directed by the lieutenants of Fred's barbershop. Cell phones were only mounted in cars at this point, so Paul quickly, with encouragement of the other barbers and with his own perceptible relief, saw me accept his clunker of a phone from behind his work space where he dialed Dad's home number, prompted by my quietly calling out the numbers. Paul swung his pivoting barber's chair 180 degrees with me aboard toward his counter workstation and handed me the receiver. In Fred's barbershop, privacy was not possible.

Dad answered with his deliberate and calming, "Hello."

I immediately came right to the point of my call, noting to Dad that I was placing it from Fred's barbershop.

"Dad, I'm at Fred's. Pete and Paul suggested I call you," I stated.

He knew them well.

"They think Rob has an injury in his arm that might have happened at Neighborhood Hardware."

Dad said, "Tell me what happened that would cause them to come to this conclusion."

I began recalling the sequencing of events ten minutes earlier. Dad interrupted my story about seven seconds into it and said, "Bob, you dislocated his shoulder and it has probably come out of the socket as a result of the trauma you caused by pulling on his arm, hence his extreme discomfort and well-deserved tears."

This was an absolute bombshell to me, and now I was in total shock that I could have done such a thing to my oldest son.

Dad quickly said, "I'll call the office and tell them you are 'popping' over in two minutes."

He used humor to relax this tense situation. I was close to his medical office building, located just two blocks from Fred's. His partner was working that Saturday morning and could attend to Rob immediately. Paul and Pete said they would keep an eye on Dave as I rushed Rob over to Grandpa's office to see Dr. Pierce, his pediatric partner. Out the door I went with the still-crying Rob tenderly in tow. My adrenaline was now pumping, wanting a resolution to Rob's pain, and mine.

Marcie, one of Dad's nurses, greeted me at the office lobby and said that Dr. Pierce was in Room 2 and expecting us. Sure enough, Dr. Pierce, in his long white doctor's coat, greeted us with a serious glance over his half glasses and asked us to come in to the examining room. In a matter of five seconds, without removing clothes or even forewarning us with counsel, Dr. Pierce smiled at Rob and took both of his doctoring hands, placing one on Rob's shoulder, the other he used to quickly lift Rob's left arm and said something like, "Abracadabra."

Rob's tears instantly subsided and a smile soon flushed over his face; an expression of total gratitude and thanks replaced the previous twenty minutes of pain. Dr. Pierce looked at Rob said, "Your Grandpa and I do one or two of these dislocations and resets every week."

He then turned and chastised me, suggesting that there was a more appropriate way of picking a child up from the floor. Bill wasn't quite as much fun as Dad was in his pontifications.

I learned then, and later from Dad, that my particular series of actions joined playground swinging of arms as the most prevalent root cause of the majority of these dislocations. Simply, the muscle and cartilage are still developing and are very flexible at this particular age and such strain causes this dislocation quite frequently in children under five. I purposely just used intellectualism to defend my unintended actions. In reality, it is still an awful feeling that makes me weak even today.

I started home in a total trance, emotionally spent. Rob was quiet but in total relief and had moved into a happy and blissful state. It was near their elementary school, halfway to our home, that Rob called out, "Dad, Dad, we forgot Dave at the barber shop."

Oh boy, this parenting is harder than I first supposed. I turned around to head back to town and retrieve our little Dave. I may have looked like a police cruiser turning around to pursue a speeder. Thankfully, Rob noticed such subtleties as a missing sibling.

We returned to the barbershop and parked in our spot. Rob was all smiles, though clinging to me for extra security, as we entered the back hallway to the more-than-interested barbers. Rob's eyes were still red from the earlier trauma. I looked down and noticed that Dave was still sleeping on the floor in his car carrier, right where I had left him. I found out that Paul, always a comedian, had been telling customers that the child had been left at their front step. The intensity that had filled the air of the room earlier was now replaced with lightness and smiling faces. Rob joined his little brother's space and was beaming with a warrior glow as he sat in the waiting chairs being congratulated by all the relieved barbers. Rob also had candy suckers galore, at least a dozen (we knew where they were inventoried at Grandpa's office) in both hands that he was going to show off to his little brother. Rob related the story to the barbers about Dr. Pierce fixing his arm and that funny Dad was half way home when he had to remind me that Dave was at the barbershop. The barbers laughed at how resilient Rob was, as he fully recovered from the depths of discomfort.

I soon hopped back into Paul's chair and thanked him for the firm nudge thirty minutes earlier. I certainly needed it! All was good again with the Adams Boys. After my haircut we headed to the school to romp on the playground.

◁ ◁ ◁ ◁ ◁

To forgive is divine.

CHAPTER 7
BOXING GLOVES FROM DAD

MAINTAINING A STIFF UPPER LIP

WE WERE AN UPWARDLY MOBILE FAMILY, the post-World War II generation of educated and consumer-driven households. I think all of my siblings, including me, by definition, are Baby Boomers. Or, at least, we are near the cusp of the defined dates. My parents, from the winding down of the war, to the early 1950s, miraculously expanded their family: three boys and two girls born between 1944 and 1952. A plethora of domestic pets including dogs, cats, bunnies, parakeets, and tropical fish (they're ferocious!) also joined the mixed menagerie and rounded out their booming household.

My dad, as a young doctor and Navy lieutenant, and Mom, as his wife, were stationed during the end of World War II in Marquette, Michigan. Assigned to a garrison organized to defend the upper Great Lakes from either an invasion off of Lake Superior through Canada by the Japanese, or as legend stretched, perhaps by the Nazi's who might utilize the vast St. Lawrence Seaway and invade from the south. By all accounts, neither event took place, at least not during this particular world conflict.

I hope this memory is credible, as I only know that Dad's Navy duty was noted in his obituary and somewhere this scenario became established in my cognitive recollection. After the war ended, Dad spent nearly two years in Baltimore, Maryland, as a civilian attending Johns Hopkins University for additional training under an advanced pediatric fellowship.

My parents finally arrived back in Birmingham in 1947, where just ten years earlier Dad had attended high school. Birmingham was midway between Detroit and Pontiac, connected by Woodward Avenue. The highway was named for one of the turn-of-the-nineteenth-century architects who envisioned an expanding Detroit that would radiate from a central downtown hub. An electric streetcar system was quickly conceived and built after the war. The tracks actually followed right in the middle of paved Woodward and then up the median, where these two very different modes of transportation competed with one another. Eventually Woodward Avenue became exclusively a thoroughfare for gasoline-motorized vehicles, as the electrified transit system failed from lack of funding and scarcity of riders, likely succumbing to the boom in consumer spending that was chasing Detroit's personal automobiles.

Detroit had been designated the Motor City since just after the turn of the twentieth century. It was the Midwest's epicenter for many of the country's automotive building enterprises that flourished, failed, merged, and survived. Dad began his childhood in Detroit, moving to Birmingham in the 1930s, the result of a bankruptcy masterminded by his father's ill-timed venture into housing that wiped them out financially (no wonder Grandpa Adams and I got along so well!).

Both parents were familiar and comfortable with their greater metro-Detroit experiences. Birmingham was selected as being most desirable to support both their expanding household and would also become home to a family medical practice where Dad literally hung out a shingle to announce the location of his practice. Knowing Mom and Dad, this was thoroughly discussed and very much a joint decision. They had two kids on board and three more were soon on the way.

After a short stint living with Dad's in-laws, my parents took up residency in a small house in south Birmingham near Fourteen Mile Road, on 1885 Washington. After six years, the living arrangements were such that my parents were sleeping on a foldout couch in the den (a hide-a-bed). We three boys slept in an upstairs dormer with our metal-framed beds lined up in a nice row, reminiscent of a hospital ward or military barrack. I remember clearly the wooden stairs to our dormer making a definitive noise as we walked up and down. The stairs had a distinct resonance, as if they were wood blocks in an orchestra's percussion section, best remembered as the clip-clop of horses' hooves featured in many Christmas tunes. I can still hear them today. Other clear benefits derived from this quirky staircase: no one could quietly sneak up to frighten you under the pretense of a surprise attack. The echoing sounds from the wooden stairs simply could not be muffled. My two younger sisters slept in a first-floor bedroom. Our family of seven shared a single bathroom with its combination porcelain tub and shower. This bathroom crowding created the necessity of an emergency urine bottle for us boys; and surprisingly it was not a bedpan, but a glass milk bottle in the back hallway. I can't even imagine. How fun.

The Washington house was our home until 1954. I had attended Pearce Elementary for nursery school in 1953. Here I would enter the side door under the orange awning, walk up three steps, and take a deep breath to gather courage and force my way through the extremely heavy wooden door. It was a challenge every school day and I repeated this routine the following year for morning kindergarten into the fall of 1954. I must have become stronger in the subsequent year, as the routine of opening the massive door seemed to become an easier undertaking over time. My fears about school had diminished and I felt quite comfortable; I had learned the ropes and gained confidence.

We were literally busting at the seams in the Washington house and were told by my parents that we would be moving to a larger home on the west side of town. With great anticipation we would head over weekly to watch the building of our new home during the fall of 1954. From my five-year-old perspective it was a huge house, measuring 2,400 square feet.

We moved in early December with the Potter Moving Company handling the details. The move was almost as remarkable an event as a neighborhood fire, when we would watch the Birmingham fire department trucks parked at a curb, attending to their various fire duties. At least, I saw the connections. The diesel fumes also shared similarities. My adrenaline was pumping and the large moving van shadowed the small brick bungalows, dwarfed by this behemoth moving van. The neighborhood kids watched the move in progress and it was very exciting to be the center of attention with the neighbors milling and watching the progress of the move, even with the cold and biting temperatures that greeted us that early December .

It took a good part of the day to load the cargo space with my family's earthly possessions.

The change in neighborhoods brought a vast new setting to me. The new homes in Bloomfield Village were being developed rapidly. They dotted the landscape on nice, winding roads that meshed with the hilly terrain and characterized the subdivision that was once a productive apple orchard. The excavated lots shouted out their presence and were laden with vast pallets of colored bricks, cement mixers, framing wood, and piles of dirt. A building boom was in full bloom, the result of the Korean War having ended a year earlier with no nuclear bomb deployed. It was a prosperous and exciting time.

The brand-new house was a beautiful colonial-style home ornamented with the perfect red/orange brick that soon would be contrasted by medium-green shutters. It was being built and completed on over three-quarters of an acre of land. The property had two backyard levels, with many mature trees that would be further complemented with formal sweeping flower gardens, split-rail cedar fencing, and a large rectangular vegetable and cut-flower garden.

My immediate interest was the hastily installed Davey Crockett (four feet by five feet) wooden cabin placed in the designated play area. Our tribe would join Dad by hovering over his many home projects during the weekends. All these activities began the following spring after our late-fall move, and all improvements were in various stages of completion during the next couple of years.

Of special note was our much-beloved lower backyard that gave way to a large skating rink in the winter. We began preparations every year during the week or two before Christmas. It was an engineering feat and we sought new approaches and fine-tuned in its construction every year. There was always a new theory on better establishment protocols and techniques. It was always a work in progress.

It brought great joy to us kids as we made it an annual family project with some wonderful successes (hoses, hoses, and more hoses, hot water and broken pipes); all necessary essentials leading eventually to great surface ice. If only our dear neighbors, the Ludingtons, that shared their real estate and rink duties with us, would have cut down their fifty-year-old maple tree, which was located right smack dab in the center of the skating rink, it would have been near perfect. Even with the tree stuck in the middle of our man-made skating rink, it was fitting for an Olympic outdoor skating venue, reminiscent of a Currier and Ives winter scene. This was especially evidenced after a snowfall when our rink-clearing duties were in full strength after the night's deliverance of the sparkling white snow that had to be removed those mornings to accommodate our willing and eager daily skaters. The kids came to skate from all over the neighborhood.

◄ ◄ ◄ ◄ ◄

We learned early on that Christmas at the Adams' household was not the platform for receiving a plethora of lavish gifts, presented to us deserving kids. Mom announced every year that she and Dad had carefully allotted a sum of money to be spent on each of us. They welcomed and encouraged a Christmas list from us. Somehow, twenty-five dollars seemed to be the inflation-adjusted budget throughout my childhood. The lists from all of us often overshot this target at least fivefold, more likely tenfold. Mom always referred to the imagined money tree in our backyard when one of us would earnestly request some materialistic need. She would quip that we just needed to pluck the dollar bills from the money tree to pay for our wants and desires. All along, even an eight-year old would understand that the money tree was a myth. We learned that Christmas was not about accumulating vast caches of goods, at least not in this family. We were learning some basic rules and customs of being part of our family.

Frugality, even in a sea of prosperity, ruled the Adams family roost. In the overall scheme of things, life was quite good. My parents personified these conscientious values of being thankful and demonstrated thrifty temperaments in their everyday living. They were happy, and it simply showed in their smiling faces and in their positive demeanor that they brought to each day.

We were very settled into a wonderful routine in our new house and met an abundance of new young families, all living their dream in Bloomfield Village. The holidays in 1957 brought the traditional, cut Christmas tree to our home with needles lasting three days at most, caused by being placed in front of the roaring oil furnace air ducts in our knotty-pine family room in Mom's undisputed perfect corner. It was where the tree belonged, no question.

My anticipation for gifts of some note was floating in the holiday air that year. Hopefully, this would be the year that my parents' latent affluence would finally break through the twenty-five-dollar ceiling that had always been our limit. Hope does spring eternal, as they say.

What I recall was Christmas morning 1957 and the community gift for us boys. It occurred later in the morning, as we made it through the ritual of the passing of gifts and waiting patiently for everyone to take their turn. Dad was quite delighted with his creative newspaper wrappings on many of the gifts. We boys were advised that morning to open the identical-shaped special gifts at the same time. So sure enough, Fred, who was thirteen, and Dick, who had just turned twelve and I, who was all of eight, waited in anticipation until the sign came forth from Dad's energetic voice. When we heard the word, levels of laughter joined shreds of torn paper that were soon scattered all about the family room. Our mutual efforts unearthed three identical sets of Wilson boxing gloves. We quickly learned from Dad that he had special ordered them from The Varsity Shop in downtown Birmingham. Vince was the owner of the shop, and my parents and he had attended the University of Michigan in Ann

Arbor about the same time; this was their common link and added to the special status of the boxing gloves. They were genuine leather with very revealing stitch lines and white laces for firm tightening. Actually, they looked quite nice in the cardboard display boxes that housed these padded wonderments.

As further background to this creative gift idea, and our introduction into the world of boxing, Dad would venture off into sports other than golf to likely add a well-rounded exposure to his brood. In golf he was a legitimate two-handicapper at this point in his life. He also had a fascination with boxing. I researched why 1957 was the year he decided to give his three boys boxing gloves. In putting the pieces together, it dawned on me that his motivation likely came from a few sources spinning in his universe. First, in the summer of 1957, Floyd Patterson had defended his heavyweight boxing title with a come-from-behind win against Olympian Pete Rademacher. Also, and Dad would have liked this statistic: a year earlier Patterson was the youngest-ever heavyweight champion, beating the aging Archie Moore. Finally, establishing Dad's interest and appetite for boxing, the Motor City was famous for being hometown to the legendary Joe Louis, aka The Brown Bomber, who reigned as heavyweight champion for nearly twelve years in the 1930s and 1940s, right when Dad was in his youth.

The fascination with boxing was in Dad's sights for years and fit his Detroit upbringing and allegiance. His three boys were going to have fun in the new house's large basement that he had just finished tiling with speckled linoleum squares. Late on Christmas Eve he apparently applied masking tape to outline a ten-foot square that would establish the imaginary ropes marking the perimeter of the boxing arena. We were being introduced to a new sport that we had not yet quite comprehended. My mother was thrilled that her boys could do something together as a family.

I began to assess what our community present sitting at my feet in our family room represented, and what it was to portend. Curiously, as often happened, it was not even on my Christmas list. This led to my first clear and definitive thought, now recognizing some concern about our group present. I remained stiff-lipped, always watchful of the older brother's take on things. Little did I know that stiff-lipped was soon to describe, both literally and figuratively, a condition that defined me over the next several weeks.

God loves my parents, as do I. However, what parents in their right minds would group together an eight year old (me), with two adolescent brothers four and five years older, with boxing gloves? This was my first inkling that though my parents attended great schools, they could not have finished near the top of their classes. I resolved, much later in life, that their overriding thought was a family that plays together, stays together, and I accept that as their likely justifiable reasoning for these gloves. Additional options have also surfaced at various times over the years. Perhaps, Vince gave Dad a deal on a set of three gloves? Very doubtful, as he was a doctor. Or, maybe I was neurotic? Neurosis is defined as imagining or demonstrating an irrational fear. I don't think this applied in this case.

So, in our flannel pajamas, secured further by our white cotton briefs, and led by our eager father, we headed to the poorly lit lower sanctum of our already musty and mildewed basement. It was as if Madison Square Garden had been transplanted into our basement. I recall very little after this initial scene. I do recall vocalizations from Dad that would simulate the ringing of the bell, and he would also announce, in an obvious New-York dialect, "Round Three," bringing further realism into our boxing matches.

During the mandatory training sessions, Dad's large hands would only partially fill the boxing gloves as he taught all three of us the differences between jabs and hooks. I believe he had a fantasy that even in his late thirties he really might give Patterson a run for his money. Well, you know, Dad was a strapping man and in pretty darn good shape, but I'm sure Patterson would have nicely set him down in the second round in our basement boxing ring.

My last memory here, before my mind developed defensive coping mechanisms, was glancing across the dimly lit ring at Fred and Dick in the corner of the basement, both with comedic smiles firmly implanted on their faces. They looked gleeful and determined, not a good combination was my quick assessment. I was soon to be bloodied, more than once.

CHAPTER 8

LAUGHTER

MY SWEATERS AT THE GOLF COURSE

I WAS IN MY VERY EARLY FORTIES, and after ten-plus challenging years of marriage to my second wife, an event happened at a parent-teacher conference that brought with it the realization that I was not going to grow old with the person I was married to, even if she was the mother of our two beautiful sons.

Oh crap, now two marriages in my life, ugh. The culmination of this bitter struggle was, of course, a divorce, and at about the same time my newly minted ex-wife had a garage sale where many of my sweaters and belongings were sold at very depressed prices. The sale was not an event I was invited to, nor would I have attended. It is how I learned of the clothes' new owners that created a belly laugh of some proportion and helped me become a total advocate of "laughter as man's best medicine."

The school conference referenced above was one of those life-changing occasions that forever can alter one's world. In hindsight, it was the straw that broke the camel's back and ironically, my former wife will likely never remember this school meeting that changed my course of actions toward our nuptials. I will take half of the blame for not finding a resolution to our issues in addressing and resolving the wounds that were now hemorrhaging in so many spots in our marriage. The concept of corrective action is so prevalent in most of life's dealings, but not here. Anger breeds more anger.

I was brought up in a household of two people who were truly in love, and their respect for one another was revealed in simple everyday words and actions. Their union, and respect, got them through some rough times in their parenting partnership. Unfortunately, this modeling did not help in my particular case. Or so I thought; in hindsight, it did!

The boys' elementary school was the learning epicenter for both of my sons. Quarton was one of the older schools in Birmingham and it was on these same school grounds thirty years earlier I played many of my Little League baseball games. Parent-teacher conferences were in full swing that fall and the parents of all these exceptional and brilliant children were dressed to the tee, scurrying in hallways to greet and meet with their children's teachers. The game plan was to get the scoop on one's child in ten-minute intervals. The teacher would explain all of the newest educational concepts they were employing at Quarton, and also explain the philosophy advocated in the greater Birmingham school's vision of excellence to bring out the potential that our children most certainly had. Especially with the taxes we paid.

This was my first meeting with Ms. Lisa Agabashian as my son David's first-grade teacher. She was quite striking in appearance and I was impressed with her basic constitution in approaching us (Mr. and Mrs. Adams, David's parents). A firm handshake and engaging eyes met us as we entered the room for our 7:10 to 7:20 p.m. allotted time-slot. I liked the atmosphere of the room and immediately felt that Dave was in good hands with Ms. Agabashian. The room and setting had a solid institutional feel. What a great environment for my David to be in for the school year, I thought.

I had heard rumblings a couple years earlier that my wife was unhappy with the assignment of a new teacher to our older son, Rob. I overheard many phone calls to other parents that got the pot stirred and I believe a meeting with Dr. Matthews, the principal, may even have taken place. I was not in attendance, nor part of this particular struggle. The outcome was that no change would take place in teacher/student assignments, as I recall. My theory was that the administration did their best, and even if a quirky teacher was assigned for a year, welcome to the real world. There was always something learned from newbies, and even from the union-protected and tenured teachers. This had been my expressed position for some time and remains a strong tenet in my belief system today.

The next five minutes began a series of discussions about Dave's early reading and cognitive development skills. All indications were quite normal, and his writing and drawing projects, though a bit sloppy, were mostly acceptable for a boy, especially taking into account the vast range in six-year olds in gender-differential skills. My wife, who had many advanced degrees and was trained and armed in the latest educational jargon, started on her intellectual banter to impress and make it known to Ms. Agabashian that she wasn't facing a stereotypic wealthy mother from Birmingham, and that they shared a collegial status as my wife taught at a private school in the area. She thought it was a bonding gesture, when it really was one-upmanship at its best. My wife expressed some deep concern about Dave's abilities as compared to our older son's more diligent approach to reading and task completion. Ms. Agabashian calmly and assertively stated that David was doing quite well in his development, and not to worry, she would keep her eye on him throughout the school year.

Ms. Agabashian shared with us that Dave had a special place in her heart. She explained that her classroom had two integrated, special-needs children this year, and Dave was unbelievable in his compassion and helpful ways to play with and assist these classmates in completing their projects. He acted as their advocate and protector. Lisa Agabashian stated that this was an unusual trait for a six-year old, and that many others under her charge shied away from this type of interaction. She was totally impressed with our David, the sentiment coming from her heart. I was so touched by this observation and her open disclosure; it created a brief welling in my eyes caused by the emotion that these comments brought out in me, especially the pride I felt as a parent.

These comments, however, did not sit well with my wife. I watched her reaction that first cautioned and then lectured Ms. Agabashian, advising that she wanted Dave to have the teacher's undivided attention because he was not progressing to standards, and his time and involvement with the special needs children was something she wanted reduced. I was aghast, and then I was pissed. The tension in the room was intense. There was a brief reprieve in the pressure as my wife backed off a bit, pretending to be gracious and mentioned that Dave was indeed a good boy, but her true position was stated and she did not care about his good deeds in Ms. Agabashian's classroom environment.

We all stood abruptly after this sobering exchange, ending the conference. I was thanking God that the school scheduled only ten minutes of this folly. I recall looking at Ms. Agabashian and with my facial expression tried to convey to her that I was so appreciative of her influence on my son and was personally very thankful for her teaching skills and comprehension of her task at hand. As you may have guessed, this was not a collective parental position from the Adams. Though Lisa was in her mid-twenties and still very much a rookie teacher, she had progressed admirably in my book.

We rode home in utter and stark silence, though some relief was gained in my thoughts as I had made an enormous decision about my life's direction.

◄ ◄ ◄ ◄ ◄

The following year, after months of divorce negotiations and proceedings, I found myself on a weekend prepping to play a round of golf. I had for years played on Sunday mornings with other young fathers who wanted to get a round in early in the morning so we could devote the rest of the day to family. On this fateful morning, with late-summer dew glistening on the manicured grasses, I arrived at the country club's grillroom for coffee and donuts and waited to see who I would be paired with that day. Our club had a tradition to make random assignments of playing partners so we would get to know other club members, particularly during a round of golf. This morning I was grouped with three other members who I knew through the social and pool scene at my club; however, I had not yet played golf with any of them.

The club also had a strong practice in promoting their caddy program so by decree and ritual I always had a caddy assigned to my golf bag. In hindsight, and now at my age and station in life, I realize this practice was a convention I went through that actually annoyed me. Having a caddy usually required a keen vigilance and a constant supervisory and training mentality. The kids often stood in the wrong place, moved at the wrong time, and were an annoyance during one's round, especially during one's swing. Back then I wanted to focus on my game and it took immense concentration. Training a twelve-year old in golf etiquette was not high on my list of interests or skill sets.

Our foursome introduced ourselves and began the morning custom of practicing one's putting. The starter would announce the names of the players on the public address speaker to alert all the foursomes of their relative position in their pending, on-deck tee times. Yes, for you non-golfers it sounds much like the ritualistic and spectacular lineup of horses in the paddock for the beginning of the Kentucky Derby. Actually, it was darn similar, though we didn't announce numbers, just names.

It was a gorgeous morning with sunshine prevalent and only a few large clouds dotting the western sky. We had a nice time getting to know each other in the group and learned what our various interests were; we offered the latest jokes and observations about this and that; and we were always courteous in pronouncements of "nice shot" filling the void during golf's glorious four-hours on the verdant grounds of our beautifully manicured club.

We began the back nine, noticing on the tenth tee that the sky was looking a bit suspicious with darkening clouds looming in the west. Thirty minutes later, as we were nearing the twelfth green, the now-very dark clouds were rumbling and began to spit moisture. The air cooled considerably, dropping some twenty degrees in just a few minutes. We looked at each other with a sense of unspoken premonition and moved toward the caddies with commands to get into the zippered golf bags to secure clothing and rain-protection gear. The distinct sounds of zippers and Velcro pierced the air, meeting the rain and wind that now had kicked up in intensity.

I was not a fan of full rain suits as they restricted my swing and were hot, so I often slipped on either a cotton/polyester sweater or a thin shell that had limited rain resistance, yet could still breathe. In less than a minute I was donning my weather garb and ready to continue our play.

When I looked up and around me, taking in a 360 degree scan, I saw on two of my fellow member's sweaters that looked curiously familiar? It took some mental maneuvers and I quipped to Mike and Dan, "I use to have sweaters just like those." Yes, the ones they were wearing for rain protection.

Smiles lit up their faces, and then a surrender of facts and truths came from Mike.

"Bob, the reason these look familiar is our wives bought them at your ex's big garage sale."

He then proceeded to pull out other sweaters, held them up and offered further evidence of my past possessions and identity. He threw them on the fairway and we looked again at each other and began laughing uncontrollably. Mike pointed with both hands to the heap of clothes lying on the fairway and said, "All of these for five dollars."

The three of us had fallen to the ground and could not stop laughing. The caddies were clueless in our uproar and playfulness. The beauty is the joke was on all of us. We knew each other before, and got to know each other during the round, but when those "familiar" clothes came out of the pockets of their golf bags, it was something none of us will likely ever forget in our lives.

◄ ◄ ◄ ◄ ◄

In sadness, one finds that laughter helps big time.

CHAPTER 9
SIMPLE ACTS OF KINDNESS

SENDING SEEDS TO NORTH CAROLINA

IT HAS AMAZED ME AS I'VE BUMPED AND BRUISED and soared through life, how one person's act of kindness can bring about such strong feelings of happiness and overall contentment, and serve as the fuel for such profound and lasting memories. My three-day connection with a gracious and wonderful black waiter in the mountains of North Carolina created a lasting memory that serves as the topic of this chapter.

The old proverb, "it is far better to give than receive," was often quoted as I grew and matured under my parents' watchful eyes. This adage was especially true with Mom's gentle reminders during Christmas gift giving. This was solid advice. However, my additional and expanded thought here is that life is a two-way street, and in our daily interactions, respect for our fellow man is warranted in 99.5% of these dealings. So, adding to this first rule is a second rule: "Do onto others as you would have them do onto you." It seems most appropriate to offer a one-two punch in proposing wise adages and verses that go hand and hand. Perhaps combining these pearls of wisdom might have created a hybrid saying such as, "Offer kindness and respect for your fellow man, and it will come back to you in multiples."

I believe these old and newer proverbs are very much the cornerstones for a happy existence, it's that simple. Reaching out, actually going first, takes some effort, but it seems to always be returned with this multiplying effect; at least that has been my experience. Happiness, in my book, is derived from acting pleasant in life's interactions and carrying a positive attitude. It can be unleashed through a simple nod or a friendly facial expression. Happiness can be found, initiated and conveyed in such settings as a line at the bank, in a supermarket checkout, or in a country inn in North Carolina. This essay recounts a three-day visit to such an inn, where I met a man that moved me, and our reciprocal acts of kindness served as a lesson in life.

It was springtime in 1975 when I visited Tryon, North Carolina, home to The Pine Crest Inn, a charming retreat that evolved from a collection of stone outbuildings nestled in the foothills of the Blue Ridge Mountains. Tryon was located just north of the border of South Carolina, in southwestern North Carolina, in the southern end of the Appalachian Mountains. The area was home to many equestrian enthusiasts and additionally noted for its crafts, featuring oak and hickory woven baskets sold in several of the mountain cabin stores dotting the beautiful landscapes in the area.

The inn and its cottages had their actual beginnings in the early twentieth century as a sanatorium to care for those suffering from tuberculosis, or consumption. One could easily picture, fifty years earlier, this small and exclusive retreat catering to well-healed clients, offering an atmosphere with fresh air as its basic tonic for restorative rehabilitation. Nutrition, under the credo of "let food be thy medicine," was also a cornerstone to this therapeutic treatment popular for several decades. The founding tenets for healthful rest were well in place and established when antibiotics came on the scene with their curative nature, forever changing the treatment approach. For the inn's own survival, it began a transformation to embrace tourism as its own prescription for health and prosperity. Even with the inn's shift from patients to tourists, relaxation and fine food served as its core offerings and our family was delighted to be catered to as its pampered guests during our brief spring respite.

My first wife, Cindy, and I were now living in Illinois, and joined my parents for this quickly conceived three-day weekend in these splendid mountains of North Carolina. We actually had our trip sanctioned as a business expense as I crafted a meeting with my regional counterpart in his southern district territory, which included the Carolinas. We landed in Charlotte, coming from Chicago. Sam, my work associate, and I talked business for a total of about ten minutes in the airport prior to us driving west to the town of Tryon. Sam and I sold improved turf seeds developed from U.S. and European plant-breeding programs for a company named Northrup-King of Minneapolis, Minnesota. Golf courses were our primary customer focus, with their demanding requirements and keen interest in improved turf varieties to enhance golf's playability.

My parents came over from Pinehurst, North Carolina, where they were golfing and were thrilled that we were only a morning's drive from each other.

The trip came together and we quickly arranged lodging and golf games with my associate, who was joined by his delightful wife, Margarette. We scheduled our golf round to be played at Red Fox Country Club some five miles from the inn.

Four years earlier my parents treated me to a trip to these environs when I was in recovery from a serious bout with mononucleosis and hepatitis during my junior year of college. This was when I was introduced to Tryon and The Pine Crest Inn with its gorgeous stone cottages with large fireplaces; the crackling fires worked to take the chill out of the evening mountain air.

It was in this idyllic setting during my second visit to The Pine Crest Inn in 1975 when I met Thuron, an elderly black man who was a waiter by vocation. He tended to our small group with total attention. He dressed to the nines, outfitted in a dark gray formal suit with long tails, complemented by white cotton serving gloves and a light gray trimmed vest. The vest's front pocket served to house his gold heirloom watch, safely connected by a looping gold chain. His coattails swung gently behind him as he gracefully maneuvered around the expansive wood dining table.

The dinner-place settings had a foundation of white linens ornamented with tableware of a practical style, and in the center was a vase of freshly cut yellow and blue flowers arranged with care. The setting invited us to snuggle up in our padded leather chairs, simply relax and take in the bounty that we would soon experience. The fragrance from the flowers floated around the table, offering waves of their sweet essence. It was a near-perfect dinner setting.

My family assembled here each of the three evenings during our stay. Thuron attended to us at our table ever so skillfully, with his careful manners and soft speech. His haberdashery-inspired clothing complemented the local antique furniture that was strategically placed around the inn and dining room; it all added to creating a special southern elegance in this very charming and quaint dining room in the main lodge of The Pine Crest Inn.

I imagined that Thuron was a very proud man, and he was ever so careful as he attended to us. He was quite fastidious in his table-side manners, partially the result of his advancing age, with his deliberate and careful shuffle, and partly with his sheer character, offering a gift of seasoned attentiveness. An aura of respect defined him, and I fictionalized that he might have been a character from the antebellum nineteenth century—a favored indentured servant working for a benevolent gentry-class landowner, and yes, a slave owner. This certainly could have been a logical assumption about his family's lineage 120 years earlier in these pre-Civil War counties of the western Carolinas.

It was under this background that a gentle and kind black man, whose eyes sparkled with magnificent beauty, entered my life for a brief moment and would forever leave a gentle mark. As my youngest sister Holly would remark today, "He was your little Buddha." A gift from the universe. Yes, Thuron was that gift.

I can still see his twinkling eyes, especially when I close mine, almost forty years later. His eyes defined pure, unspoiled goodness. There was no evil in this man, and I believe his inner heart could be observed through engaging just his eyes. It was under this innocent transaction, that of a waiter to his guest, which allowed me to reciprocate with my own act of gratitude, and both of us forever became bonded. It was his thoughtfulness in graciously serving my family that initiated the transaction that played out in the week that followed our wonderful hiatus in the foothills of Tryon, North Carolina.

Bob Hull was the owner of The Pine Crest Inn and, through our normal dialog as guests, we discovered some interesting tidbits about his life. He too had been a guest of the inn a couple of years earlier and had an earthly revelation that brought him back in a new form, as its lead protagonist, this time as its owner. Through a mid-life calamity, that involved a total redirection, usually called a crisis, he left a very powerful executive position with Chesebrough Ponds, stationed out of Connecticut. He chose to come back to this lodge and become its owner and working innkeeper. Bob was both appreciative and yet watchful of Thuron's ability to serve the inn's guests. While I related to both men on different levels, it was their own bond of being tied at the hip, as employee to employer, which helped bring the magic of this reciprocal event to a wonderful conclusion.

During the second evening of our stay, our table talk was directed for quite a while on the thirty-year-plus career of Sam with Northrup-King. He was a consummate salesman, in the truest and most positive sense, having worked in various divisions of the company during his tenure of employment.

As a brief history, the company was the largest general seed company in the U.S., having origins from the 1880s near the headwaters of the Mississippi in the Minneapolis area. One of the divisions was the home-garden division that sold small seed packets at retail centers across the U.S. Though Burpee Seeds was the leader with their greater brand awareness, NK was a close second in sales volume. Every year our territory account managers coordinated the collection of unsold inventory of last year's garden seeds that would be shipped back to the company's warehouses to be basically consolidated and then destroyed; yearly dates and lot numbers were required to be printed on each seed packet by the USDA to guarantee freshness and quality to the consumer. Reality was such that most garden seeds would germinate without issue even after years of storage, but politics were politics and our government was here to protect its citizens. So through this regulation, pallets and pallets of last year's seed packets were stored and tucked in my warehouse in Illinois waiting to be destroyed by fire in the city incinerator.

This background and story became integrated in our table talk and we began engaging Thuron, as he was refilling our coffee cups after serving homemade fudge chocolate desserts. We learned, through some probing and courteous discovery, that he loved gardening and spent the majority of his days nurturing the expansive garden at his home in South Carolina.

"Yes, ma'am" and "yes, sir" came from Thuron as he bobbed and weaved around the table. We queried about his gardening methods and then learned of his practice of tilling his soil and tending to his young plants every day at sunrise. We gained further knowledge of his absolute love of growing anything that was edible. Of course, this garden practice was borne from necessity, but true joy was at this senior citizen's pleasure in gardening, now mostly as a hobby. He shared his gift of tending to his garden, knowing he had a most appreciative and interested audience. He carefully cleared the last of our oncefull dessert plates, now very messy from the remaining frosting and melted ice cream, and filled our nearly empty coffee cups from a silver serving pot.

Bob Hull, always watchful and quietly present, added that Thuron was one of the inn's valued purveyors of fresh greens and vegetables in the summer months, to the pleasure of their very eager chef that appreciated the additional talents of Thuron. The immediate scenario had me visualizing the abundance of garden seeds sitting in my Illinois warehouse and a thought developed that I may have just found a home for seeds with Thuron.

Under my breadth, away from Thuron, I checked with Sam for his insight into our company's policy on donations and he strongly supported my idea and suggested that often there were several damaged displays that could be added to last year's stash with newer seeds and newer cultivars that all could serve as the makings for a thank-you gift package. So in the dining room that night my thank-you gift was conceived, and after dinner I approached Bob Hull to garner his support for my plan in thanking Thuron for his three days of splendid service. Bob was appreciative of such a thoughtful idea from his seed-company guests.

I arrived home late Sunday night on a North Central Airlines flight from Charlotte to O'Hare. The next morning I related my great Carolina experience to Lloyd, our branch manager, and asked for his sanctioned support in packaging a gift of hundreds of individual seed packets for Thuron. He saw the infinite wisdom of my idea and obliged. We both had fun embracing our unusual task of raiding the seed racks in the warehouse, quite a different start to a normal Monday morning at work.

Initially we unearthed and gathered seed names that suggested a southern zone of adaptation to them. Mustards, kale, eggplants and okra headed the list, and we grabbed many packets of each. We then went to sweet corn and selected five varieties that were housed in small cardboard boxes. One of the varieties was a proprietary cultivar of corn named NK 199. I had been told that it was the hit of the year for the fresh roadside markets because it remained sweet for two days after picking, not just hours. It was one of the first of the coming generation of sweeter sweet corns.

Lettuces, spinach and kale rounded out the classification of greens. Frankly, I didn't even know what greens were in my mid-twenties, and especially clueless to their relevance in black southern cuisine. The sturdy shipment carton was gradually being filled with seed packets of many additional vegetable types, which included squashes, pumpkins, cucumbers, tomatoes, beans, and carrots. I remember the beautifully photographed images on each pack displaying the future bounty that would surely develop after the contents germinated and were tended to in one's garden.

I literally collected hundreds of these seed packets and smiled, imagining Thuron opening these down in North Carolina. The office prepared the UPS paperwork and the shipment was accompanied with a handwritten note from me to Thuron in which I wished him well and hoped he would have pleasure with the many seeds I had enclosed. I further noted not to worry about the expiration dates as they meant little and he could use the packets for many years. This was my little thank-you tip to him for the attentive service he performed for my family and my business associate during the previous weekend.

The next week I received a letter in the mail. The envelope had a printed logo and the address of The Pine Crest Inn, Tryon, North Carolina, 28782. It was nicely typed and was addressed to me, but was from Bob Hull. I thought this was a bit odd, but collected my thoughts as I quickly opened the letter. It was a typed letter from Bob Hull thanking me profoundly for the seed packets for Thuron. He expressed how surprised and elated Thuron was at receiving such a bounty of seeds for his garden. The last paragraph explained that Thuron could not pen a thank-you note, as he had not attended school during his rural upbringing. I realized then that he had not learned to read or write.

There were two signatures at the bottom of the letter. One from Bob Hull, with his executive flare and crispness set in blue ink. On the opposite side of the page was the typed name Thuron L. Mills and just below it was a very acceptable and legible mark by Thuron, proudly displaying an attempt at his signature with the same writing pen.

How wonderful was that! My heart still feels the happiness that was embodied in our simple act of exchange and thank you.

◀ ◀ ◀ ◀ ◀

My referenced illness during my first Tryon visit entailed a six-week memory fog that included a brief hospital stay and led to an extended period of rest under the care of my family in Birmingham. I missed a semester of college, but through artful negotiations, spearheaded by my skillful dad, the dean of the college helped to keep me on track to graduate in four years. I finally buckled down and doubled up on classes and got serious about studying, and yes, about graduating on time; nothing like a serious illness to wake one up to the task at hand. I still have nightmares about not graduating.

CHAPTER 10
INTENTIONS—SKIING WITH DICK IN PETOSKEY

SORRY, WRONG GIRL

MY SECOND-OLDEST BROTHER DICK IS A UNIQUE PERSON. He moved to the Upper Peninsula of Michigan (the part connected to Wisconsin) a generation ago in the 1970s to begin his lawyering ways. He's extremely principled, an especially rare quality in the legal profession. As a county prosecutor, he "bleeds" when a jury concludes that his careful preparations for trial are simply viewed as government harassment of an accused. He steadfastly pursues justice representing his constituents, nailing the bad guys; he hasn't found a judge whom he really outright respects. Dick is tough-minded and very much his own person; he has much to offer in life's lessons. He was often accused, by unnamed family members, of having a bit of an attitude. My parents frequently referred to Dick as "Sunshine," a name that represented quite the opposite of his special character.

He was almost four years older than me (still is!) and had many interests that I didn't share, but I liked hanging out with him as he was an older and wiser brother. There was much to learn from him even if it needed some refinement. This was my general attitude when having to work around his prickly nature when we were kids. He taught me about mechanics, model building, glues, and skiing. He also loved and shared winter encampments that were part of his rugged outdoor life and was our true wilderness brother, especially versed about the rocky and tree-lined bluffs overlooking Lake Superior's gorgeous southern shoreline. All of these capabilities and interests are qualities that helped define Dick and I am thankful to have experienced our times together.

Dick battled cancer earlier this year, and though he's missing most of the right lobe in one of his lungs, he remains committed to daily outdoor exercise, hiking into his "back forty" that is nearly heaven, especially if you have a Thoreau or Emerson-like desire for heaven on earth, which we both do. I advised him a couple of years back that I spotted a wolf in his backyard environs down by the river, but he thinks I'm nuts, seeing things that don't exist. We'll see with time whether it was just a neighbor's scruffy dog playing in the woods, as Dick insisted.

His memory was quite spotty until about his thirtieth birthday, when things seem to have remarkably cleared up. It is the ideal state for his little brother to fully manipulate his weak cognitive skills for this essay. I've recently approached Dick to verify the "facts of the case," as I was prepping for this story about when we met up with his two lady friends for a ski weekend during college. He has only a vague recollection of the ladies, basically admitting he could be of no help in the details. He does recall something involving a freezing motel room, an abundance of beer cans, and lots of pizza in 1968 or 1969. This memory block is quite ideal, as I can set up the story for a new family legend, perhaps suggestive of the likes of Paul Bunyan, or maybe James Bond. Yes, Bond, that would be more apropos in this instance. So, bottom-line: his memory, or lack thereof, is great news as I can make this story much more risqué than it likely was; a dream come true in writing a memoir.

Fred, Dick, and I, also known as the Adams boys, snow skied together as kids, beginning in Gaylord, Michigan, at a place called Otsego Ski Club. My parents were members of the Ski Club, and it was our winter vacation destination for several years in the 1950s and early 1960s. Otsego Ski Club was a fusion of some developer's dream to make money and cater to the upper-middle-class families that were finding winter skiing suiting their fancies. It was frequented mostly by suburban Detroit families, and was a winter wonderland of skiing and frolicking with other kids whom we rarely saw in our downstate environs. This was because most of them were enrolled in private schools in the greater Detroit suburban area, and that environment of private schools was quite limited to kids networking with their own kind.

When Dick and I were still living at home in Birmingham, we regularly would enhance our winter's enjoyment and ski locally. The two ski hills I recall in southeast Michigan we frequented were Mt. Holly and Alpine Valley. Both ski hills were about twenty miles north of home. We would, on occasion, quite dishonestly split a lift ticket to save money at the ski areas and staple the split tickets to the dangling strip of previous ski tickets. We'd let them cascade from our jackets' zipper pulls. It was as if we were displaying earned battlefield medals. The fear of getting caught, now that I look at it, was not worth the risk; however, we never did get caught. Dick was sixteen and I was twelve, and he would drive Mom's green Buick Special wagon that had one of the first production aluminum-block engines in the U.S., whatever the hell that meant. Dick knew.

As we would head up to ski in the late afternoon after our school day, we would stop at the first fast-food chain I ever remember visiting. This was the Red Barn out on north Telegraph Road heading to Dixie Highway, near the old Pontiac State Mental Hospital. For nineteen cents you would get the thinnest—notice I did not say tiniest—best darn hamburger topped with onions, mustard, ketchup, and pickles. For sixty cents, you'd have an entire meal of some substance. We had fun those couple of winters skiing after school before Dick headed off to Northern Michigan University. Yes, I lost my ride upon his departure and never replaced it in the local ski scene.

Skipping forward a few years, Dick and I were home from our respective colleges for the holidays and planned a January outing to Petoskey to ski the expansive Boyne Highlands. We hadn't teamed up to ski for a few years, so I was quite excited about our weekend plans. Dick had mentioned that he may have some female companions from a dorm in East Lansing join us. I was likely getting over some girlfriend, so this seemed most interesting, and probably needed. I looked forward to the upcoming weekend of skiing with the ladies.

Dick always surprised me with some of the girls he dated. I remember one, a hairdresser that was a few years older than Dick. One evening I recall she wore a bejeweled miniskirt and fancy, white, knee-high leather boots. Dick either took her, or was just hooking up with her, in the aftermath of seeing the Beatles at Olympia Stadium in Detroit. She appeared late that evening in the back driveway of our home, absolutely ecstatic about seeing the Beatles. I wondered how in the hell Dick competed with John, Paul, or George? She was giddy and titillated. At fifteen, I was amazed with her urban sensual appearance and found something erotic about her without understanding the emotion that she was stirring in me. I did not see how Dick had a fighting chance for her affection, competing with the likes of the Beatles. I avoided women that were wowed by rock stars; too much competition was my applied logic.

Dick and I arrived in Petoskey in the late afternoon and rented a room in a local no-name motel on the strip along the main thoroughfare off of US 31. Dick called the girls from the room phone while I was doing duty in the ice-cold bathroom. I overheard a conversation that was quite truncated. The phone's handset was placed quite forcefully on the massive receiver and Dick announced, perturbed, that they had decided to come up the next morning and would meet us at eleven o'clock out by the ski racks at Boyne Highlands. So much for female action on a late Friday night, I thought, without commenting. Our first evening consisted of drinking Coors beer (just in from Dick's Colorado friends) and splitting a pizza with pepperoni and cheese (Dick was not into vegetables). It was an evening of just us brothers catching up on family things.

The next morning, after a restless night caused mostly by the distracting and unappreciated noise from the intermittent humming of a floor-based heater, we headed to Boyne Highlands, using Pleasantview Road just on the outskirts of Harbor Springs. Anticipation was in the air both for a day of skiing, and also for hooking up with the ladies that Dick kept assuring me would arrive.

We did indeed finally meet the girls, and they were only one hour and twenty minutes late, not bad for two blondes just off a two-hundred-mile morning drive. They looked to be curiously attractive and both were very nicely packaged in their brightly colored ski outfits, appropriately called jump suits, designed for the woman skier. Dick did the courtesy of introducing his little brother to the ladies in a brief and non-eventful first encounter. We quickly made our way as a group to one of the many chairlift lines that sprinkled the hills in front of the lodge. The scene of pure white hills to the west of us and the effect of sunshine created a spectacular visual sensation. The Saturday crowds at the lifts reminded me of congregating ants enjoying a cube of sugar.

I don't remember how I ended up first of our foursome to glide into one of the two lanes that fed the chairlift loading area. Blonde A came to my left and was immediately beside me, focusing not on me, only on the readiness and preparation it took to arrange oneself for the ride up the chairlift. One had to hang onto the poles in one hand, grab the center tubular bar with the other, and then gracefully sit on a thinly padded, red vinyl seat cushion. Somehow the goal was to mesh one's girth into this automated miracle they called a chairlift. I was always amazed that everything somehow seemed to come together on chairlifts, mating the chairs with one's buttocks. Usually the launch occurred quite uneventfully. Women appeared to be much more graceful at mastering this act than men.

I didn't know which of the girls Dick had an interest in, as his disclosure of intentions was never one of his strengths and I didn't think to ask during the previous day. They both seemed friendly and were joking with Dick and making references to how cute his little brother was. They were MSU coeds, and I really didn't have a clue how old they were? Their bond with Dick made me feel unfortunately like a little brother and troubled my maleness, just a bit. I didn't know the expectations, or the rules; I just showed up with my big brother. They say that showing up is three-quarters of the battle.

When Blonde A joined me I assumed she was not Dick's love interest. In a matter of one minute, while we were in line and jostling to move to the platform for the aerial lift, she instantly got cuter and cuter and it was becoming clearer that we were in for quite a day. Alcohol would soon become part and parcel to our day on the slopes.

I've been at bars where several beers were needed to make a girl pretty. This was not the case here, whatsoever. These girls were legitimate keepers and they got my adrenaline pumping, even without the effect of alcohol that was just minutes away. They were daytime drinkers and announced that they were here at Boyne Highlands to have fun. I thought that this was a bold and provocative statement.

I realized for the first time, having just completed the pairing to the chair, that I would need to say something clever to engage and impress Blonde A. The problem, as I assessed, was that I would be with this gal for an eternity (the three minutes up the lift) and my first utterance had to hit the nail on the head. A miracle happened: she made it very easy for me and initiated the conversation with such gentle grace and uttered a simple statement, "Gosh, I am so happy to be here."

She possessed a certain mature quality with her forthright manner. She was complimentary of Dick and impressed that we hung out together as brothers. The three minutes up the two-person lift sent me figuratively to the moon. I was mesmerized and remained in this spell for the next 24 hours.

We truly hit it off.

We did the normal routine of a few runs on the slopes, and then the girls had to go to the bathroom, which as I suspected would entail a lengthy process of peeling off layers of clothing, peeing, and then resetting their hair and hats and the always-needed touch up of lipstick and facial powder. It was an act that may have taken about as much time as their drive to Boyne Highlands that morning. Of course I am kidding, but rest assured it took some precious time, it always does.

While the bathroom stop was in progress, Dick and I had headed to the lounge and ordered of all things, beer. I was nineteen and looked all of seventeen-and-a-half. The Michigan legal drinking age was twenty-one. I was well prepared with my recently acquired fake ID I'd gotten for twenty dollars. The phony ID was developed from a Tennessee-based driver's license board in a fraternity brother's room using a Polaroid Land camera and an electric iron for laminating. The 1947 birthdate on the license worked most everywhere, including Boyne Highlands.

Our server commented as he handed back my license, "There are many of you from Tennessee today."

Always thinking on my feet, I responded, "Yes, that is our tour bus," pointing to the front of the resort to a fictional diesel bus running in the vast parking lot.

The girls returned and Dick and I began in earnest an afternoon of drinking, which would include beer and wine. The ladies also had to show ID. I noticed that their licenses were from Michigan, so I immediately deduced that I was indeed dealing with older females. I'd had a few dates with upper-class women at Albion, but they already knew me and it was mostly a group of friends of friends. These girls were definitely at least twenty-one years old. Seasoned coeds, was my conclusion.

The afternoon progressed and beer was consumed in some quantity, both at the lodge and in Dick's VW Bus. We made it to the hill repeatedly and continued the consumption of alcohol in the form of a burgundy-colored wine in our leather Botas.

Our afternoon involved more skiing, more beer in the lounge, and then more Coors beer back at Dick's mini bus. We were having a great time. The laughter continued as we stumbled into the night.

A community brainstorming session among the four of us came to the consensus that the girls wanted pizza for our late dinner; Dick and I said absolutely nothing about our previous night's meal. Privately, we wanted the cheapest meal possible. We proceeded in the VW to the pizza parlor, where we had picked up our Friday night's pizza twenty-four hours earlier, and ordered a new pizza for Saturday's players. To our surprise the establishment also served beer, which was banned in East Lansing restaurants. Gosh, backwoods northern Michigan had beer and pizza in one spot? More beer was consumed from several pitchers and we exited the parlor fully satiated and quite drunk into the bitterly cold night. We found ourselves in the parking lot bathed in rising clouds of our own breath, mixed with several plumes from vehicle exhausts. We piled into the mini-van to escape both the frigid night and the dirty air.

The only thing I remember after our eight hours of drinking was ending up back at our room where, thankfully through the evening, we had negotiated splitting the twenty-eight dollar nightly charge with Blondes A and B. The rationale was it made sense to bunk up together so we could keep drinking and partying.

I remember ending happily on my bed with Blonde A, and quite purposefully put my arms around her. She met me with very eager lips, responding to my gesture with a full-fledged and ardent series of slippery kisses; we were making out. The evening was just seconds from being over. We all were fully clothed, minus the jackets and ski gloves and hats that were tossed around our now very crowded motel room.

It was all that would come off our bodies in this group setting that frigid night in Petoskey. It was simply time for sleep, and little more.

The issue with this particular pairing, I would discover, was that Blonde A was the intended love interest of my miffed brother, not Blonde B. I did not know this until the next day when laughter was not the highlight of the day. We were hung over to beat the band, another full-fledged victory for alcohol. My resolve was a developed belief that one needs to let the people you're with know your intentions. An adjustment could have been made, though not easily. Isn't life grand!

As I look back and tap into the best of my memory, I can honestly say that I assigned the letters A and B to the blonde gals to differentiate them only as two separate ladies, not for the purpose of protecting their identities. In the two weeks that it has taken me to write this chapter, I was sure their names would come back to me. Nope, not even a hint.

Perhaps I should speed up the hours devoted to my writing to complete the memoir project before dementia slowly robs me of my memory? Not a happy thought, and oh-so-sobering in my sixty-third year. The obvious final assessment was that these gals were but a one-night stand. I never saw A, or B, again.

◄ ◄ ◄ ◄ ◄

Dick and I moved into other directions and interests and we never spoke about the weekend in Petoskey until just recently. He now thinks they might have been brunettes and I finally had the nerve to ask him how he fared with Blonde B. There was no response, but not because of chivalry—because of no memory.

CHAPTER 11

COMING OF AGE

BEER AND WOMEN: A GREAT COMBINATION

HOW DO YOU EXPLAIN TO YOUR MOTHER after she drops you off with a friend at the entrance of the World's Fair in 1964 in Flushing Meadows that you spent your allotted five-hour window in a beer hall, called a Rathskeller. I was fifteen years old, and my good friend was seventeen. No one in the beer concession ever once asked for ID. There could be no mistaking that I was under the age of eighteen, which was the legal drinking age in New York. I barely shaved. I guess the World's Fair operated under an international code ? In other words, they turned their heads when it came to underage drinking. Good for them.

It was an early-summer trip that involved Mom, my two sisters, and my childhood friend, Phil Laux. This trip's highlight was the fair, but it was also partially slated to visit my mother's childhood stomping grounds. These included Flushing, and then Scarsdale, where she spent her life through high school before she ventured west to Ann Arbor for four years at the University of Michigan. I recall she was also arranging for my grandpa's casket, with him in it, to be transported back to White Chapel in Troy, Michigan. Here to finally join her mother, who had passed away earlier in the year. Mom showed us all around her neighborhoods and reminisced quite openly to all of us as we drove around. It was odd to imagine my mother as someone other than my mom. Do you know what I mean?

I had learned tidbits about Mom's early life, especially when she was a teenager, but she was very private about most events. When she attended the University of Michigan she worked in the business staff office of the University's newspaper, *The Michigan Daily*. The late 1930s were an interesting time on college campuses because the U.S. was trying so hard to remain an isolationist nation. It worked for a few years, but that ended on December 7, 1941, when the Japanese bombed Pearl Harbor. This contrasted with my own college experience, which was more about the negative perception concerning our involvement in Vietnam. The conflict was literally ripping our nation apart in so many ways. There was no one single unifying event that rallied the nation like Pearl Harbor in Mom's college days: it was the ever-present video and the newest technology in portable cameras that brought the bloody conflict back to us on our televisions. Revisionist patriotism has changed the perception that I certainly remembered about Vietnam during my college days.

Mom told us of losing two male high school friends in Europe in the war, and I know she was particularly fond of one of them, a sweetheart killed in France. She shared that with me earlier, during one of her reflective moments, usually surfacing as she was going through a trunk of her possessions in our basement's infamous "locked room." A room that was never locked, I might add. I had always thought it the best place to hide my glossy Playboy centerfolds. I often tucked them away for future viewing among her family articles or in drawers to avoid detection.

We drove by these dead boys' houses in Scarsdale and Mom reflected back some twenty-five years earlier as if it had just been yesterday. We had gone to her teenage house and she pointed out places she remembered from her youth. She also took us to the train station that her dad would board, taking the daily commute to his offices at Domino Sugar in the city. My friend Phil mentioned during one of our evenings at the motel that he didn't realize how cool my mom was, as we talked after our day of sightseeing and commenting on her reflections.

Every once in a while a story would surface about her romance with Tom Harmon, "Old 98," the legendary football player from U of M. This was mostly teasing from Dad. She never revealed much about her romance with Harmon, which took place in 1939 and 1940. She had just met Dad in 1940, and, as the story goes, she announced to her father, who was hosting Harmon at the Downtown Athletic Club in New York, that she had fallen in love with Fritz Adams (good old Dad!) and was moving on from dating Harmon. This was all transpiring while Tom Harmon was being awarded the Heisman Trophy in New York City. Tom Harmon was losing her to Fritz. Dad would just smile at the mention of his coup.

To complicate matters and add even more intrigue, Dad's unrequited love a couple years earlier at Albion, Ruth Brown from St. Ignace, was dating Harmon's teammate, Forest Evashevski, whom she eventually would marry. He had been the quarterback for Michigan the year they beat Ohio State 40-0 and was great friends with teammate Harmon. Imagine all the intrigue around these lusty college kids. In today's parlance: OMG! Mom and Dad actually kind of reminded me of Donna Reed and Jimmy Stewart in *It's a Wonderful Life*, another great story from their era.

Phil and I had traveled together a couple of years earlier to Boston with his family. His dad was also a pediatrician and our families were close. We visited a famous restaurant in downtown Boston where President Kennedy ate when he was a senator, the Union Oyster House. Another night we had dinner at a stonewalled and wood-planked restaurant that had a pond with the ugliest ducks I have ever seen, something like The Old Mill. Several tourist spots made up our wonderful five days out on the East Coast, and they all are much of a blur to me now.

During this Boston vacation we headed to Rockport, Massachusetts, to see the Atlantic Ocean, eat lobster, and look up artists. The art was of particular interest because Phil's mom had learned how to paint in Kansas. She had some dependency issues and painting was part of her therapy. The Lauxs had her paintings all over their house, but they were not very good. There was one that scared me as a kid: it was the blue-hued painting of their dog with a trident. Devil was his name and the painting really captured this image of evil and torment. Maybe she was a better artist than I gave her credit for? I do recall the exhibits and booths in Rockport's coastal town. Sitting in them were the artists. They were the strangest lot of characters, nothing like our midwestern artists.

In our Rockport spin, I hooked up with a threesome of many-starred generals who reluctantly accepted me as a fourth to join them for golf. It just sort of happened. I had enough socialization because of my own exposure to our private country club, and offered jokingly to the golfing generals that this was their lucky day. They politely smiled and said, "Come along, young man." I had the best round of the year, in the mid-eighties, and was congratulated by them with my first recruitment solicitation mixed into the praise. Little did I know that this outing was a prelude to years of such activity from our Selective Service.

What a difference a war and a couple of years can deliver. Coming of age carries new perspectives, often in contrast with the expected norm. I always pictured these generals leading battalions of soldiers in Vietnam, and could never quite get a handle on the surrealism I found imagining them either wearing golfing attire or combat uniforms. I'm not sure which was more becoming.

My thinking was that Mom likely felt an obligation to the Laux family for their nice gesture a couple years earlier, and thought I'd like a companion joining me with the females of my clan. Phil was invited to join our half-band of Adams. Phil was two years older than me, and I suspect that this age difference, in combination with my two brothers' early influence of beer consumption in high school and college, was the foundation for my early exposure and indoctrination to intoxicants. Not only do I suspect it, I know it.

Laws that govern drinking have been bantered and bamboozled over my cognitive fifty years, and sadly they are simply used and reused to support national causes. I never understood the states having so many different ages of consent. There was a movement afoot in our nation, as Vietnam was spinning out of control, that if you could die fighting for your country at eighteen, why couldn't you legally drink? My parents were total believers in this rebellious notion. Once we went to college there was never an issue about having a drink with them at the dinner table or on their back porch. Michigan was slow to vote for lowering the legal drinking age, but just as it was finally enacted as the war was winding down, a new enemy surfaced called the drunk driver. It became the new national cause. Michigan's legislators did an about-face in a matter of six years, moving the drinking age back to twenty-one in 1978. The drunk-driver faction was the winner of this ongoing issue and continues to be here to this day.

The acceptability of beer as a national drink in northern Europe was legendary to me even at fifteen. The servers in their dirndls, and something about the lure of intoxicants, all played into one of my coming-of-age experiences. Coming of age often is associated with a boy or girl's first sexual experience, but I would like to challenge that narrow definition and broaden the definition. Coming of age is an all-encompassing concept where an event makes an impact and forever carves a place in one's memory, and hopefully moves them nearer adulthood or, at least, to a more seasoned perspective. The visit to the beer pavilion was a story of the contrast in morays and laws, cultural acceptability, coming of age, and that beautiful day in June, all intersecting, giving me a new gift.

I do recall that the beer hall was near the entrance Phil and I had come in that late morning. It cost two dollars to get into the Belgian pavilion. We had passes from a neighbor in Birmingham for us to see the Ford exhibit that had 50 new Mustang convertibles on display. We reasoned that the Mustang was from Detroit, and we had already seen several during the last year, as several of the Ford brass lived in our neighborhood. The nation however, was in love with the Mustang and outer space. The theme of the World's Fair was "Peace through Understanding" and in about two hours, Phil and I would be repeating this every ten minutes at the beer hall thinking we were funny as hell.

We were happily seated at our first venue, which also proved to be the last; it was the 1500-seat capacity Rathskeller below City Hall in the Belgian exhibit. As soon as we sat down, the prettiest waitresses approached us. They were Belgian, German, and likely Irish, too! They wore dirndls and their numbers were plentiful. They seemed to be particularly attracted and attentive to Phil and me, which was even nicer. I did not know what the outfits were called back during the World's Fair. I just remembered how their crisp cotton shirts were filled out with their upper endowments and the bodices were securely cinched with laces at their waists, accentuating their young and voluptuous curves. They were a sight to behold, and as I visualized dancing and frolicking with these maidens, my attention was riveted to their every move. My head and eyes moved for the entire afternoon tracking our ladies. There was no subtlety at my age.

My socialization, frankly, was about respecting beauty, and it was everywhere, hovering around me for nearly four hours in pure joy, all accompanied and matched with mugs and mugs of the finest beer. This was my coming of age, and I enjoyed every minute of my experience. It seems that beer and females became a wonderful theme in my life, and I have always been grateful to Mom for dropping Phil and me off at the entrance to the 1964 World's Fair. I'd do it again in a heartbeat.

She was surprised at our giggling as we lightly got into her Oldsmobile 88 at the designated four o'clock meeting time. In my family's approach to things, you giggle and laugh, and tell the truth.

She wanted to know, "How did you make out?"

This was a consistent inquiry from Mom, especially during high school when I arrived home. She was genuinely interested in my outings. This was no ploy to smell my breath, or check my eyes, or delve into my success with dates.

I responded, "Mom, it was beer and waitresses, that simple." I saw Phil flinch just a bit.

"That sounds like fun."

That was Mom, and she genuinely meant it.

I looked at Phil and smiled, confirming that we were not at all in trouble. We went to bed very early that night after that wonderful day pretending we were in Belgian bosoms.

◁ ◁ ◁ ◁ ◁

The 1964 World's Fair is often described as the last major venue showing optimism for space and technology. Soon, our nation would be dealing with the aftermath of assassinations and war, and civil rights became the nascent call. The winds of change were fast upon us, even if we weren't at all ready for them. It meant so much to me in such a smaller cosmos. The Belgian beer garden introduced me to a world window of females, festivals, and fun.

CHAPTER 12

LOVE THE ONE YOU'RE WITH

EVEN MY HUMOR HAS NOT SOLVED THIS ONE

IT SEEMS I HAVE ALWAYS BEEN ATTRACTED TO MY FIRST LOVE, Karen Kieppe. She makes my heart flutter when I see her, and that feeling remains with me even now. The good news is we have never married one another to deaden that feeling. I've developed relationships of a loving and intimate nature outside of Karen; it was a recipe for moving on in life and hopefully not getting caught in the chains of unrequited love, the shackles of which can be very powerful.

From the minute I first saw Karen in the junior high school hallway, wearing a plaid cotton dress and a button-style open sweater, she struck my fancy. She was the most beautiful girl I had ever seen. Patty, Dana, Linda, and Sue weren't bad either, but Karen was the best. Karen grew up in Birmingham on Stanley, one block from my Washington Boulevard childhood home. She and I were baptized, side-by-side, at the Presbyterian Church on Maple Road when we were in high school. I recall us both laughing at the water running down our necks, in disbelief that our parents felt this was a necessary requirement for our lives. We took a class to qualify for our delayed baptism. I guess accepting the resurrection was our parents attempt to help in our own ascension to heaven.

I am not the one to clear up, or expand on this issue, whatsoever.

It wasn't just Karen's looks, or her laughter; she was and still is a very special person to me, with a list of endearing traits. I really liked Karen because she didn't play the games of other young teens or hang out with them with their giddy, girlish and groupie ways. That was one of the things that appealed to me as life was revealing itself, first in school, later in college, and then years later as we reconnected. She is a mystery to me, but I believe it is part of her own plan, and perhaps, deep down, part of mine. It allows a game of checks and balances in my own constitution.

Karen was and is a lady. She also was very athletic: a cheerleader and accomplished downhill skier, I also played tennis with her and had some very tough matches. Thank goodness she was not a golfer. She was a friend, almost a lover, a heartbreak, but also a confidante. Through it all, we still like each other very much.

I recently asked, when staying overnight at her house, a night when wine was freely consumed by the two of us, "What happened to your breasts?" Another one of my observations in life is that, unfortunately, I have a habit of verbalizing. My friend Ed calls it being charming. Her breasts were still very perky, just smaller than I remembered.

After I fumbled and bumbled and delicately elaborated on what I meant, she responded quite matter of fact, "More than a handful is a waste, Bob."

This shocked me, and perhaps, with her age now sixty-three, it might be a sign she is coming out of her guarded shell, or so I thought, without having a clue what she was suggesting. I have been studying my hands intensely since her comment.

Karen still has a figure of an eighteen-year-old female athlete. She is very graceful and bouncy. She has her mother in her constitution (Shirley was a very beautiful woman); her headstrong father is also in her gene pool. She is feminine, but also has a deep voice, much like her dad, whom we called the Bruiser. She was never a smoker. Her distinct voice was the result of inflections and intonations learned from one's tribe. It makes me smile.

We both laugh together, not the nervous laughter from our teenage days, but we find things in our everyday universe that make us laugh. The laughter comes deeply from our inner beings; it likely helps mask our various wounds. I know we both allow the other a measure of vulnerability, which is nice. We feel safe when we hold each other, but she is afraid for us, as I am always seconds away from total bliss, so this too has to be monitored.

This pretty well describes, but never explains, my deep feelings about Karen.

She is in my inner circle and knows of this memoir endeavor. She knows of my losses and triumphs and is helpful with encouragement. She has advice that she passes on occasionally that is very appropriate for me. One saying that she offered a couple of years ago from her repertoire, "The further you fall, the higher you bounce." This was one of her mom's favorites. It was her pep talk to help me get up and rebound as I was having trouble and in the doldrums.

We have continued to communicate for almost fifty years, now opting for occasional emails.

There were times during our respective marriages when decades passed without us conversing. She had become a mother of three, had married a couple times, and I hadn't seen hide nor hair of her. She asked me to make her "saucy" in my memoirs. We both knew she was not saucy, except once. Such liberty she has granted me, in contrast to another high school honey, whom I have written about in these memoirs; unfortunately that one threatened to sue me. Such an odd reaction, I thought, especially for such a compliment when I compared her high school breasts to those of Ursula Andress. I changed her name to protect her rights and will add a legal disclaimer in the Introduction. That is my gesture to this other old high school girlfriend, supporting her forever dream of chastity. Life's too short for such nonsense.

Karen's admission that she wished she had been a little saucier in her youth threw me for a bit of a loop, and I recently emailed her asking, "What? Now you tell me." I still can get absorbed into Karen's brown eyes and near-perfect figure and dream of holding her in my arms, all in the buff. This is a girl whom I've slept with over the years just because we were tired. We danced together most the night at our senior prom when she was crowned queen of our hop. I held her many times on the dock in St. Clair during the months she dutifully attended to her dad while he was slipping into his final episodes on planet Earth.

Yes, this is a tale of almost blissful connecting. It is a tale of almost-love. I must try to never say never, or I wouldn't be Bob Adams and the fantasy might end. There are times I am weakened in my emotional state, so I choose not to see her. I have learned that distance helps in this game of the heart. Can you imagine that Karen thinks I'm a romantic?

Karen was likely a near, final straw that broke the camel's back in my third marriage. She and I became reacquainted as I visited her dying father at their forever summer cottage on the St. Clair River, where she was dutifully caring for him. I fell deeply in love all over again. It took but one evening of cocktails, dancing, night swimming, and holding one another. Trust me, this camel had more burdens than just Karen. Hopefully, with time, perspectives will change and deliver the glorious power of healing to my third wife, and to me.

I appeared unannounced at the Kieppe's doorstep in St. Clair during the summer of 2009. Regardless of the reason I was there, I was available, and I was happy being at the summer cottage with all the family. In hindsight, I desperately needed this reconnection more than the four Kieppe girls or their dad did. The grace that transpired those few months was divine. It was all so heartfelt and real. It was an awakening for me; it propelled me forward on my new path of discovery and recovery.

Karen has cautioned me to not take her dad's final week at the nursing home with much credence and credibility with his deathbed request of me. She did not want me to be burdened by his powerful wish. We were sitting in the dining hall visiting with Dick, joined by several patients from the nursing home, enjoying their afternoon supper and dessert. They were all babbling. Yes, that would be an accurate description of most of the characters' utterances and represented their conditions for admission. Karen was the only female present and she charmed many of the old and feeble men with her caring ways; she was not at all flirtatious, but the Bruiser's new acquaintances sure were. Her ease at conversing in a group setting was apparent. Her act of civility toward the beleaguered men was all it took for pure happiness to fill their souls. Sadly, they were all objects of measured time, too many pills, and lack of attention.

Karen's dad, during the end of this visit, lifted his head, opened his eyes quite purposefully, and smiled. This affect had been missing for weeks, and with a verbal directive of some depth and clarity he looked at me and asked me in a loud voice, "Are you back to take care of my Karen?"

Oh shit, was I embarrassed, but reached out for his weakened hand and looked at Karen, offering a reassuring wink, and quickly turned to Dick and said, "Yes, Bruiser, I am."

Karen was embarrassed and her eyes darted to the ceiling with mild annoyance. She also appeared happy as he showed a momentary spark of life. I suspected that Karen probably thought this was all she needed, her Dad burdening Bob Adams with a last request. She was astonished by what had just happened. Death's door brings strange requests, and often delivers surprises. He was gone within a few days after this dining room incident; he slipped into a coma and quietly passed on.

He was a good man and helped me for years connect with the automotive purchasing kingpins at many GM divisions. We played golf for a couple decades in my early business career; boy, could he play the game. He was a great competitor and was Karen's not-quite-perfect dad. His dying plea was completely understood: a father facing his final fears, simply attempting to get the house in order for his beloved daughter.

◄ ◄ ◄ ◄ ◄

The summer after my senior year in high school is one of my favorite memories of Karen that involved my dad. I have retold this story many times, as it was also a glimmer into Dad's character and beguiling humor, probably not totally appropriate for a respected family doctor, but still very funny. Times were a bit more innocent back in 1967.

It was an early summer dinner in my parents' dining room. Mom was trying to have both nicer and more conversational dinners with the three remaining children (me and my two younger sisters, Sally and Holly). In a free forum, often supported with newspaper or magazine articles, we would sit at the dining room table and use these clippings to start discussions on newsworthy events, with each family member taking their turn. Mom must have read that this was a good thing to do to support the bonds of unity for the family. In hindsight, it really was. Good for you, Mom.

On that memorable evening, when it was Dad's turn, he produced no clipping, and he introduced his topic as something of a side note. He announced that he had just seen Karen at his office, not more than an hour ago. My younger sister's both wooed, knowing I was smitten. I ignored their mocking of me; I did not acknowledge their existence in the room. I responded to Dad, "Yes, she had mentioned that she was going to see you."

This was of little news to me as Dad had been her pediatrician for years. In fact, as most everybody I knew went to Dad. I said, with no deep concern, "How is she?" It was just small talk, nothing more. I probably thought it was a bit of a private matter, too.

He leaned over, coming closer to me, and said, "Karen is on her way to MSU this fall and I gave her a physical exam today."

My eyes must have grown to the size of saucers as the realization came over me like a lightning bolt that Karen was just at his office sitting on one of his painted wooden exam tables only in her bra and panties. I was trying to deal with this news, and further with the fact that I had become instantly jealous. So many emotions clouded my brain.

"That is one beautiful girl, Bob. You are one lucky guy," he continued.

One lucky guy? What in the hell was he talking about? I had dated her for a couple months and we finally shared a kiss, or two, on prom night a few weeks earlier. On the other hand, here's my physician father, my flesh and blood, examining her in her underwear and checking for moles and bumps and whatever the hell else you do during a physical exam. I still shudder at the thought. She was a nearly nude, seventeen-year-old female that Dad had just touched, and she was my girlfriend to boot. Who is the lucky guy? Doesn't he get it? These were the thoughts that raced through my brain.

My face was red and I believe Mom was now chiding Dad that it was time to go on to other topics, supporting her newly enacted family-dinner discussions. She knew I was throttled by the news. So much for doctor/patient confidentiality, I thought. I imagined that Dad was actually touching and viewing what only had been a dream of mine.

I didn't like my dad very much that night.

I was devastated and depressed. I retired to my room early, suggesting to my parents as I walked up the steps that I had to get up extra early for my morning golf course maintenance job. All I wanted was to curl up in a ball and think of Karen in her underwear. If there is a modified Oedipus complex for dads and sons, I had one for sure. Dad could have Mom all to himself; I only wanted Karen.

◄ ◄ ◄ ◄ ◄

My life of dating and romancing continued off and on throughout college, and Karen and I went our separate ways, as often happens after high school. Occasionally we would see each other and have our small forays at each other's campuses during weekend parties, but nothing of great note; that was the extent of our continued involvement. Then finally, in 1970, the "saucy" night to remember finally gripped both of us, moving us in two new directions as a result of an evening on the river.

It was early August, Karen and I had finally both turned twenty-one. Life was good, and we had begun to see each other sporadically. This likely resulted from her younger sister's near death and medical condition that involved surgeries and rehab, during which my dad was very much leading the medical interface in assisting Karen's parents deal with the trauma.

The entire Kieppe family was up north vacationing, stationed at the Holiday Inn in Traverse City. I was invited to join them for a couple of days as I lived quite close, just south of the city on the Boardman River. I was working several gardening jobs for wealthy ladies whose permanent homes were perched overlooking the West Bay of Traverse City. My own summer residence was shared with a college buddy. The residence was a modified and dilapidated former school bus parked on the riverbank. It had been painted dark green.

It had two makeshift bunks and no indoor plumbing. We used an outdoor latrine dusted with lye and bathed in the river.

The two days of planned fun included canoeing in Glen Arbor, climbing the sand dunes near Empire, and enjoying a round of golf with her dad—just the two of us boys, at a famous golf course named Crystal Downs. Dad had arranged our golf game and starting time using his vast connections. Karen's parents thought the world of Dad and me. I was able to shift my job schedule around nicely to spend time with the Kieppe family and be with Karen to see where this newly invigorated interest might take us. I was to pick Karen up at the Holiday Inn for our evening date after her day at the beach with her family.

We planned to have a few beers at the bars in Traverse City then head out to my river spot for a late grilled dinner, more beer, and whatever else. She wore a yellow-and-orange trimmed sundress and flip-flops, the shoe style of the day. She had her swimsuit and beach towel secured in a woven straw carrying case, ready for the river swim I had suggested.

I picked her up in my 1962 Chevy II that had previously been a Consumers Power fleet vehicle. It had too many miles and no functional seat belts, as they had slipped between the cracks in the seats and became irretrievable. I had learned to touch up the rust spots and nicks with a can of spray paint that almost matched the original paint; unfortunately it was glossier, a lot glossier. The clutch was acting suspicious and I loved what I called my "three on the tree" column shifter. I put nearly as much oil as gasoline in the green machine. It was the first car I owned. It worked and had a huge trunk for its small size, allowing for many sets of golf clubs, or beer coolers.

Karen and I, having both turned twenty-one, now had our true Michigan driver's license IDs stating we were born in 1949. It was fun to order drinks and get carded when we could show the real thing. It was a rite of summer, both of us coming of age. We hit a couple of spots in town for quick beers and then headed to the river for our late dinner. I had asked my roommate to stay in town that night at his parents' house so I could romance my high school sweetheart. He understood. He, too, had a high school flame he was reconnecting with that summer; it must have been contagious.

Karen absolutely loved my summer living quarters. She was in a great mood. The riverbank was covered with greenery including peppermint, watercress, and newly appearing Joe Pye weed. They all created fragrances that were an aphrodisiac for me. My little spot in heaven also had a fire pit, which was surrounded by a dozen chain-sawed tree stumps used for seating. As I prepared both fires, one for grilling and one for romancing, it dawned on me that this might be a breakthrough evening, as she was accepting my touching advances by lightly touching my hands in return. I hoped this was the new Karen.

The Weber kettle charcoal grill was my source for all great cooking that summer. I grilled the hamburgers to perfection and also placed the river-soaked husks of corn on the grill, a perfect complement with the burgers. I even had fresh butter and salt. Karen was impressed with my culinary skills. My stereo speakers hung in the windows of the bus and broadcast the popular songs of our day. We had consumed many additional beers at the encampment and were well into a second six-pack that had been chilling in one of my many coolers. It was a perfect summer night's setting and darkness crept in unnoticed.

After dinner Karen and I began to cuddle with each other in front of the splendid fire. I was seated behind her and draped my arms over her shoulders. She responded by weaving her arms into mine. I touched the back of her hair and then moved slowly and kissed her neck gently. I felt warmth from her body and took in the glorious fragrance of coconut and banana oil from her summer's lotion. We sat quietly for many minutes, just taking in the surroundings. The crackling fire with its ember sparks became the focus of our anesthetized brains. It seemed like an eternity had transpired as we cuddled with our unexpressed thoughts. Then Karen broke the silence, jumped up unexpectedly, turned to me and announced that we needed to go skinny dipping in the river.

"Let's just do it," was her exhortation.

This was an out-of-the-world invitation at my river home.

Leaving our campfire, we headed to the bus and scurried up the steps, adrenaline pumping. We entered the main aisle and moved to the center of the bus to my sleeping quarters. We disrobed on opposite ends of my bed, careful not to sneak a peek as there was soft light coming from the campfire, aided by the illumination from the crescent moon. In our modesty, we grabbed our towels and wrapped them around our bodies, hopped back down the bus's metal grated steps, and tiptoed down to the very dark riverbank. Nervous laughter came from both of us, but it was exciting as we plunged in the swirling cold river. This was my morning swimming hole where I usually bathed and shaved, but tonight it was to be my place for romance.

It was extremely sobering. I was in disbelief of the events that had transpired. I was in the water nude with my high school sweetheart; she was also nude and had led the charge to disrobe. It just happened, likely alcohol induced? We mostly expressed how absolutely spectacular this was, as we looked at each other's silhouetted heads bobbing above the water. We were barely able to see each other because the moon's illumination was faint. Our bodies were huddled under the water, with a single focus to conserve our rapidly escaping body heat. I was responding to Karen's lead, as this was totally new turf to me. I had only dreamed about this, never imagining this would happen with my Karen.

We stumbled up the bank of the river and covered our trembling wet bodies with our beach towels that had been tossed onto my sandy little beach, where they had quickly become moist from the evening's damp air and were further full of sand. We ran back to the summer heat that was thankfully still captured inside the bus. We were continuing our joyous giggling and reentered my sleeping section where we had earlier disrobed. With our short sprint from the river to the bus and the chilling effect of the river, we were both breathing deeply, almost gasping for air. We quickly sat on the two beds, looked at each other and smiled.

I reached for Karen's hand and she responded by coming over to my berth. I kissed her lips and we both slipped horizontally onto my bed and continued kissing, now enthusiastically. I was careful to hold her to share our body heat in the act of recovering from the shock of our cold river plunge. We both responded nicely to this sharing of body warmth. We continued, opening our towels and sharing our cold bodies; it seemed appropriate and effortless. I recall the resplendent beauty of her stretched-out figure below me, and her soft and fragrant skin. We were enjoying a level of arousal that was new for us. I treasured caressing her breasts and touching her buttocks. We continued our ardent kissing and touching. The very late night began to slip into the early morning hours as we acted almost like lovers.

What I recall toward the end of our amazing evening was the sand that had been shaken from our towels. It was everywhere, on Karen's stomach, breasts and legs. It finally became her focus and was upsetting her. This distraction, coupled with our utter exhaustion, brought our ardent encounter to a screeching halt. I blamed her body lotion for the sticking sand. It hadn't bothered me too much, perhaps just a little. Her skin was covered with the lotion and sand, but it sure smelled wonderful.

We dressed hurriedly and headed out to my car. Thankfully it started. I drove on the wooden bridge over the river and back to Traverse City and the Holiday Inn. It was very late and we were now sober and very spent. The drive was quite effortless and we arrived at the hotel well after three in the morning. We ended our evening with a gentle kiss in the car as I dropped her off at the entrance to the hotel. I reminded Karen that I was to be back at six-thirty to pick up her dad for our early golf game at Crystal Downs. We both chuckled, as it seemed like a nearly impossible feat and she assured me she would not see me at that hour, only later in the day. I sped off totally happy, but had an air of concern. I would need to come to terms with our evening in the near future. I calculated that I would likely get ninety minutes of sleep if all went well. I reasoned that the short night was worth it, and headed back to my bus on the Boardman for sleep.

I picked Bruiser up right on the dot at six-thirty at the Holiday Inn, and he was excited about our day. We placed his clubs in my trunk, moving one of my coolers to make room for his large leather golf bag. He was happy to be away from all his girls to join me for our twosome of golf at our fabulous pre-arranged venue. I remember him seated next to me, his stubby fingers rubbing the sleep out of his eyes. It was very early for most of civilization. The fishing boats on the bay were announcing daybreak as we drove toward Lake Michigan's dunes and their many sites to behold.

I was worried that Mr. Kieppe may have had an objection with me keeping Karen out so late, but there was no indication of that during our almost hour-long car ride. He laughed at my modest car, and reminisced that he had had some real winners, too, while in the Navy stationed in California and getting started in his married life with Shirley. I drove because he left his company car for the girls for their day's activities, and we would rendezvous in Leelanau County after our round of golf.

The first tee at Crystal Downs excited me with its breathtaking elevation and panoramic vista, including woods and water that were spectacular. We were about to play one of the great gems in golfing design, truly a golfer's dream. As I peered down the first fairway I briefly reflected on my two conflicting emotions: I was both calm and elated, the aftermath of the evening activities with Karen; my body and soul were occupied with these two opposing feelings. Calm prevailed.

We were the first group off at 7:30. The greens were being mowed in the distant landscape, prepping the course for our assault. I one-putted the first hole from 25 feet to salvage a par and Dick and I laughed, noting my good fortune. Nobody one-putts the first green, we remarked. The day progressed and I kept making exceptional shots; my putting was unconscious. I couldn't believe my luck throughout most of the round. I carded a seventy-seven for the day, even after sadly double-bogeying the seventeenth hole under weird circumstances. After hitting the flagstick with my second shot, the ball ricocheted into an unplayable lie in a green side bunker. The golf gods can be brutal. I will never score like this again with my few years remaining of playing golf. In twelve hours I had two of the most memorable events occur in my life: a passionate night with Karen and the golf round of my life with her dad the next day.

After our round, we went to Glen Arbor to join the rest of Dick's girls for the afternoon activities. Canoeing, climbing and hiking dunes, ice cream, and laughter were all included. I was a tourist in my own town. There was a perceptible remoteness coming from Karen that alarmed me, and I immediately surmised that last night might have violated our covenant of friendship.

Karen and I returned later that month to our separate colleges, fresh from our two days in Traverse City. I attempted reconnecting both through letter and phone, but there was a serious detachment happening, with too many pauses during our telephone conversations. Our passionate experience did not move our relationship forward as I had hoped. Ironically, our new dating interests that began that fall for both of us turned into our first marriages. Had we scared each other?

The beauty of this fantasy about Karen is that it can remain just that, especially as we check out the time left in our own existence. We both know that familiarity breeds contempt. Unfortunately, I am a series of chemical reactions. As hard as I try the chemistry kicks in and the machinery of emotions and feelings come alive and then, bingo, I am in total lust caused by six million years of inherited genes that serve as my fuel. Aren't women just wonderful!

I simply remind myself to love the one I'm with and move on.

Bird hunting with Dave and Jon

CHAPTER 13

DELIVERING AMBULANCES

I'VE NEVER BEEN WITH DAMN YANKEES BEFORE

COLLEGE BROUGHT SO MANY WONDERFUL FRIENDS AND EXPERIENCES. It was a great period in my life, one of the happiest, except for the one area that delivered way too much stress: classroom tests and term papers. Devoting time and energy to these pursuits was not one of my strengths, at least not through my junior year. That was the year when it dawned on me I needed to get my act together. A proverbial late bloomer, it finally occurred to me that I needed to buckle down. Or, in retrospect, was it buckle up? Yes, both.

I announced to my parents at the beginning of my sophomore year that I was interested in shifting to a pre-med curriculum. I prayed that the general disciplines that made up my freshman year, which produced a remarkable 1.88 GPA and probation, just weren't suited to my DNA. I concluded that the classes might not have challenged me, now opting for microbiology and organic chemistry. Would this magically unearth a latent aptitude? It sounded good and had the wholehearted support of my physician father when he said, "Good luck." I never looked at his face to ascertain the veracity of his well wishes. That may have told all.

I lasted three days.

On the third day, after much distress and introspection, I stared out the window of the old chemistry building at the large rock on campus that students painted nightly, and asked for help.

The syllabus shocked me the first day. The people I met I had never seen before at my small college. Likely they studied religiously, and consuming beer was a low priority. It was the first chapters in the textbooks that really did me in. My genes delivered a clear message: time for flight. I was in a total panic and by the end of the third day decided to cut my losses. The embarrassment was to be mine, with yet another new career announcement. It was awful and I can still feel my stomach churning.

My counselor always wondered aloud how he was assigned me, with our constant change authorizations and late registration paperwork. I reminded him that we came together because it was an alphabetical assignment and he had the A – C surnames in his office for academic counseling. He was a professor of economics, and at a small college the faculty wore several hats. We decided that psychology and economics would be my new direction. This summoned visions of becoming a powerful businessman running a large company with a strong background in understanding numbers and people. It was nearly a perfect fit, bringing direction and relief.

During my senior year my counselor and I again met, this time in an econometric modeling class he was teaching. I was thankful that I had opted for a pass/fail designation; it was so close. A meeting at the end of the term, and great salesmanship, made it clear to him that he alone might alter my graduate school plans. I was a senior and we were both done. Thank God he loved me. Bless the Dr. McCarley's of this world.

◅ ◅ ◅ ◅ ◅

Dave Bowen and I were friends at Albion College. He was an excellent tennis player and was from Oconomowoc, Wisconsin. I was so proud that I eventually could pronounce his town's Indian name without stuttering. His college highlight was the misfortune of cashing a check that ended up in his mailbox from our college's contracted food service. It was made out to another D. Bowen, in a different fraternity house. He obviously felt that it was close enough to warrant cashing it. Though he did not literally work for the food service, he ate their food, so perhaps he reasoned that it was a rebate. This indiscretion resulted in suspension for a year. I guessed that was better than prison, as it stayed within the college's jurisdiction. Our various struggles with school and women helped us bond. I was very happy when I heard his parents supported his return to Albion after his time-out year in Wisconsin, during which we kept in communication, mostly by letter. How bizarre that seems now, writing a letter.

During our junior year, Dave and I discussed an opportunity that presented itself: deliver two ambulances to a small town, west of the mighty Mississippi, in eastern Arkansas. It would be during our 1970 spring break, and net each of us one hundred dollars. A company owned by George Squibb, Dad's good friend, made the ambulances in a small factory in Troy, Michigan. They were always looking for responsible drivers to deliver their ambulance and hearse conversions around the country, or to ports, like Miami, for far-off global destinations.

I knew George quite well. A year earlier I had worked at his conversion shop for five days around Christmas to earn some extra money for college. I had little idea what my job was to entail. I just knew they were busy, needed a couple more workers, and welcomed my brief involvement. In one week I learned a few lessons and earned some desperately needed funds.

I was assigned to install secondary heaters in army ambulances that were specified for the rear of G-Vans under a large army contract that the company had secured. I was opposed to the war in Vietnam, but reasoned that these ambulances were for our wounded troops, so spent little time worrying about value conflicts. Plus, I was again out of spending money, so was strongly motivated, war or not. The ambulances were headed for a U.S. military base in Japan and we were under a Tuesday deadline, two days before Christmas, to have all the conversions completed. There were eighteen ambulances scattered about the factory floor and in the company's snow-swept parking lot, all in various stages of conversion. My morning job the third day was to install rear heaters which required drilling holes through the flooring and underbody. I'd had little previous training in fabrication, except for my Boy Scout Soap Box Derby creations. I tackled the assignment with vigor. The first step was to drill one-inch holes through a template that, unfortunately, was handed to me upside down. Quite sadly, I did five other vehicles just like the first one before discovering that the copper tubes at the base of the heaters did not fit through my fabricated holes. I went to my supervisor to disclose my troubling discovery.

"Goddamn it, that's all I need this morning," John barked. "How did it happen?"

I explained the upside-down template that had moved the holes about an inch out of alignment to the sidewall trim in the back. John was the individual who earlier handed me the template. He was a bristly character, under much pressure, so I did not remind him of the actual upside-down hand transfer of the template, along with a notable lack of instructions given for its use.

He said, "You can't read, huh?" He knew I was a college student.

John showed me some black arrows and notations on the other side of the template that meant absolutely nothing to me. Hieroglyphics, I thought.

"Watch this." A glimmer of hope had come over his determined face. "We must get these goddamn units built."

He took a heavy rubber mallet and pounded away at the two five-eighth-inch copper tubes and then grappled with the thirty-pound heater, guiding the repositioned lead tubes into the two holes I drilled earlier. John proceeded to stomp on top of the heater, first with one work boot, then with the other. With his torso bent over just below the van's ceiling, he used all his weight, and then some, and the heater finally bottomed out on the floor of the van. It fit perfectly, snug as could be. The only problem was, as John was stomping on the heater box there were all kinds of sounds, like metal breakage, and maybe cracked brazing. I suspected that the force and stress of his solution to the installation had shattered the heater's innards. John looked at me when I cringed at the noise and advised, "That's to be expected, just needed to adjust a little to fit your mistake."

Then he summarily barked, "This is government work and we have less than two days, goddamn it."

He handed me the rubber mallet and strongly suggested that I follow his lead and get on with my job. I did, and have always wondered if wounded soldiers ever got the benefit of heat in the back of those six vans. I did complete the other twelve later that afternoon and there was no more stomping on the heaters. They fit nicely and I connected the rubber hoses underneath the vans, using the coolest hose clamps and pliers.

One other quick lesson was learned that week. A lesson that was so obvious: do not accept a Christmas ham when you are a temporary worker.

The ham was presented to me by George Squibb during the brief late-afternoon Christmas party and almost created a walkout by the shop's unionized workers. After I learned of my malfeasance, I gave the ham to one of the nicer workers whom I had worked with two days earlier. With several mouths to feed at his home, I knew he could use the food. The hams were only for the permanent employees, or at least that became the new rule at the company that afternoon. The union had just been voted in that year, and year-end cash bonuses were replaced with a ten-dollar ham. I suspect I may have been used just a bit for rubbing the workers' noses in their new contractual relationship. Change is hard. I have always thought that a turkey would have been more appropriate.

My final conclusion on this assignment: I liked delivering ambulances much better than building them.

◄ ◄ ◄ ◄ ◄

Dave and I were quite fortunate that the two ambulances that needed to be delivered in the South occurred in the same timeframe as an opportunity to drive a new, metallic-blue Volvo 144 GL from Mobile, Alabama, even deeper in the South, to Milwaukee. The Volvo was a vehicle Dave's dad was buying from his brother. These logistical opportunities were all coming together during our spring break from college.

Dave's uncle was the first Volvo dealer in Alabama. The real logistical issue we had to solve was navigating the considerable gap of 350 miles between the two cities in the South. Dave and I figured we could hitchhike down the Mississippi as part of our adventure. I possessed a really cool road atlas that was a gift from some insurance company. We looked at it almost nightly in the late winter, preparing for our expedition, learning and studying highway routes we had never been on. We were so excited about what lay ahead. We didn't even consult AAA for their famous TripTik maps. Such an adventure we were soon to have.

Dave's uncle lived right on the Gulf of Mexico and we were going to stay there on his house boat for a couple of days after we delivered the ambulances in Arkansas. Part of the developing itinerary was our curiosity to observe the aftermath of Camille, the powerful hurricane that had pounded the Gulf Coast, centering on Mobile, the previous year. With all our driving planned, we also wanted to take a few days to really soak up the sun and its warmth after a long Michigan winter full of gloom and little sun.

Our contact in Arkansas was Mr. Bud LeFave. He owned the Chevrolet dealership and was also the mayor of the little town of McGehee, with a population of 4,000. As mayor, Bud LeFave was the authority that secured these brand-new ambulances for their county emergency services from Automotive Conversions. Dave and I were independent contract drivers. We wore our hair long, quite representative of the times. Infrequent haircuts saved money for more important pursuits, like beer and peanuts. It represented the rebellious times of the 1970s, except in Arkansas, we were to soon learn.

Our trip progressed without incident, and we had just passed over the great Mississippi River and were on the outskirts of McGehee. Per our instructions,

I called a phone number on the bill of lading supplied to me from Automotive Conversions. When I called, the voice I heard was not at all familiar in its dialect. It was quite a surprise, and I concluded that it was very southern and rural in its style.

"Welcome to Arkansas," were Bud's first words over the pay phone I located at our rest stop. It was like the resonate voice of a Hollywood actor combined with my impression of perhaps, say, a Tennessee molasses hauler?

"I'll meet you boys at the dealership right off of Highway 65 in about twenty minutes."

He advised us to just pull in the front lot, and because it was Sunday we would be the only game in town and we'd get the transfer done quickly.

You would have thought Dave and I had delivered two of the finest gifts from the factories in Detroit. In hindsight, Bud probably had been fighting for funding for ambulances in his city council meetings, and these two polished gems were the outcome of a year of political wrangling. We jumped out of our respective vehicles to shake hands. Mr. LeFave welcomed us to Arkansas and to his town of McGehee. He noted that he was so glad we had arrived on a Sunday so he could devote some attention away from his business duties. We were equally pleased because we heard that Sunday was church day in the center of the Bible Belt. This caution had been the only warning from my parents about our trip when we left their driveway on Saturday afternoon for our fifteen-hour excursion to Arkansas.

Bud remarked, "Had you been here yesterday, it would have been hell greeting you." He explained that the nice weather brought in the customers. "We were busy and sold ten cars and trucks. It was hopping mad."

He examined the ambulances with their large rack of red lights, sirens, and very basic emergency decals. He walked around both vans, inspecting them to make sure nothing had been damaged on their newest county assets delivered 900 miles from the North. Most of the expense of the conversion was on the inside of the vans, but he didn't even look.

We presented the transfer documents that needed his signature, and I explained to Dave, showing my seniority and acquired skills, how to get the three signatures and keep the one to return to Automotive Conversions for proof of delivery. Bud was like most businessmen I knew; he just signed all of the paperwork as if he knew everything contained in their written text. He was much more interested in chatting it up with us.

"Where are you boys headed?"

I took the lead and told him we needed to get to Mobile as we were on our spring break from college, and also would pick up a new Volvo to deliver back up to Wisconsin to Dave's family. I stammered a bit, then announced, "We are on an adventure and thought that we would hitchhike along the Mississippi and end up in Mobile for our next assignment."

He said, "Why, bless your heart."

I found out quite later in life that this was a common southern expression meaning that we were clueless, with no offense intended. It was interpreted by me that he was happy we were staying in the South to enjoy his part of the country. He moved our conversation quickly to our next step in being welcomed to Arkansas.

"You boys will first come to my home for Sunday dinner with my family."

He added after a brief pause, "I am not a fan of you two boys hitchhiking." He did not explain his concern or why he was reluctant.

We proceeded to hop into his Suburban C-10, a behemoth of a vehicle containing lots of steel, rubber, and huge seats. We had driven all night and now sported a few whiskers, and felt that a meal was a great idea. Dave and I smiled at each other with the thought of being placed under this man's seemingly gracious wing.

The short drive was uneventful and we chatted about our schooling, interests, and car dealers we knew. We were searching for common threads. We arrived at his house within five minutes, in a rural Southern neighborhood.

Spring had definitely come to Arkansas. I bet it was a full month ahead of Michigan in leafed trees, with annual spring flowers and perennials all in full bloom. The warm weather was welcomed after a cool night of rain and fog in the mountains. The scents of chemical and fertilizer residue filled the air, likely sprayed earlier in the day on the emerging corn and soybean plants around Bud's property. The house was sand-colored brick and sported several large shrubs around the foundation. The yard was nicely maintained; the Zoysia lawn still tan from winter dormancy had hints of green just starting to show through.

After parking the Suburban we walked into the house and immediately found ourselves in the middle of the kitchen, noticing three women at various countertops. We were introduced as, "The boys that brought the new ambulances down from the North." They acted as if we were relatives and the ladies greeted us warmly. They were wearing their finest Sunday dresses under their aprons. We shook their outreached hands as they curtsied in their own kitchen. A Southern habit, I surmised.

The smells of the kitchen matched anything I had ever experienced, even at the holidays in Michigan. I could see a pie and a cake and waiting dishware on top of a mammoth server in the adjoining room, ready to be filled with the offerings from the pots on the stovetop, where steam carried familiar smells of potatoes, vegetables, and gravy. There were some unique aromas unfamiliar to my senses, but they all smelled great and suggested that we would be fed extremely well, and quite soon. Mrs. LeFave handed us washcloths and towels and scooted us into a bathroom down a hallway to freshen up before meeting her children and the rest of the family and friends. It was an Arkansas Sunday family celebration for sure.

Dave and I emerged from the bathroom. We both had shaved and washed up and laughed quietly behind the closed door about ending up at the mayor's house for Sunday dinner. How funny was that we shared? Such an adventure we were on.

Back in the family room we met the entire family; there must have been a dozen in total. Dave and I showed real well, except perhaps for our long hair. We were gracious, as were they. Bud's youngest son had a small flash camera that he was sporting and I caught his eye several times as we exchanged little smiles. We were both playing face games, sharing exaggerated expressions intermingled into the adult discussion comparing life in Arkansas and Michigan. He was a cute little boy, but you could tell he was a hellion in tennis shoes.

After about six shots with his camera, squarely aimed at Dave and me, I asked him, "Why all the pictures?"

"Ever hear of show and tell?" he responded in a southern drawl.

"Sure," I said, thinking back on my grade school experience, just fifteen years earlier.

The group laughed and thought that was curious. The attention of the room shifted to our developing conversation and then the bomb was dropped.

"I have to bring something into class this week. I will show them pictures of you two. I've never been with damn Yankees before."

Boom!

And briefly silence.

These represented for the little tyke his last words of the afternoon.

This was a major faux pas. I knew it immediately, as soon as this six-year-old boy uttered the phrase.

Bud moved with an authority and speed that I was surprised he had in him, the speed that is. I bet he was nearing fifty years of age. If "ass and elbows" is a good description of what happened to his youngest, it is likely the best picture as the boy was led from the family room toward the back of the house. I assumed to his bedroom, where he would go without the benefit of Sunday dinner.

This was a major social breach.

All the LeFaves recovered nicely and we enjoyed a wonderful dinner. Grace was delivered by Bud, now in a very calm and reverent state. In the blessing we were welcomed under God's eyes and grace. He also got in the county's appreciation for the delivery of the two new ambulances. The food was spectacular; Grandma LeFave had made the biscuits and was praised by all who sat at the table for her skills in the kitchen. I ate at least three biscuits and learned to use a wooden honey dipper to slowly release the nectar onto my biscuits.

The conversation was very complimentary of Grandma's baking skills and she was so proud to be recognized by nearly every family member. We got the picture at the dinner table: keep Grandma happy, she likely owned the dealership's buildings.

◄ ◄ ◄ ◄ ◄

After our most appreciative thank-you and goodbye to the entire family, which did not include the little boy, we hopped back in the big Suburban. Bud had made reservations on a bus in Greenville, Mississippi, that would take us into Mobile, Alabama. It was about a forty-mile trip from his home back across the Mississippi to Greenville. We chatted about so many things. He again apologized for his little one, now remarking candidly that he was simply echoing what he learned every day from his surroundings.

Bud surprised us with his candor. He explained that hitchhiking the back roads of Mississippi and Alabama was dangerous for three reasons, in no particular order: we were college students, we had long hair, and we were from the North. He explained that those were three enormous strikes against us with the bigotry that manifested itself in the small towns in the Deep South.

He admonished us for such naivety, and asked us if our parents knew our itinerary? I answered, resoundingly, "Sort of." Thinking back, Dave and I were a bit sketchy to both our parents as we laid out the trip, and though they were excited that we were excited, we suspected that the 350-mile gap between our two delivery jobs might have gone in a low-disclosure mode as we prepped for the sojourn into the South. I realize today that adults never want to know too much, anyway.

"Boys, I didn't go to college, but I have worked hard and have had some nice breaks along the way." Bud explained that he had more worldly experiences than 99% of his neighbors, and wondered out loud that we surely must have read about the problems in the South?

"What are they teaching you in your college? There is an awful tension and too many outsiders are trying to tell us how to live. It doesn't work."

He went on, "Most of my neighbors are four generations removed from the Civil War. Now compound this with the Northern-controlled federal government's building high-rise homes in the cities for the Negroes."

He particularly espoused the belief that "Urban Renewal" would destroy the family structure of the American Negro. He believed all the "Northern do-gooder" solutions are far worse than the perceived curse they were trying to correct.

We were driving a back road, rural route to Greenville and he was pointing out wooden shacks, gardens, donkeys, and black figures off on the horizons in both Arkansas and Mississippi. We peered out the windows of the Suburban, taking in all the views and all his words.

Bud explained, "These people are solid citizens, these are their homes and they are happy and a great people. You can't develop high rises and stuff them in and hope that providing government welfare will ever help the American Negro. It just doesn't work like that."

He warned, "Once we get the Vietnam War over with, there will be hell to pay in our cities, you watch."

The frustration, yet sheer integrity that Bud demonstrated during the forty-five minute drive was our price for his hospitality. In his fifty years he had learned much and he had something to say, and used Dave and I to get some issues off his barreled chest.

We were twenty years old with very little insight. No college classes we had taken could replace the history lesson and perspective that this man was giving us. This was the Deep South and their voices and points of view were not a favorite of the North and East Coast-controlled media outlets. The contrasts were incredible. We focused on Bud as if he were lecturing in a classroom. We truly listened.

I was thoroughly impressed and thankful that our ambulances found such a worldly man. I was in conflict because he loved a way of life and he was not a bigot, but yet he was. This was adding more confusion in my attempt to define our changing world.

◄ ◄ ◄ ◄ ◄

In all honesty Bud may have "saved our bacon." I learned that expression on our trip. He paid for our bus tickets and gave us each an extra ten dollars for snacks on the way. The Arkansas lecture resounded in our minds as we found ourselves on the bus heading to Mobile to enjoy the sun and fetch a blue Volvo.

Bob, Sally, Fred, Dad, Mom, Dick, and Holly 1977.

CHAPTER 14
SANTA, CIGARETTES AND ALCOHOL

THINGS REALLY, REALLY HAVE CHANGED

MY PARENTS WERE BLESSED with a strong constitution to do things as a family. They balanced their young parenting life by developing annual traditions with old friends and neighbors, and their offspring. It was great modeling at socializing their brood. One of the traditions that we as a family enjoyed was Christmas Eve at Mary and Dean Beier's. Interestingly, two vices, alcohol and tobacco, were intertwined in these festive evenings and characterized how these were viewed so differently sixty years ago. This is simply reporting and I'll try not to judge harshly, as I have two differing views today on each. The closet smoker, or closet alcoholic, is becoming much more common today, as behaviors have gone underground to avoid detection and chastisement.

Interwoven in this wonderful and festive evening, we saw intelligent people enjoying the pleasures of alcohol and tobacco. It wasn't even an issue in the celebration with our families; young and old accepted them. There was absolutely no controversy. There wasn't even a dark cloud. These vices have become such a story today and are lead stories in a new society that is about restrictions of many kinds. These will be explored here with the strongest of convictions. Lost in the just-stated theme of this chapter is the night I discovered Santa was a phony. Now, that was an issue in the 1950s, at least it was for me.

Please give me the liberty to detail the evening of discovery of the truth about Santa's existence before we discuss booze and cigarettes. It was just awful.

The Beier's annual party spanned nearly fifteen years, at two houses in Birmingham in the 1950s and 1960s. It was a wonderful evening of games, socializing, dinner, and then always a visit from Santa Claus, who kindly showed up at the house during his nightly rounds on Christmas Eve. The adults would party and celebrate, and all of this was recorded on Dad's Bell & Howell 16-mm camera for us to watch for years in the future.

The group consisted of a few good friends of Dean and Mary, including the Christiansens, Everetts, Straights, and Adams. These families made up the annual guest list. It never expanded, nor contracted. I assume they were from the old neighborhood, or college acquaintances. Dean went to law school in Ann Arbor and Mary was from North Dakota; they met in Ann Arbor during graduate school. She was a very nice and beautiful woman. They had four children, but I was particularly attracted to an older daughter, Kathy, that I had a little crush on. Kathy was four years older than me, so I was not in her universe of potential suitors from her perspective, whatsoever. From mine, it was another of my long shots that I seemed to savor. She reminded me of an Indian princess with beautiful dark hair and great white teeth. She never appeared moody and seemed to naturally smile. She was a keeper.

Mom was always responsible for supplying goulash for the party. It was her noted dish to pass. She placed an enormous mass of flat egg noodles, tomatoes, onions, celery, ground beef, and paprika in a bright-red enamel serving casserole for the event. It weighed a ton, but Dad always lifted it with such ease from the trunk of the car. It was one of the many dishes that the moms brought. Each dish joined a diversity of comfort foods such as Jell-O (red and green), Sloppy Joes, leaf salads, warm buns and rolls, and more of the like. There were also carrots and black, pitted olives. Mrs. Beier always worked hard to make the evening special for all. The adults were dressed in their best Sunday clothes; no blue jeans for this generation. All the ladies helped Mary clean up before we left for home. Traveling back home from the Beier's always involved viewing the colored lights that decorated most of the houses and yards, in full anticipation of what the next morning would bring. Santa was on his way. There would be lots of snow, too!

It was 1955 when I discovered the shocking truth about Santa at the Beier's Christmas Eve party. Mr. Straight was dressed in the familiar red-and-white-trimmed suit that defined Santa, handing out gifts to all the eager guests. It was his year to play Santa, and it was my year to discover that it was all make believe.

I became suspicious while gifts were being passed, first noticing the very hairy arm reaching in and out of the sack to retrieve the wrapped presents as we were anxiously waiting for our name to be called. It hit me like a brick:

only Mr. Straight had arms that hairy. I tried to deny my new understanding, not wanting this heartbreak. A very troubling feeling came over my stomach; it was my first recollection of a bodily experience described as "butterflies." It was not a good feeling. I dug deeper into the mystery of Santa and focused on his disguised deep voice, and the eyes, and then his face that was under the makeup, and white beard and mustache. Sure enough: all signs of Mr. Straight under a disguise.

Life was going to bring some big surprises and it began that night.

Santa had been a ruse.

I was very quiet that night on the way home, wanting to return to my pre-evening giddiness and I was soaked in a veil of denial. I couldn't wait to get home to my security blanket and figure it all out.

SMOKING

Here is the scene: Dad's camera catches all of the women sitting together on a long cushioned bench along the family room wall at the Beier's Christmas Eve party. It is 1952. The camera pans back and forth, keeping the scene as steady as one can while performing a handheld sweep of the subjects. Dad knows to go very slowly for the best cinematography. In a brief thirty seconds, we learn that all five ladies wore bright red lipstick, held Manhattans or highballs in one hand, and displayed lit cigarettes between the index and second finger in their other hands. To add further to the scene's clarity and complexity, two of the ladies were very pregnant, and one was my mother. They were all chatting and semi-posing for the lights and camera, all having a great time, all with bright smiles.

What now strikes me, in hindsight, mostly about the mothers, were the vices that they displayed during this festive event. I have taken almost sixty years to gain a perspective and deliberate over the observations of these behaviors. It simply was a different time and health issues were viewed so differently, under so many different settings.

Let's put this in a modern perspective. What are females doing drinking and smoking while pregnant? This must show a total lack of knowledge about the effects these behaviors had on the health of the newborn, not to mention their own health. These were college-educated women, to boot. Some were married to doctors. It made no difference. It is a comment on changing values and norms, and brings with it many questions. I won't even comment on the bright red lips, allowing only that it was the style of the day. I have noticed that recently it is back in vogue. God forbid!

Now back to the evils of smoking.

Both of my parents smoked for years and it was accepted. My brothers and I, and one sister, smoked. We all have stopped; one died. The fact is nicotine and its chemical offshoots are powerfully addictive and harmful to life. Pretty simple, it just has taken years to gain this perspective.

I quit cigarettes nearly thirty years ago for several reasons. They were to do with women, a new son coming, and only finally, for my own health.

The first agent of change was my pregnant wife and her morning sickness. She was frequently sick in her first trimester, and my smoking contributed to her nausea. This created an incentive to be free of the habit with new life soon to be under our charge, and it would reduce complaints from my wife, always a worthwhile goal. I also had a female GM buyer that I would have lunch with every couple of weeks and she was very vocal about the awful smells of my car and that I should "Quit that silly habit."

I was terribly addicted to smoking cigarettes, and loved them with coffee in the morning and cocktails at night. Having two significant women in my life show me the way to finally tackle this addiction, which it clearly is, was monumental.

I took a cessation course at St. Joseph's Hospital in Pontiac in the fall of 1983 and was in disbelief that a five-day Smoke Enders course could work. It did. I have never had a cigarette since that week of operant-based conditioning. To this day, I have little understanding as to why I was able to remain cigarette-free. I didn't want to quit, but I did.

I have empathy for the pangs and pains of smokers. But, in reality, I have very little tolerance for cigarette smoking today. I am a reformed addict and now have moved right of right and look down my nose at people who smoke. Until recently, Michigan law allowed smoking in bars, but on May 1, 2010, all public places banned cigarette smoking to protect the Michigan citizenry. Secondhand smoke represented the rallying cry for the majority of the voters. This was the eventual tipping point for its ban under new legislation. The will of the majority wins again. I am fully in favor of this new law and find the smell in casinos, clubs, and tobacco lounges to be offensive. I am now fully on the side of the "ban cigarettes" police. I find this curious, given my general nature of low tolerance toward any intervention by do-gooders—as even more offensive than wanting to reject any law that governs our behavior.

But not here. Smoking sucks.

What I am having trouble comprehending today is getting my arms around the proliferation of young smokers, especially female. Even with the expense of over five dollars a pack and the known health effects, cigarette addiction seems to grab teenagers and lower socio-economic females and wraps its seductive arms around them. They're set up for a life of addiction, and then handed for decades the long-term side effects. Guys who smoke are just idiots, too.

I even surprise myself at the strength of my stated position.

ALCOHOL

How about alcohol? Now that's another story. Here I come up on the other side of the coin. I am back in vice's grip with my very positive position here. The balance of life's vices is evidenced.

Many wonderful evenings have taken place under the comfort and consumption of alcohol. It falls into the human desire to relax and seek intoxicated states to eliminate pain of all kinds. Now, what in the hell is wrong with that? It is simply satisfying humankind's most basic desires and yearnings. Sadly, it is wrapped in hundreds of years of politics and biases. It is used to control attitudes and is so political it divides friends and families.

As we are all aware, there's a progressive national campaign to curb alcohol for its negative health effects. Add to this the rallying cry for curbing drunk driving—a goal that has near-unanimous support as safety and death on our highways is something that has affected us all. My tales are not at all meant as whistle-blowing. Fifty years brings about societal changes in attitudes, and in a free society, they are supposed to evolve. They certainly have.

This elicits a fond memory of my childhood that depicts our changing attitudes about open use of alcohol, flashing back a half century to my junior golf days when I simply needed a weekly ride home from golf school. Dr. Keeffe was our chauffeur and he was one of Dad's very best friends. He was a radiologist, you know the guys that read x-rays, seeing things that no one can decipher without at least eight years of college. He was a very strange man and, giving him the benefit of doubt, he meant well. He reminded me almost as a caricature of Jack Nicholson, the actor. The hair and facial expressions were all there. They could have been brothers. I could easily replace Nicholson for Keeffe, in the lines from the movie, *As Good As It Gets*. Nicholson, who plays a writer, is just leaving his publisher's high-rise office. The young buxom receptionist asks Nicholson, "How do you write women so well?" He replies, "I think of a man and I take away all reason and accountability."

On Thursdays, Dr. Keeffe's day off, he'd get sauced up and do his fatherly duty by coming back out to Orchard Lake Country Club in the early evening to pick up his son, Scott, and me after our 36 holes played in our junior golf program. He was very proud of his 1962 Bonneville convertible with a 421 V-8 and a four-barrel carburetor. What was even more remarkable, he had his own manufactured and mounted gimbaled cup holder, commandeered from a yacht builder. It was attached to the instrument panel in the perfect spot so he could access his gin and tonic, always in a glass, right next to his sliding metal ashtray, which he also used all the time. He was a Kool's man.

The club's bartender would make him his favorite gin drink with a slice of lime served in one of the club's monogrammed glasses. I suspect that it was heavier on the gin than the tonic. Scott and I would practice golf while Dr. Keeffe had a couple refreshers in the Men's Grille. We were too young to be allowed in the grille, so we just practiced our putting. There wasn't room in his trunk for our golf clubs because it was filled with sturdy cardboard cartons of empty glasses that needed returning to the club's kitchen to be washed and re-inventoried in the bar's glass shelves. I guess he often forgot to carry them in, or would do it when we children were not looking. We always held the clubs with us in the backseat between our legs.

The Keeffe family had the first ice machine in the kitchen at their home on Williamsbury. It was incredible that this stainless-steel contraption could automatically make small ice cubes and had a scoop that could fill a large ice bucket in no time. In contrast, my parents had little metal trays in our freezer and you had to flex them with their lever arm and run them under the water faucet to get the cubes to pop and release. I thought back then that someday I was going to have an ice machine, even if the carpet was constantly wet from condensation dripping off the Freon-filled coils.

As we headed back to our neighborhood from junior golf, Scott and I would sit in the back seat of Dr. Keeffe's Bonneville holding our canvas golf bags, watching Dr. Keeffe's drink in the cup holder. It would lean left and then right, always swinging opposite to stay level as we sped over Old Orchard Trail to Bloomfield Village. Even if the glass was full, there was not a drop lost, except for his own clumsiness in bringing the glass to his waiting lips. The road had dips and curves reminiscent of a fantasy ride at an amusement park, and not more than five feet from us on the side of the road were mammoth trees.

No seatbelts for this crew.

Dr. Keeffe remained calm, and though he was totally pickled, his demeanor was relaxing and doctor-like. This gave me the assurance that he was in total control and would get me back to my neighborhood so I could catch a late dinner before retiring for the night. I had to get up early for my paper route duties. There were times that Mom and Dad would invite Dr. Keeffe in for a drink. The Beefeater's gin was kept in a special spot below the bread drawer, marked just for Dr. Keeffe. He would come in for a quick one, sitting on the back porch with Mom and Dad. Scott and I would hit wedge shots into one of mom's woven wooden yard baskets as they visited and laughed in the background.

◄ ◄ ◄ ◄ ◄

Much later in life I gave a lesson to my boys on what not to do with your vehicle after having a few toddies. I discovered I did not quite have the skill set of Dr. Keeffe. I think I also may have been subject to the proverbial double dare thrown in for good measure, which was categorized under the definition of poor judgment. Darn, even at forty-five, I was a sucker for that challenge.

I suspect that my immaturity may have been a good lesson for all, kids and adults alike. So, there was some good that came out of my only experience attempting to drive on an old horse trail in the middle of the woods, in my new truck, on my new farm. In fact, lessons are part of life whether you're twelve, forty, or seventy. Alcohol does in fact alter your judgment, as evidenced from the view of my new Suburban. My sons and their buddies saw a grown man use poor judgment. They all knew that I screwed up. I admitted it then, and I do now.

In the summer of 1996, my son David had a couple of friends up to the farm for a weekend of exploring. They were ten years old and full of the dickens. Their play included water balloon fights, making popcorn, and egg tosses. Carol, my third wife, did a marvelous job at being like a favorite aunt to all these boys. There was always some game, or adventure, or video that they packed in their weekends at our Leelanau farm. I'm sure someday they will look back fondly at these memorable weekends at the farm with the Adams Family.

It was late afternoon on Saturday and I had worked most the day weeding and preparing plots for my demonstration gardens of ornamental grasses. Their presence in landscapes had fascinated me for a couple of years and I was going to learn about them from a hobby point of view, especially their showy seed heads. I suggested to the boys, as I was having my first cocktail, that we should drive the perimeter of the farm and check things out in the four-wheel-drive mode of my new dark blue Suburban. We planned on it, and I announced that I was first going to jump into the pool to cool off, and then we'd go. Time got away from me just a little and I had a few vodkas in my favorite blue plastic tumbler. I was relaxing and enjoying the gorgeous early summer weather in the upper yard.

The boys came up thirty minutes later to fetch me for our ride. They had discovered many new relics from the farm's past in the woods. The boys had an array of artifacts including rusted horseshoes. They were amazed that horses once were the power that ran the farming in these hills. They were ready to take the late-afternoon spin in the new Suburban. Carol announced that she would accompany us with her youngest daughter, Jessica. All the kids hopped in to the "Kaburban" (a name that young Jessica tagged). Seat belts were buckled and we were off over the hills of the "back forty." In our case, it was the back fifteen. I had a few little spots around the farm where I knew that I would nearly max out the heavy-duty suspension. Sure enough, warning them added to the thrill, as we met the bumps and let the Suburban roll with the terrain. All the kids giggled in sheer joy. It was a total blast.

"Mr. Adams, Mr. Adams, let's go through the old trails." These words became the battle cry from the backseats. Dave helped bring it to a crescendo, by suggesting the famous, "Double dare you, Dad." He knew my weakness for such a challenge.

I announced to the carload of occupants, "Hang on, here we go."

We proceeded up the hill in the four-wheel, positive-traction, locked mode. We drove up our cleared sledding hill with nary an issue. This was a beast of a vehicle. Then we went into the woods, where horses once galloped and deer now roamed nightly. The power steering and V-8 handled the ruts and years of nonuse with ease. I had never "four wheeled" in my life. I was like a young teenager with his new dirt bike. My vodkas certainly helped create the adrenaline to handle the challenge with confidence. Laughter filled the cabin interior.

The path narrowed, which I knew, and Carol cautioned that we had likely gone far enough.

My own guts told me if I went slowly, I would be able to weave around the tall maples and oaks and we would soon be on the wider descending trail, back down to the upper garages in my paved driveway.

Not even close.

In two seconds the mirror on Carol's side disappeared, I overcorrected, and in less than a second my mirror also disappeared. The sound of flap, flap, now comes to mind. Next, there was the door bumper stripping peeling off and sheet-metal sounds of crinkling. Then silence.

In fifteen tense seconds the "Kaburban" emerged from its maiden voyage into the deep woods and trails at Overby Farm. She was clearly damaged. Had she been a ship she would be taking on water. We were not laughing. There was tension in the cabin among all occupants. I parked on the driveway and we quickly disembarked onto the pavement. Six of us walked around the blue monster, and after a brief assessment, I said, "Well shit."

Still silence.

One of Dave's buddies couldn't hold it in any longer and began the famous nose snorts, trying like hell to hold it in. The laughter began. It became contagious. All were now laughing hysterically. It finally hit me, and my tears of laughter joined those of the rest of the survivors.

An hour of fabrication and temporary repair was needed to make the Suburban roadworthy for the 250 miles back home. I drove with the mirrors in a revamped state, using twenty feet of gray duct tape and wire. After three days and $1,800 at Fisher Body in Troy, it was like brand new.

The technician asked, "What happened?" I told him, "Poor judgment," and we left it at that.

I'm not perfect, and neither was Dr. Keeffe, thank goodness! As I said earlier, the balance of life's vices are surely evidenced here.

Grandma, Jessica, and Grandpa 1998

Sara and Jessica Jones 1999

◄ ◄ ◄ ◄ ◄

CHAPTER 15

DAVID MERRILL ADAMS

WONDERFUL SON AND CURIOSITY

MY SON DAVID MERRILL ADAMS was born on March 25, 1986 in Royal Oak, Michigan, at Beaumont Hospital. Like his older brother, he too was delivered by cesarean section. The baby was planned in every detail. We also had a Dachshund who did not know how to share his food with human babies. The humans remained, the dog was soon history.

We delivered our first son, Rob, almost two years earlier. I had reluctantly, but dutifully, earned my Lamaze certificate, allowing entry to the delivery room. I carried the certificate with me in case I was to be carded. After a short period it became readily apparent that I was doing everything wrong and that my further participation was not at all appreciated. After considerable effort, with little results, the decision was made to perform a C-section. In hindsight, it was not one of my favorite outings.

Men attending childbirth was a new trend that I did not understand, and it still mystifies me. I recall a comedian describing a caesarian section as utter confusion with hoses, fluids, lava, tubes, a rainbow of colors, and, somehow, a large-headed creature emerges from all of this goo. However, when Rob emerged his features were delicate, his eyes so very blue, and the color of his skin so perfectly pink. He had the cutest nose I had ever seen on a newborn and a radiant glow on his face. Yes, Rob was nearly perfect in all features. This sentiment, shared by many in our family, remained even days after his birth.

Dave was quite another story.

Honestly, he was just about the homeliest baby I had ever seen. Measured on a bell curve, we experienced the two possible extremes in appearances that we could possibly have created.

The delivery room was very similar and the surroundings matched my first experience. Machines, monitors, gowns, and stainless-steel surfaces were everywhere. I was brought in for the final moments of the section. The doctor, from behind his mask, said to one of his many assistants, "Strap him in." It was me he was referring to. Apparently, fearful of both my pallor and my disposition, the doctor did not want any complications under his watch. Or, was I wrong and this was mandatory? I did not remember this with our earlier delivery. Regardless, I did not like being strapped in, and it was unnerving to be secured in this little side chair right next to the entire cesarian procedure. Christ, I was nervous as hell. My vast experience and own medical roots did not seem to matter to this attending medical team, or to me.

The doctor pulled an object out of the goo, with all the attachments still in place, instantly I saw this dark gray, deformed head. It also had a protruding snout. My immediate thought was this baby was not ready to be delivered, perhaps underdone or something? Dave resembled an extra-terrestrial from the movie *ET* that had impressed moviegoers earlier in the decade. They had much in common in surface appearances and texture. I was confused.

"God almighty, what is this?"

This was my first barely audible reaction. I looked at his mother and there was horror in her face. I tried to decipher her expression, and the source of the pain that was clearly evidenced in her face. Was it from the incision and the delivery aftermath, or, was it from getting a good look at our new son? I was convinced it was the later.

In a split second I tried to understand what had been delivered to us. We looked at each other, sharing our stunned expressions. It was visible to the medical team. We were dazed. No words from them could possibly help explain, or rectify, the apparition we saw. I'm sure we were remembering our Rob's cherub-like first appearances. The differences between the two were incredible.

One of the nurses was an acquaintance of mine and she knew we were in shock. How could loving parents admit such a fact about one of their creations? She handed a swaddled Dave to his mother for postpartum bonding and held my hand to keep a physical connection among the birthing team. She did this to comfort me and said nothing.

It was very tense in the delivery room. I was wondering how his head could be shaped like this with just a C-section? There were no forceps, or plungers, or wooden mallets used. I did notice that a brighter color had begun to appear in Dave's face, and perhaps the tide was turning. There was hope.

I tell this story occasionally and the fact is I have embellished it to add a little drama here, but not by much; in fact, by very little. You need not worry, as David became a beautiful baby after just a few days. Both boys could be considered quite handsome, "real hunks," as my friends say.

If any men will listen, or have a choice, I do not recommend delivery rooms.

◄ ◄ ◄ ◄ ◄

As Dave grew, we went on many junkets to the various playgrounds in our hometown of Birmingham, Michigan. Most of the time I managed to collect both boys and we ventured together for our fun outings. One playground was by our house, but the playground equipment was, honestly, old and boring. We usually would take the time to head over to what would become the boys' grade school. This playground had a mix of old and new equipment that was pretty impressive.

I was particularly fond of the metal merry-go-round that was a testament to ball bearings, die-castings, pipes, and centrifugal force. It was older, and built like a tank and very sturdy. It had both mass and a nice feel to it. A week earlier, I had taken Dave on it, his new teeth just emerging, and he grinned and laughed as he experienced that great sensation of whirling in a circle. I hung on to him to keep him safe and secure. He just loved the merry-go-round. Dave became so animated with his giggles and grins. It made us both smile.

A new camcorder was in my wife's sights, and Panasonic had introduced a sleeker model to compete with Sony. It was a seriously researched item, by my wife. My business was progressing nicely, and affording such luxuries was considered a necessity, especially with our role as doting Birmingham parents. I was ready to get some great footage at the playground with my boys; a term I now realize was a remnant phrase from dad's 16mm and my Super 8 film days.

Rob was now over three years of age, and he loved the playground's chain swings with black rubber sling seats. Dave was almost fourteen months and had begun to walk and run. After his newly mastered mobility, he was always trying to escape any containment plan by adults.

He had a really well built stroller that was collapsible and had many new design features that were quite innovative for the day. It had two wheels on each of the four swivel casters. The stroller was of excellent construction and quality, fashioned in complementary navy blues and grays. I would securely strap Dave in his stroller so he could not escape.

I had tried some earlier test recordings with the new Panasonic camcorder in my backyard to get used to this new device with its ergonomic touch controls. The manual was extremely complex, and I had it tucked in my rear pocket for fear that I might have to delve into it someday. I was looking forward to capturing some family videos/audios of these childhood memories. My dad had been so good at devoting time to taking 16mm color movies in the 1950s. I was going to blend new technology in the camcorder with my creative eye to produce some great shots of Rob and Dave. It was all quite exciting.

We three boys headed out on an early Saturday in mid-May to Quarton School's playground. It was a two-mile drive from our house. I had the boys fully secured in my car as we pulled into the empty parking lot at the school. I announced to the boys, trying to get them fired up, "We have the whole place to ourselves."

This was understandable, as it was just a little after eight AM. Rising early was a learned behavior, likely the result of my morning paper route and years in golf course maintenance. It was beautifully sunny, and I was encouraged by the lighting effect that the morning sun would have on the video quality of my recording efforts. The camcorder was housed in a very handsome sewn pouch, containing many straps. I was able to loop it on Dave's stroller as we disembarked from the parked car and rushed to the playground.

The playground surface had for years been covered with stone pebbles, but a new cover of chipped wood was being implemented by an agreement with the city's forestry department and the Birmingham schools. It was supposed to offer a safer surface for children who fell from the play structures. I had been made aware of this new approach to safety from an interested parent the last time we were there. She went on and on about child safety on playgrounds. It was likely her cause of the month. I tried to be polite. Her interest in safety was indeed to become a harbinger of the morning deliverance.

The boys were eager to begin their activities and Rob was careful in his engagement with the playhouse jungle-gym combo. I had some confidence in his play routine, so I let him go. My attention was directed to his little brother. Dave kept looking up at me, wondering if I was going to let him out of his stroller. My plan was not to untether him, as he could not successfully hang on to the crossbars on the merry-go-round; he was just too young to master this with the needed skill and dexterity. My judgment was well founded. Dave and the stroller would stay as a unit and be placed on the merry-go-round.

I was prepping the camcorder from behind him, trying to recall what I had mastered only a week earlier. I was ready to get rolling as soon as I could get his stroller onto the deck of the merry-go-round. At least, that was my well-conceived plan.

It almost worked.

The camcorder was placed on the ground on top of its carrying case about five feet from the merry-go-round. I placed the stroller with Dave in it up onto the deck and turned it side ways to secure it. I began the slow rotation of the merry-go-round using all the leg power I could muster to get it moving. I then shifted to a stationary position next to the camcorder, still pulling and pushing every available crossbar to gain the needed rotational speed of the merry-go-round. Dave began his weeing and laughter; he just loved this ride.

I deftly secured the camcorder, bringing it up to my cheek and eye, and pushed the standby button off. We were rolling, both with video and audio. Having just missed Dave in his 360-degree rotation, I thought this would be a creative lead-in to capturing his stroller and his delighted face as it came around the next turn.

The only problem was there wasn't a next turn.

My camcorder was aimed and fixed on the spot where he was soon to arrive, i.e. where he would come into view. A noise in the background a split second earlier alerted me to a catastrophic failure of some magnitude. The sound created a considerable thump and thud, which were heard and recorded; this was followed by the distinct noise of a child gasping for air, filled by loud shrieks of absolute horror. It all happened very quickly. I swung the camera around 180 degrees and somehow pointed it at this montage of a child and upside down stroller. All its molded wheels were spinning in the air, and Dave was buried underneath.

With no skill or intention whatsoever, I captured the negligence of the century against a child. Sadly, it was my child. I had swung the camcorder around and had the ill sense to keep the camera rolling. Later, I saw the close-up function in action where I had zoomed in on his face that was now muddy, covered with wood chips, lips bloodied, and a nose running with mucous.

He had tumbled off the merry-go-round in his stroller due to a combination of stupidity and centrifugal force. He did a header, stroller and all, face first into the ground. The stroller simply yielded to the laws of physics and propelled itself at a right angle to the merry-go-round's circularity. You know the mass and velocity thing we learned in physics class?

Not only did I have the video of the event, but audio joined the visual evidence of the accident. It was remarkably clear, containing all the background sounds that both led and concluded the event. As I played it again, and again, I could hear my voice exclaiming, "Oh shit," as the video shifted to the upside-down stroller and baby. Adding to the audio was Rob laughing in the background, and this too was clearly recorded on the new Panasonic. It was immediately apparent that while this was a serious and catastrophic event, Dave had made it through with minor trauma. The wood chips performed their intended job and their purpose was revealed, and not just for a good story.

Need I say more? Sorry Dave.

◄ ◄ ◄ ◄ ◄

Dave continued to grow and survived many mishaps. He had two states of motion. First, he could sleep, anywhere, anytime. Joining this was his second state, that of a full-throttled, talented escape artist resisting any restraints, whether a stroller, car seat, or high chair. You name it, Dave would eventually wiggle or negotiate his way out of it. He was wiry and strong, and always on the go, even as a small child. I was always catching him, preventing imminent disasters.

Early on he used a backpack to store all kinds of necessities. He seemed too young to me to need this, but the fact that his older brother had one was telling. Secondly, teachers were churning out paper trails of rules, school projects, and notifications. The backpack became a new-generation necessity, an accessory for the daily transport of paper trails and crap.

Dave loved his backpack, and it was certainly used by his mother and teachers, but he too added items that he had found in his daily rummaging. Rob's was always so neat and organized. Dave's was a mess, with a collection of every imaginable item under the sun. His backpack contained personal items, papers, books, partially eaten food, and auto parts. Yes, auto parts.

I was in the OE (original equipment) automotive supply business, and Dave observed me working on new components for GM, Ford, and Chrysler vehicles. Samples were huge in my life, and these would be at the office in my conference room, on my desk, in my brief case, in the car, and in the trunk.

My business group and I were always working on some new part; prototypes were a big part of our engineering inputs for customers.

I loved what I was doing, and Dave was always watching, and joined me by collecting samples during his daily excursions. This interest and behavior was modeled after me. I used to climb under cars on vacation to see our latest production rubber moldings of exhaust hangers and suspension bushings. Or, I might disassemble a molded air conditioning louvered outlet from our rental cars to look at samples of components my companies had produced for my customers' vehicles. It was simply a way of life for me.

Dave's backpack acted like a mini-warehouse. It contained items such as suspension grommets found on the street or in the gutters on his walks, or metal brackets that had rusted and fallen off old cars after hitting potholes. He was particularly fond of rubber muffler hangers as evidenced by his backpack payload. He also would find parts on the playgrounds as he played. He was always collecting samples for me to help in the cause of competitive product reviews. Just about every day there were new finds from his scavenging efforts. A teacher questioned his odd interests in collecting these "dirty little items." She would never have understood, so I just smiled.

During his childhood, Dave often combined his natural curiosity with what was new in vehicles and his fascination of what constituted the inside of cars. Most people loved styling and chrome, not Dave. He liked the molded shoddy used as trunk insulation, or metal fender pencil braces. It was the guts of vehicles that seemed to fascinate him.

I recall an event in the back driveway at my Wooddale Court home. Dave, around four years of age, peered into my new Buick's broken and shattered front grille, the result of my car hitting a deer just a day earlier.

I had driven early one morning from Traverse City to my Birmingham office on my way back from a fun-filled weekend. I made sales calls in Saginaw and Flint on my way in. I had a new Park Avenue that was about a week old and, unfortunately, it experienced the bane of early morning back-road drivers, hitting a deer. It was like slow motion as I watched the deer leaping over a wire fence and bounding in front of my Buick. My new ABS antilock brakes had not yet awoken as I was pushing the accelerator, and the bang from the crash made a resounding thud.

After hitting the deer, two distinct visuals presented themselves. First, I saw in both side view mirrors the deer rolling and tumbling to the side of the road, mortally wounded by the impact, no question. Second, about three seconds later as I slowed the car down, I put my arms up, fearing the late deployment of my air bag. I was relieved when the white air bag did not deploy. I was told later by one of my GM engineers that I should stick to sales, as air bag technology did not quite work the way I imagined, and he felt that taking the time to explain it was not in his job description.

As I came out to join Dave in the rear driveway next to our newly installed cedar fence, I observed him peering into the large opening in the front of my vehicle. It was formerly the grille, now missing. He had his head well inside the front impact zone. The vehicle now had a wide gaping appearance, almost like an arcade game that you would toss bean bags into. I cautioned him to be careful of the shrapnel as he examined the damage.

Dave announced to me, "Not here."

I asked, "What's not here?"

"The deer" he replied.

It did occur to me that the gaping hole could have likely absorbed the carcass, and I explained the rest of the events so he would understand why the deer was missing. He noticed tufts of tan fur that verified my story. This finding actually surprised me.

He then added while pointing, "Dad, I see two rubber parts in there."

It must have been by sheer luck, but the radiator and AC condensers were cushioned by two new parts from one of my companies and were clearly visible to both of us. How brilliant was that!

◄ ◄ ◄ ◄ ◄

That was Dave's world, such wonderful innocence and curiosity. Today my advice is to stay curious, as it is the cornerstone of a productive and happy life. Keep finding stuff, keep rubbing your nose in it, and keep trying to improve things!

I love you Son.

Webster and David Merrill

Dave, Webster, and Rob 2011

Dave, Rob and Liz Portsmouth, NH 2013

CHAPTER 16

NORTHERN MICHIGAN WINTERS

OTSEGO AND COMFORT FOOD

AS SO OFTEN HAPPENS IN WRITING MEMOIRS, there are many changes, edits, and endless suggestions from significant influencers. This essay was taken from earlier efforts as I was trying to develop my own style and unearth the mystery of writing. Thankfully, the tutorials I embraced encouraged me to just let the writings unravel, to let them flow. Two ladies, Julia Cameron and Judith Harrington, encouraged this helpful insight into the art of writing. Their call was to be bold and courageous in penning one's thoughts, and reminded one to "show versus tell." Mistakes are allowed and even encouraged. I did just that here, and rebooted the many paragraphs into this chapter on Otsego Ski Club in Gaylord, Michigan. It focuses not on any great single teaching, or proverb, as some of my early chapters did, but describes the environment of the ski resort and the foods of Northern Michigan. Of course, to keep my recovery theme going, I unearthed an insight at the end that surprised even me.

Reflecting on the vivid detail of the lodge, or cafeteria, or the ski instructor's voices, simply allows these impressions and recollections to describe a period from fifty years ago through a young boy's eyes. It was an era so different from today, remarkable in its modesty. It delivered impressions that have been recounted by me, now a senior citizen. As I recollect and muse with today's newly formed synapses, I'm surprised as it seems clearly to me that it was only last winter's experience. It is indeed not.

Otsego was a setting in which we learned and experienced the joys of being a family during winter vacations. I do know that life must become an adventure, and one should balance their life between work and play. The vacations that were made possible by my wonderful parents contributed to my learned appreciation for both the beauty and sanctity that surrounds me. Minimally, it was a break from routine, but there also was a reduction in stress that came when siblings played together during vacation, a bonding that could not be achieved at home. It was harder to capture this feeling under the roof of routine; hence the vacation and its value in offering a balance in one's life: a lesson my parents acted on. The natural environment they chose was their choice and it became ours. They passed it on. Family vacations always involved the immersion into the out of doors, with woods, water, and earthly offerings. This was all gifted to me and my siblings, from my parent's love for one another and love of the family they produced and nurtured by their own accord. They were fully in charge.

◄ ◄ ◄ ◄ ◄

Author at 11 at Otsego Ski Club 1960

Otsego Ski Club was the northern Michigan winter resort and holiday skiing destination for the Adams family for nearly a decade in the 1950s and 1960s. Otsego is an Indian name meaning "meeting place," and regardless of this his-torical note and tribute to the natives, the ski club was conceived and built to cater to the demand in downhill skiing that had gripped the U.S. during and after World War II. Otsego's design and layout was fashioned to replicate a village in the Alps. It lacked only the mountains and the snow, but who would ever notice—we were Midwesterners.

The main lodge at Otsego Ski Club was constructed from huge, round cedar logs. The beams had the shiniest finish I had ever seen. The atmosphere of the lodge was nicely enlivened with its several high-mounted, outdoor speakers playing Swiss folk music. The speakers were shaped like stout cones, and the sounds that came forth always included a zippy accordion and ringing bells. The music helped create the atmosphere of a European mountain resort, though it was interrupted quite frequently for announcements, either beckoning ski school attendance, or paging for a lost child. I guessed they did that in Europe, too. Somewhere in the village's striving for authenticity, characters would occasionally appear in Lederhosen, and one chap even yodeled. It was all so foreign to me; I'm not sure if they were real or costumes, likely both.

The terrain at Otsego Ski Club was gently rolling, with the addition of a few man-made bluffs. To the delight of most skiers, the owners created an illusion of steep and treacherous slopes. The ski resort was mostly equipped with rope tows mounted and looped on telephone poles, using a collection of spinning metal pulleys powered by electric motors. No gasoline engines were used at this fancy ski resort.

I'm sure electrical safety codes did exist in the 1950s, but likely not enforced at the ski area. It was my introduction to black electrical tape and its remedial nature. I smile as I recall tattered and frayed cords often exposed to the winter elements that were quite frequently tripped, resulting in an immediate stoppage of all the skiers on the tow line. The entire line of skiers would often collapse abruptly in their own tracks caused by an "event" tripping the infamous safety line. It was quite a sight as the skiers appeared like a game of spent dominoes.

I was reminded early in learning to ride the towrope how to react under a lost-power condition, quickly turning a single ski transverse to the slope to stop a traumatic backward slide. When the power was restored the towrope magically came alive, inviting you to grab onto it to right yourself and propel you back up the hill. It was not the most nimble reconnection scene. Attention and physical dexterity was required to avoid being run over by skiers behind you. I never quite mastered this reconnect, letting the brute power of the tow simply drag me up the hill, skis nowhere in alignment, depositing me at the top of the hill. It wasn't the coolest-looking action, but I didn't really know too many of the kids, alleviating the potential for embarrassment.

I also learned one morning that my normal winter gloves could be shredded to pieces in less than three minutes. It was a lesson on friction generated by the slip-stick of the ropes with my regular gloves. I finally succumbed to Dad's insistence that the bulky black ski mittens had a functional role and I needed to get use to them with their tougher construction. Somehow, this tow system worked, not at all well, as my beautiful powder-blue ski jacket also had problems with the effect from the tow ropes, marked with black scuffs on each side under the arms. They were quite permanent. It was all simply part of the Otsego skiing experience on towropes.

The Otsego Ski Club was additionally famous for their ski instructors born in Austria, Switzerland, and Germany. Names such as Karl, Hans, and Gunter filled the instructor ranks. Their Germanic accents were quite pronounced, and they were oh-so charming, especially when they taught the women, a.k.a. our mothers (which were one in the same in the 1950s). When their responsibility shifted to teaching us, the charm diminished noticeably. Images of Hitler's brown shirts came to my mind as the instructors barked out their commands. What the heck did "shush, shush" mean anyway? I also have to admit that parallel and transverse directives never made sense to me. I was not a fan of this type of instruction, or the bellowing instructors.

My brothers were much more proficient at skiing. They were a few years older and had experienced the benefits from ski school and had partaken in programs offered for the club members. Most of my early recollection of learning to ski was being with Dad, starting up the towrope on the Panty Waist hill, secured between his legs. I was learning to master the art of ascension. Gosh, he was a very patient man. I actually liked skiing with Mom and Dad a lot better than the group classes, as they, at least, laughed.

Of particular note at Otsego, adding further to the ambiance was the ski hill's maintenance crew. They dressed for warmth and duty in their oil-stained World War II coveralls that included tattered winter coats, when needed. Always they wore huge, unbuckled rubber boots and overalls. Style was a secret even to these souls. The men were quirky and cold and this translated to being grumpy and disconnected as their basic nature. They frankly had trouble dealing with our playful antics as we kids waited in line to grasp the whirling tow rope for our sixty-second ride up the hill. The maintenance workers and the resort kids kept a distance from one another. There never were conversations, or even so much as a greeting; mostly just grunts and groans coming from underneath their covered heads. I suspected they had faces, but I cannot recall ever seeing them.

The workers use to ride up the hill on their upside-down coal shovels used for grooming the slopes, forever covering dirt and grass with a shaving of white snow they artfully crafted from the existing banks. I always wanted to ride up the hill on one of those shovels. Today, my knees and back would likely not handle the stress of such a physical act, and I have also lost interest; a fact of aging, I suspect.

The lodge had an expansive cafeteria located in front, or rear, depending on which door you entered. The girded and beamed hallways nearer the ski slopes led the way to the cafeteria. It served the best hot cocoa. The cocoa had a sweet, yet deep and dark chocolate taste that was near perfection; the whirring cocoa machine filled the white porcelain mugs to the top. The cool down of the cocoa was a critical attribute in the sensual taste experience. One needed to learn the fine art of timing the intake of the hot liquid. The cup of cocoa would move from scalding hot, to tepid, in a matter of seconds. It was indeed a very narrow window and took some practice and luck to hit it just right. When you did, you would be in "chocolate heaven."

I could never quite balance the filled hot chocolate cup on the cafeteria tray and walk at the same time; it always was subject to spilling. I attributed this problem to a lack of coordination, blaming my heavy, metal-toed, leather ski boots. In reality, I would have spilled the cocoa even wearing flexible tennis shoes. The porcelain cup was not meant to be placed on a cafeteria tray by a child; especially with a room full of random motion-makers with their darting bodies making up the crowds. The cafeteria was always packed and humid and smelled sweaty. Most days after visiting it, I would head back out onto the ski slopes with blotches of chocolate on my powder-blue ski jacket. If I looked straight ahead, I wouldn't even see the stains.

Mom would wash out the powder-blue nylon ski coat nearly every night and let it dry on the shower rod in front of the heater outlets in our very warm bathroom in our rental chalet. This simple act of ingenuity involved a bar of soap and water that prepared my jacket for the next day's visit to the cafeteria. I think now that she might have been embarrassed for me, but never hinted at my weakness for hot chocolate.

Food seemed to be a constant theme interlaced in our outings, and it helped bond our family together during those winter holidays and adventures. The North woods delivered the cold and darkness. I now believe this created a survival reaction that focused our family on the necessity of eating lots of carbohydrates. The fare was always so different from Mom's healthy attempts in her home cooking. The only flavoring in Mom's kitchen was salt and pepper and packets of sugar. That was the extent of it. So, when we were let loose to sample the offerings in the North, we unearthed a whole new world that brought with it flavors and smells that were delectable, despite being not at all healthy.

Dad loved hot beef or pork sandwiches, the sliced meat placed in between soft white bread. Joining his meat of choice were mashed potatoes and corn, all smothered in real gravy. The four boys in our family enjoyed this diet only when Mom was not with us. Dad always found the spots that served such fare, and there were plenty in Northern Michigan; around every turn as we would come into a small town on our eating adventures, either lunch or dinner. The chosen place had to offer milk, which was by far the beverage of choice with Dad. He was not a beer drinker.

Gaylord, which was about three miles from the ski resort, had the Sugar Bowl restaurant. It was a dinner venue for our entourage of Otsego kids. I had my first slice of pizza ever there, and frequented the establishment over the years during our Christmas breaks. I smile, reminiscing about our booth of kids with hands and arms lifting pizza slices just out of the oven; hot pizza held high above the round elevated metal serving tray. The cheese would cling to the pieces that remained on the pan and we would all watch the elongating and dangling strings of mozzarella form; such fun, and what a mess. I remember being introduced to dried oregano and garlic flavors so sumptuous in the pizza and so foreign to me in contrast to Mom's basic approach to flavoring a meal.

Otsego and its surrounds were the perfect venue to vacation and learn skiing during our Christmas holiday breaks, and that we did for about ten years. On special winter weekends later in the ski season, Dad would take us boys to a different spot to save money on lodging; the resort was meant for the very well healed. Dad's economy choice was the more rustic Ken-Mar Motel on Old Route 27, five miles south of Gaylord. The motel spent most of their paltry profits on the blinking fluorescent sign on top of the hill where it overlooked the old highway, always announcing a vacancy. I remember looking out the frosted window in our cabin at three in the morning, wondering why the light was still blinking when the owners were fast asleep.

The motel was a collection of smaller log cabins joining the owner's larger cabin, where every morning they served the best homemade fry cakes (donuts) in all of Northern Michigan. Again, our adventures always found food that was not in Mom's kitchen, nor in her vocabulary. I remember vividly Dad seated each morning at the owner's substantial kitchen table with a cigarette pressed in his lips and his muscular hands grasping a mug of coffee. He was always chatting with the husband and wife owners of the motel, mostly about how their life's journey got them to this place. Dad loved conversing about life's stories, and he highly valued and was invigorated by the redirections they often took.

Just now, remembering Dad's civility and true interest in people's life stories makes me cringe just a little, as my late-in-life redirection might have surprised him if he was still living. Yes, still a father and son, forever in psychological contracts. My humor at first blush would have him rolling over in his grave about my losses, but in reality, he would be proud of me, after hitting bottom, I totally downsized and was developing new products to once again benefit from our free enterprise system. And writing? That would have him smiling.

The theme of my memoirs is about life's lessons, the bounty that is delivered in every moment of our existence, and the need to constantly recover. I named it "Rebooting," and that is acceptable and seems to have just now freed me just a bit as I write here. I just answered my own fears and considerable disappointments with the positive outlook and spin that Dad would surely have offered. He loved redirections, and I am in the midst of a major one.

◂ ◂ ◂ ◂ ◂

Yes, I believe he would be proud of me.

CHAPTER 17
LEELANAU PENINSULA

THE INN IS GONE. THE FARM HAS NEW OWNERS. I HAVE GREAT MEMORIES

THE GREAT LAKES CONSIST OF FIVE FABULOUS BODIES OF WATER, and my life has focused primarily on two of the lakes: Michigan and Superior. They offer such contrasts in shoreline scenery, created by a combination of their geological formation and the prevailing westerly winds. Glaciers came from the Arctic Circle through Canada and chiseled out the basins that soon would be filled with water as the ice moved into its liquid phase. Sand and stones were deposited as the glaciers moved, and lakes formed from the melting ice. I realize people spend a lifetime studying this phenomenon, but this explanation and background will need to suffice, as it is all I know. These wonders helped create the gorgeous Leelanau Peninsula, which is the setting for this essay.

Leelanau County is a peninsula in the lower mitten of Michigan that peeks out into Lake Michigan. It is often displayed as the tip of your hand's pinky. Its agriculture and tourism blend together, usually without complications, to the respect of one another. In the last decade locals have coined the peninsula's offerings, calling it an "agri-tourist" destination. I think this fits, and was the basis of my lure, first in my childhood, and then later as an adult.

The fruit orchards, especially cherry, are everywhere. Wine grapes and wineries have been the push for the last two decades. Now coupled with fine dining in Traverse City, the two have created quite a buzz for the region with its exceptional land-to-plate fare.

We vacationed summers in Leelanau in the 1950s and 1960s, and even back then I said that someday I would make the area my home. True to this dream, in 1995 my third wife and I, after a string of business successes, bought a historic Leelanau farm on 27.5 acres, perched on the bluffs of Lake Michigan. Neither lasted; thankfully the bluffs and farm buildings are still there.

◄ ◄ ◄ ◄ ◄

Bob at 50 Next to Mammoth Tree at Old Orchard Inn

Our summer vacations were a family affair that began first with Mom and Dad sampling a few Northern Michigan spots in the late 1940s and early 1950s, then happily settling in 1953 on the gorgeous Leelanau Peninsula in North-west Lower Michigan. It was home to the spot we vacationed at for nearly two decades, named The Old Orchard Inn. The inn was located on the west side of Glen Lake, twenty-five miles from Traverse City, Michigan. It was further surrounded by the Sleeping Bear Dunes National Lakeshore that comprises much of the county's western border on the shoreline of Lake Michigan. The national park was voted the most beautiful place in all of America in 2011 by ABC's *Good Morning America*. That is some observation and honor. It certainly echoes my thoughts.

The decision to vacation at The Old Orchard Inn would have been very much Mom's doing. Always concerned about the wellbeing of her boys and girls, she was also correctly selfish about her own rest and relaxation. She, too, needed to unwind while on family vacations. Water and sun were the prerequisites; after that some compromises were in order, but not many. She knew what she wanted.

Mom demanded clean floors and crisp sheets in our summer cottages. Rounding out these basic necessities was her requirement for great food. Heading this list was fresh whitefish, green beans, and homemade Thousand Island dressing on iceberg lettuce. Daily cut flowers also needed to embellish the dining table and, of course, laundered cloth napkins. These were her basic requirements, and I almost forgot, the five o'clock cocktail hour for the adults. Yes, these necessities were defining year to year, and made The Old Orchard Inn quite remarkable with its consistent offerings. I also remember as we children aged and became teenagers, the cocktail hour both started earlier and expanded later in its time slot.

The Inn likely was sought by Mom as an embodiment, or replica, reminiscent of her childhood when her own family vacationed in the Finger Lakes of New York and the mountains of New Hampshire. These were Mom's experiences in the summers with her family in the 1920s and 1930s. We use to elbow her about her affluent upbringing in Westchester County, New York. She would just stoically smile, with "no comment" imprinted right on her forehead. We knew she had the class in the family, and she knew a gem and value when she saw it. I can see her walking the Inn's grounds, relaxed in her navy blue Keds and powder-blue sunglasses, pulling up a recently painted wooden lounge chair to just sit and take in the view of the Inn's grounds and Glen Lake.

On our first night's arrival for several years, we would take metal flashlights loaded with brand-new Eveready D batteries to the apple orchard just 150 yards north of the Inn to literally spot deer's eyes in the early evening amongst the old trees. It was as if we were in Africa tracking lions and tigers in the evening bush. In reality, just deer in an old orchard, but it was still so exciting for us suburban kids. It dawned on me this is likely where the Inn got its name from—Old Orchard Inn. How brilliant is that? Eureka.

The rental cottages were very meager, revealing a single overhead light bulb in the bedrooms, and often a single porcupine trapped under the crawl space. I can still smell the woods where the rental cottages were nestled—so invigorating, especially as we disembarked from our station wagon without the luxury of air conditioning after the nearly seven-hour trip from Birmingham. We parked right next to our rental cottages, taking in the earthly smells of pitch from the white pines and the musty fragrances from fallen needles joining last year's oak and maple leaves that lay on the sandy ground. The trees' perimeter near the cottages offered a great location to dig for hidden worms under decaying leaves and rotting wood—the worms we used for our annual fishing on Big Glen Lake. Even with our efforts to collect local worms, Dad still bought night crawlers from Fainting Phil Kroll's marina in Glen Arbor so we could land the big lake trout up near the narrows on Big Glen.

The mention of the porcupine elicits a memory that changed my life when I was twelve. Jack was the wonderful "ice boy," appropriately named by the adults for his daily routine of dropping off ice buckets of oddly shaped cubes inside the front screen doors just in time for the folk's nightly cocktail hour. Jack and I were playing a morning match of Pingpong in the game room. The game table was located in an old open garage, just north of the main inn. The garage had better lighting than the cottages, which was quite helpful in our game. That particular morning Jack noticed movement in a back storage space, and to our wonderment we discovered a single porcupine tending to his destructive labor. Jack and adrenaline were not a good combination, as a call to arms found a shovel in my hands and Jack encouraging me to kill the pest. It was a manly thing to do in these North woods.

I did kill the porcupine after countless blows that seemed to never end. I caused the death of this young porcupine. He kept looking at me as blood came from his mouth and head. It was unnerving and I retired to my bed in the cottage and threw up my morning meal. I vowed to not be a hunter, or a human that did such deeds. It changed my life.

The inn itself had the perfect balance of amenities, led especially by the food. Mom, with her pedigree, required this, but interestingly, it also was a nice compromise, respecting her developing Midwestern values of thriftiness. I suspect that this had been shaped by the Great Depression, World War II, and marrying Dad. The Inn and my Mom were both absolutely charming.

The main lodge and inn were quite substantial in size, and could seat approximately 90 guests at a single full seating for the evening meals. It had rental rooms on the second floor, but we children never saw them as the ground's perimeter of rustic cottages was our domain and the upstairs at the inn was considered off limits. The inn was of wood construction, and had an expansive, windowed front porch for the guests. The lodge and inn were definitely built for summer-only accommodations. The porch housed games and books, wicker chairs, and chaise lounges. It had a hodgepodge of small tables, and various chairs in the long sunroom sitting areas, always inviting the guests to lounge and relax. There were lamps of all shapes and sizes dotting the gently slanting wood floor. Jute rugs and woven cotton throws were placed and spaced at both interior entrance doors and covered the wood flooring along the long porch. Paintings and framed pictures of all categories dotted the walls. As I listened to the adults converse, I learned that the Inn's owners had acquired the art during their extensive winter travel. Audubon lithographs were plentiful on the paneled walls.

The interior glass windows framed the long dining hall, and the polished maple floors were nicely worn from many years of use. Several coats of light-green paint covered the dining room tables. The tables and chairs were heavy and well grounded, serving as a good omen for our back-room antics, where we families were confined and isolated from the more profitable daily dinner guests. There was a workstation in the secluded back dining room that supported the five tables that made up the eating universe for our group of families. The cloth napkins and fresh-cut flowers were the foundation to the lasting impression of the dinner settings. The food was exceptional; had it not been, I assure you we would have ended in a different venue for our summer vacations. Knowing Mom, we would still be looking for that perfect place.

The newspapers were scattered all around the porch area, and I remember distinctly the Sunday *Chicago Tribune* seeming so foreign to my Detroit roots and my universe at the time. The inn seemed to attract Illinois residents who opted to summer in Michigan, rather than Wisconsin, likely to get away from other Illinois residents. But not their Sunday *Tribune*; it was their umbilical cord long before the Internet and cell phones.

Bingo was the Thursday night organized game, and we children attended enthusiastically and with great anticipation. The winners were allowed to cheer ever so loudly at their good fortune, breaking the tension as the game progressed to completion. I remember Mr. Wrisley calling out such numbers as B-12 and G-50, as if it were just last week's game. Cash prizes with many silver quarters and fifty-cent pieces were always the reward and the elixir. These winnings could then be cashed in for candy bars and gum in their messy office.

I remember walking on the crushed-stone service road with its grass median to cross to the kitchen area, located in the back of the inn. The trash and food wastes were just outside the kitchen behind a swinging gate. Flies and odors seemed to go hand in hand with this spot we frequented. We would lean over and peer down into the kitchen pit, talking to the cooks through the wire-meshed screens that were in place trying to cool and protect the kitchen staff and the food preparation.

Sophie, a hunchbacked older woman, was the Inn's infamous pastry maker. She was from the small town of Cedar, just up the road. The town was in its own universe, quite separate from the wealthy summer residents of Glen Lake. Sophie's Polish origins were revealed by her old-world accent and her necklace with a shiny metal cross. She loved us summer children and our own tales of mischief, which were plentiful. She would work in her space behind the screens and talk to us curious children. She had flour on her beautiful hands that were always moving, and they joined the red and blue fruit stains from summer's local bounty on her white apron. I felt sorry for her with her deformity, but also proud that I was part of her world. She was oddly an engaging person, and being in her presence made me feel happy.

Other Birmingham families joined us for our two-week hiatus. These included the Stricklands, Lauxs, Ludingtons, Barnes, and Millers, all linked with the Adams as regulars for years. There is another entire book possible with the collection of memories that took place with these families that I must reserve for another time, except for the following lasting memory, selected here in tribute to our family's Bloomfield Village next-door neighbor, Ivan Ludington. I just learned he passed to his maker in early December 2012, and this news makes me sad. He was such a spark and great friend of the family and always kind to me.

◄ ◄ ◄ ◄ ◄

It was Dad's fortieth birthday, and Mrs. Ludington had ordered a huge cake from the Woman's City Club of Detroit. She transported this creation of butter, flour, and sugar to Glen Lake for the opening night kick-off dinner at the Inn to honor dad's birthday. The cocktail hour lasted longer than normal. We children could hear the roar from the adults in the host cottage as we played shuffleboard and badminton on the front-lawn courts. I suspect the first night of vacation, combined with Fritz's (Dad's) birthday, all played into this particularly extended party for the adults. They were exuberant as they arrived to our special dining room for dinner and further celebration. The many children would all match up with their respective parents, who marched in with cocktails in hand, and we would all sit on the solid wooden chairs in our pre-assigned dining tables. The dinner proceeded that night with so much laughter that the two entry doors had to be closed to our back dining room to shield the main-hall guests from our noisy entourage.

The great finale of the dinner and celebration came when the entire room sang Happy Birthday to Dr. Adams, led by Mr. Ludington as he retrieved the heavy, frosting-laden cake, ablaze with forty-one little candles. Predictably, Ivan tripped two-thirds of the way through the song, the cake and candles all toppled upside down onto the long dinner table, two place settings short of Dad's seat. The room erupted in hysteria, already awash from the evening of laughter, and all enjoyed the disaster, except one person.

I learned that night that women often cry during the funniest events. Mrs. Ludington was devastated. We were all crying with laughter. She exited out the screen door that freely slammed and ran to the safety of her cottage. We all heard the slam, but focused on the prized cake, using our fingers and forks to retrieve and taste the smashed delicacy. It was delicious. What a great party. There was hell to pay.

We kept returning to The Old Orchard Inn for nearly twenty years for our two-week Adams family summer vacation. Our aging hosts, Mr. and Mrs. Wrisley, appreciated our coming, but especially our going. Yes, in a two-to-one ratio would be my guess. They, too, had recovery in their plans.

◁ ◁ ◁ ◁ ◁

One of the last vivid memories I have of this earlier Leelanau period was sitting on the Inn's lower-beach playground on Big Glen at midnight on July 21, 1969. Neil Armstrong and Buzz Aldrin, aboard Apollo 11, had landed safely that day on the moon, and the two took their famous steps, all somehow beamed back to earth to be viewed on television. I sat on the grassy beach of

Glen Lake and looked at the half shining moon in total disbelief that mortal men had just landed and accomplished such a feat. Or, so it was reported on the black and white television up at the Inn. It was quite an event. It was historic, and in such contrast to our summer vacation in the woods and water of Northern Michigan. It was where the word "surreal" derived itself.

The waitresses from The Old Orchard Inn loved to party with the Adams boys as we came of age, and even when we weren't. The little beach area on the lake, and our nightly fires, lured them after their evening work to take such risks, coming down the hill after freshly showering in their "rookery." Such daring ladies, even with the wrath of their employer just a small misstep away.

The burning open fire consisted of mostly freshly cut oak and maple mixed with very seasoned and dried apple and cherry. It created incredible scents that settled in our hair and cotton sweatshirts. Reinforced by beer in ice-cold cans, the evening air combined with the night's coolness, and almost always set the scene for a kiss and the touch of warm flesh from the waitresses' arrivals.

I learned that Ohio girls were much like Michigan girls, wonderfully soft to touch. Every kiss of their lips and gentle touch offered a unique and pleasurable sensation. Priorities were defined by our earthly connections to these college girls from Akron.

I hope two of my favorite and memorable waitresses at the time, Sue De-Witt and Sandy Norman, are alive and happy somewhere still on earth. The hell with landing on the moon, these girls were so much more memorable, and in full color to boot. I admit that I may be off a few years, or summers, but not on the girl's names or our friendly actions on the beach. I do recall all of this as if it was just this past summer. I wish it were.

Thank you Glen Lake and Leelanau County, you are heavenly.

The Inn was demolished in the 1980s, making room for two, large single-family homes. The razing of the Inn ended a fifty-year era for the sixty acres that made up this magical Glen Lake property we called The Old Orchard Inn.

◁ ◁ ◁ ◁ ◁

A new chapter will take place in June 2013. Glen Lake and Lake Michigan will be the recipient of my sister Sally's ashes. My siblings and I will cast them, committing them to wet storage for eternity. Sally loved these areas of Northern Michigan as much as I do, and even longed to move there before cancer delivered a fatal blow in the summer of 2012. Now, her troubled soul can finally be at peace. That is all we remaining siblings had ever hoped for you.

Peace sister.

Dick, Fred, Bob, Dad, Sally, Holly 1954

Native Lake Trout at Isle Royale 1993

CHAPTER 18
UPPER PENINSULA ADVENTURES

A VAST PENINSULA FOR SURE, EH

THE LAKE SUPERIOR SHORELINE IN THE UPPER PENINSULA of Michigan is rocky and gravel-laden. This contrasts to the hundreds of miles of sand and dune grasses of the Lower Peninsula's Lake Michigan shoreline. Both shorelines are gorgeous, and forever alluring, yet quite different in appearance and foundation.

I've paid great tribute and adulation to the northern portion of Lower Michigan throughout my memoirs. This is indeed where I have spent most my life, first as a young tourist, and then, for the last two decades, as a landowner and part-time resident. However, the Upper Peninsula deserves its own chapter, there have been so many great adventures that I have experienced.

The Yoopers who inhabit the Upper Peninsula, are unique and very hearty souls, representing about 3.17% of the state of Michigan's total population. They are mostly ancestors of French Canadians, Irish, Finns, Swedes, and Norwegians. For varied reasons, they migrated to this rugged peninsula in the nineteenth century. The majority were supported with jobs in mining and forestry. The current residents really are an amalgam of so many factors. The presence of snow and more snow, as much as their heritage, expresses their resolute character. I think they are a great example of the philosophy of my early beliefs: they are the proverbial melting pot that is America.

Imagine the scene that I have observed over the years and you can get a feel for their character. They love their Great Lakes and they frequent them at all times of the year. While half of the southern border shares Lake Michigan, it is the northern shore on Lake Superior that really gives the Upper and Lower Peninsulas their differentiation. Year-round access to Lake Superior sees swimming in mid-August as the only sane time to enjoy the water, if you are from any other part of the U.S. The water is so cold. Fishing for trout from rock jetties is practiced in the fall, and this quickly merges into ice fishing on inlets and bays from self-constructed shanties made from every imaginable material in the winter. Come spring, these hearty inhabitants are dipping for smelt all night long. Alcohol accompanies every shoreline activity, and it is rumored that the Yoopers were the first to champion and comprehend 24/7. They love their water, and their cans and bottles.

They also have accents that are distinct and cannot be described on paper. OK, I'll try.

Part Canadian Mountie, part Minnesotan lumberjack, and with a twist of Swedish milkmaid, all blended together, producing pauses in their diction that make them appear, at first take, somewhat flat and dull. Yes, that's it! Gosh, I hope in your lifetime you get to hear a Yoopers' accent—perhaps at an airport, or on vacation in Arizona; you'll detect it in a second. It is unique and quite pleasant.

I described in an earlier chapter my parents' brief exposure to Marquette, the UP's largest city, near the end of World War II. It is a city on the north shore of the Upper Peninsula. Dad was stationed there in a small battalion of Navy conscripts, prepared to defend an invasion of the Axis powers through Canada, or from the St. Lawrence Seaway system. If it had ever really been planned, it would have had to occur only in mid-August. The elements would have prevented any serious military charge except for midsummer. I suspect Marquette is where my second oldest brother was conceived as he "had to move to the UP" after law school, like a salmon coming back upstream. He remains domiciled in the western UP today as a prosecutor and outdoorsman.

◄ ◄ ◄ ◄ ◄

In 1957, at the ripe age of eight, I was sitting on a smelly, old converted school bus during mid-July's first hot spell, waiting for a very large ferry, the Vacationland. The ship was to take our bus across the Straits of Mackinac to access the Upper Peninsula. We were heading to Camp Nekana, outside of Steuben, Michigan. It was a girls' camp likely portrayed to the parents that would expose us suburban children to the outdoor life that we sorely needed. Guilt worked even for Protestants. The camp's owners did not mention that

Cousin Mike and Author Cooking at Camp Nekana

camp directly across the 180-acre lake. This meant little to me at this juncture. I later found, even with the discovery of the girls, that I was more interested in the candy bars we could get after dinner at the camp commissary. I was not ready for the female allure, but it was getting close.

The ferry was the only real option to access the Upper Peninsula, as the Mackinac Bridge had not yet opened. Air flight was an option, but who could afford that? The ferry was operated by the State of Michigan, and it certainly appeared that way. The seamen had the pace of today's U.S. postal clerks. It was gearing for dry dock, or at least some new service, with the advent of the soon-to-open Mackinac Bridge. I learned later that the ferries, by strict legis-lation, had to stop operating, and were not to compete with the $3.75 crossing fare of the new bridge. It was slated for a grand introduction for deer season later that year on November 1, 1957. They were completing the construction, which now was mostly about paving and painting. It was a spectacular view from deck of the ferry. The bridge reminded me of a T-Rex rising out of the misty waters, both the ferry and the bridge were astonishing to this eight year old.

I had to join my older brothers for the adventure of our lives with camping, fishing, and crafts planned. It was marketed as every boy's dream for fun, discovery, and enjoyment, except mine. I just wanted my parents, my blanket, my new kittens, and my own bed. Sucking my thumb was not an option, as it had become socially unacceptable. This was going to be a tough four weeks for me, but "chin up" were Mom's forever words of encouragement.

I recall being scared, as if we were being sent to a battle in some far-off land. I had my enormous steamer trunk that joined me in the back of the bus with my month-long clothing allotment neatly folded and packed away. All week prior to our departure, I recall Mom packing and whistling. That was quite rare for Mom, on both counts. I was imagining that we were really being sent to finish up some far-off war, or maybe preparing for the Soviet Union's atomic bomb, which the grade school seemed to focus on in our preparedness during the school year. Practices were spearheaded by my second-grade teacher donning a Civil Defense hardhat, imploring us children to hide under our desks with our books placed on our heads for added protection. Boy, did they have a clue, or not? Friends claim that my active imagination mistook this memory for a tornado drill. I really don't think so, although, perhaps we were preparing for the double whammy.

Thank God I was bunking with cousin Mike, and neighbor Bruce Kostere. We were assured of this through my parents' gentle prodding. (My brothers were long gone, and Fred was remaining downstate to play in Little League baseball tournaments.) My parents said goodbye to Dick and me in a church parking lot in Pontiac on that fateful Friday departure. I must have had the look as if I was in line for the gallows, or a beheading. You pick; the look matched the feeling.

"You take good care of your little brother." My parents gently pleaded with Dick through the windows of the bus, pointing their index fingers toward the front of the bus where I was sitting alone.

These were the last words from my parents, almost in unison, as they waved at us in this non-air conditioned converted school bus. I remember seeing Dad smile. Again, another fantasy and white-picket-fence image shot to hell. My older brother was with his buddies and wanted nothing to do with me, not even an acknowledgement on our first leg of the trip to Mackinaw City. I was going to have to persevere without my brothers, even if their interactions were mostly to pick on me. I did not exist in their world. Can you imagine four weeks in a wooded jungle in the Upper Peninsula as an eight-year old? Me either.

I have been getting the facts straight with my older brother, Dick, so I can tell the stories of our adventures in the Upper Peninsula. He recalled our oldest brother Fred flying up to camp a week late, after he played in the Little League baseball playoffs. It was definitely in 1957, and not 1958, as I had first contended. It was not like my parents paid for such luxuries, and I suggested to Dick that our Grammy Carpenter must have paid for this plane flight. The team needed Fred's second-base glove, certainly not his bat. When he arrived, Dick and I gave him a hero's welcome and showed him the ways of the camp. What you can learn in one week. I was a convert.

Jumping forward more than fifty years, in June 2010, Dick and his son Jon, joined me and my son David, along with our cousin Mike, where we were checking out lodging for our future father-and-son weekends planned each year in the fall. On our weekend list, we had to find the old camp, as it was near us. We former campers were at least sixty years of age and it seemed to represent a thing we needed to do. Yes, like a bucket list, I suspect.

We started outside of Manistique, Michigan, on Indian Lake in some rustic cabins. We would launch our search team to try to find the remnants of our great Camp Nekana. Dick calculated the location to be some thirty-five miles northwest of us. He had county maps, GPS, and notes galore that only he could decipher. We hopped aboard Dick's Honda four-wheel truck and learned of his research and mapping efforts. I was along only for the ride; Dick was the Captain of this outing.

We drove for miles and finally went through a virtual ghost town that had been Steuben, the little town that was the camp's mailing address. We were getting close; it was a nervous feeling as we crept along forgotten county roads before coming to a gate that warned of dire consequences for trespassers. Dick, with the authority of a prosecutor, opened the gate and we headed through it, driving miles on two-track muddy roads and came to a clearing at a lake. It was the footprint of our long-lost camp. There was little remaining that was recognizable to any of us. The place had been nuked, it seemed. Our faces were both stunned, yet inquisitive. This view was even more surprising to Dick because he lasted a few more summers than Mike and I, returning as an assistant in the craft and hobby shop with more status than just a camper.

I looked down to the lake and pictured what once was the swimming area and remembered the buddy system that the lifeguards had employed. Keeping track of one another on Bass Lake was a high priority that we all took very seriously, especially the waterfront director, my cabin's counselor. Brass tags with numbers were assigned, and each buddy was responsible for the other buddy's head remaining above water. I think I hooked up with cousin Mike quite often. He and I looked into the lake and reminisced about a dying fish we ended up calling "Frank," for no apparent reason. We played with it one evening using sticks as it floated upside down for a good hour, thinking we were the two comedians of the camp. It made us laugh from our bellies. Poor Frank, upside down and a slow tail was all he could muster. He was a goner.

Walking around instantly brought memories for all of us. Several, three-foot northern pike that we all caught, almost at will, came to our consciousness. Mike was certain he had old pictures at his house somewhere of these monster fish. Trout and walleye were abundant. They supported the Friday night fish cookout at an adjoining lake's picnic grounds with a massive fire pit and open kitchen shelter. The fish-cleaning station brought sneers to our faces, remembering the task and the odor.

I pointed to a spot that once had a cedar telephone pole that a small flying squirrel would climb up. The squirrel would look down at all of us campers for a while. Then Max, a tall handicapped boy, would coax him down. The squirrel would leap into the air, spreading his wings to softly glide around the open area and land on Max's shoulder. How awesome, a flying squirrel. Who would have ever imagined such a creature existed?

This was the same infield where Dick would fly his first model airplanes, with the whine and high pitch of glow-plug, single-cylinder engines made silent when they nosed into the ground. This was operator error most of the time. The plunge brought deep gasps from the onlookers.

We worked our way several hundred yards over to a spot that once housed the shooting range, where we learned how to handle .22 caliber rifles. I remember lying on old discarded mattresses. Thank goodness for the smell of gunpowder. All that was left was the dirt mound where the bullets would have buried themselves into the backdrop berm fifty years earlier. I reflected on capturing furry mice in the locked cabinets and pinning them by their tails to targets so we could shoot them, thinking we were some big-time hunters.

Dick was so fond of the hobby shop and the sounds of shop equipment— all distinct but recognizable—and the scents released from paint and shellac came into our memories. Dick built many planes. I built a wooden archery bow that I fabricated with much help from Russ, the older craftsman. The building that housed the craft shop was no more. As we surveyed the area, the gradual realization came over us that the camp was really all gone and there was virtually little left of any substance. Remnant steps, broken cement here and there, and our sketchy memories were all that remained.

We introduced ourselves to the couple that was up for the summer from Florida. They were fascinated that we wanted to come back to our summer camp. They offered us beer and we obliged, saying we had a cooler, too, and could join them on their screened-in porch in their modest newer cottage. It sat in the southern clearing of the property, facing the lake some 300 feet away.

Dick, with his attorney ways, offered proof that he had contacted the DNR agent to learn about the new owners of this condemned piece of property and the bidding they did to obtain it, all from county records. We had a wonderful hour visit. Amazing to us was the especially aggressive nature of the flies and mosquitos that day. They are legendary, but I had never spent time in the UP in June, and I learned that this first batch was super hungry. They were absolutely annoying beyond anything I had experienced. Thank goodness for the screened-in porch, and beers, and swatting hands.

We were asked by our host to sign a guest book to commemorate our visit. We were honored, and all three former campers signed their little book. They bid us farewell as we headed back to Manistique, fully satisfied that we had found and explored our legendary Camp Nekana. It was now relegated to a past life. We were all silent as we drove back to our weekend cabins. I'm sure we were all wrestling with childhood memories of what we had just unearthed.

The plot, however, thickens. Three weeks after our June visit my oldest son Rob called from his home in San Francisco, laughing away. I couldn't figure out why he was so giddy, and was confused until we both unearthed the unbelievable connection we had with the family that we had met at the old camp.

"Dad, didn't you recently go to the UP?"

"Yes, you knew, Dave and I and cousin Mike joined Uncle Dick and Jon in Manistique."

"Well, Dad, two of my longtime friends from MSU, Darren and Scott, were up at Scott's mom's cottage in the middle of nowhere. On the second day they looked at their guest book and noticed your signature, and it about blew their minds; they knew you were from Leland and had my exact name."

They apparently were so excited, and tried several times the next day to call Rob to expose their discovery. Losing cell service in the UP is quite common, and getting little fragments out about the happenstance took several redials. It finally came together in a clear cell.

I said to Rob after we shared more of the weekend, "This is like finding the proverbial needle in a haystack." It is indeed a very small world.

◄ ◄ ◄ ◄

Native Lake Trout at Isle Royale 1993

Isle Royale, located in the vast waters of Lake Superior, became an energized idea in 1993 with a simple comment during a winter's dinner at my parents' house when Dad announced he'd always wanted to go there. That little wish started the ball rolling to take the family to the least-visited national park in the U.S. I read that the daily attendance at Yellowstone is more than the annual attendance at Isle Royale.

Let's go with that picture as I describe the most beautiful piece of real estate, a thin forty-five-mile-long island in the middle of Lake Superior, accessible by boats from the Upper Peninsula ports of Houghton and Copper Harbor, and also from Minnesota's Grand Portage dock. A small seaplane also lent service with two flights a day. You'll see it if you use Google Maps. Hell, most people I know don't have a clue where it is, thinking it was a James Bond movie, or some place in the Virgin Islands. Nope, it is about seventy miles northwest of land, off the western shores of the Keweenaw Peninsula of Michigan.

The actual plans for the family trip took months to arrange. I had the pleasure of taking my boys on a weeklong adventure from Birmingham to Mackinaw City, taking the Arnold's ferry to Mackinac Island for a day of touristy events, just us three boys. Rob noticed that I had an expired registration sticker on the license plate at our motel the first day of the trip. I hate when that happens. After fudge and pasties and soda pop for a day, we headed to Houghton the next morning at a nice pace. It was a distance of 275 miles, and we would be staying at The Franklin Square Inn, right on the Portage River that runs through Houghton. This was 500 feet from our loading dock the next morning. Dave loved our room's view of the river and the piles of coal and iron ore at the various docks. We were definitely in the UP, with the many buildings of red sandstone and brick and wooden structures needing repair and paint.

Somehow we all managed to arrive in Houghton throughout the afternoon for the first evening. We were coming from all over the country. The Adams family was preparing the next day to board the *Ranger III*, the largest ship in the U.S. National Park's inventory of seaworthy vessels. The boarding took place in Houghton at the simple dock siding.

Dick was particularly excited, as he had heard of the legendary fishing that the island drop-offs offered. We had our sights on native lake trout. He trailered a seventeen-foot Boston Whaler, a boat he had recently purchased brand new. We all figured his lawyering practice must have been doing well in Bessemer. The five-hour crossing was wonderful as we continued to catch up on the latest happenings with siblings and cousins. The August weather was gorgeous, the waters calm. Legendary Lake Superior was not going to bring this crossing to its knees.

We landed in Rock Harbor and exited from *Ranger III* onto a very sparsely populated marina. True to the research, there weren't many tourists. How nice. Dick's Whaler was deftly unloaded with a smartly conceived frame-and-sling hoist system. We smiled as the Whaler dwarfed in comparison to the few yachts parked in the various slips. We were here to fish, not cruise.

The first surprise was minutes away. We lugged suitcases, backpacks and camping gear that we hastily secured at Meijer's the prior week. I bought hiking boots for Rob and Dave so they could become wilderness savvy in the four days we were staying. Somewhere past the marina was the only lodging complex on the island. When you're the only game in town, surprises usually accompany such conditions. I followed the signs that directed us to the lodge.

I entered the hallways of the Rock Harbor Lodge. Rob and Dave hung out with their cousins in front of entrance as I took care of the business of getting us registered. I signed in at the Lodge and expected a wonderful blend of Canadian, Minnesotan and Upper-Peninsula accents. Nope. Every employee that greeted me had a southern twang.

With furled eyebrows I asked, "Where are you kids from?"

The three in unison answered, "Tennessee."

All had nice smiles and were perfectly mannered. They were well rehearsed.

Apparently the senator from Tennessee was the chairman of a committee that oversaw our national parks. I had three Tennesseans helping me sign in. Mentally, I pictured our entire country being remembered by foreign visitors as a country whose natives had such strange accents. Well, at least at our national parks that year. I had to live with this anomaly, unless I could quickly add to our country's bureaucracy, placing these greeters under the jurisdiction of a nonnative, invasive species jurisdiction, which was a hot issue at the time. We would have to live with this constituency play. Reflecting back it makes me smile, but it was a little unsettling at the time. Their accents were best described as incongruous to the setting, so much for local content.

My boys and I settled in our rustic cottage with its kitchenette. They were so thrilled to be with their grandparents, aunts, uncles, and cousins. We were quite a group. It had been a few years since we had all been together, and these few days were already shaping up to be memorable and life-giving in continuing the bonds enabled through genetics. Lots of whiskey, 7-Up, Goldfish snacks, and beer filled our travel cases, secured in the nooks and crannies of our belongings. We unpacked and joined the family to continue the celebration.

Our first night had all the adults partying and bonding by catching up on my latest divorce. Attention quickly shifted to young Dave, who was banging on the door of our community cottage saying, "Daddy, Dad, look what I found."

He handed me a very muddy and heavy object he had found in the woods. It took a few seconds to realize that Dave had found a moose horn, or antler.

I didn't know the terminology, but yes, indeed it was a nice find. All of us watched as I scrubbed it in the porcelain sink, eliminating the dirt and moss. How cool was this! We had read in the preparation for our trip about the moose and wolves, but there is nothing like bringing home the real McCoy. Later I learned that only males shed their palmate antlers, annually. We had a gem, I would bet on it.

◄ ◄ ◄ ◄ ◄

The next day also brought a surprise that has not been matched in my cold-water fishing experiences. After a good ninety minutes of preparation and dealing with rambunctious sons, we hopped aboard Dick's prized fishing boat and began slowly working our way out of the marina. We were just heading out of Rock Harbor, located on the southeastern part of the island, when from up on the docks an odd looking fella, with clothes to match, yelled to us.

"Buoy Six East in thirty-five feet."

Dick nodded, comprehending the fisherman's message, and went out some two miles to a white buoy. He slowed the boat and let his daughter, Katherine, and my son, Rob, take the wheel as he prepped his homemade down-riggers and fishing lines to begin our trolling of the pristine waters.

The buoy warned of an underwater rock ledge. At six feet, it would be of no concern to our watercraft with its shallow draft requirement. The buoy was the referenced marker from the "hot tip" we received not seconds before departing the marina. In a matter of twenty minutes we were done for the day, lake trout beautifully tripping the lines every few minutes. A beautiful picture taken back at the marina shows our fishing group with the bounty that morning. Two nice four-pounders and two substantial twelve-pounders made up our harvest. We quickly iced our catches, and that evening grilled fish and red skin potatoes. One-dollar lemons and onions from the Lodge's provisions store created the finishing touches. Incredible tastes and satisfaction met our fishing group as all the family savored our catch and meal of the day.

◄ ◄ ◄ ◄ ◄

We departed Saturday morning after four remarkable days of hiking, sightseeing, and bonding. It blended a renewed strength in our family ties with a true American wilderness experience in a wonderful national park.

The *Ranger III* was mesmerizing as we listened to the calming hum of the powerful twin Caterpillar engines, and twenty-plus of our family sat throughout the inner cabin, all seated and prepared for the five-hour voyage. We were all relaxed, but ready to get back to the mainland.

About twenty minutes into the crossing, we were treated to a ten-minute interpretive talk by a fully ornamented park ranger in a very authoritative uniform, who was summarizing the history of Isle Royale and the pledge that the Department of the Interior, through the National Park Service, makes to the citizens of the United States of America. His charge was to forever protect the environment and holdings that are dear to us. All good stuff and no problem here, whatsoever. I liked the talk.

However, as he closed his speech, we learned that he believed that his particular authority was directed at leaving his park in its natural state. He explained to us that the park service has strict laws in leaving the pristine wilderness in her natural splendor and that humans should not leave their footprints in the sands, so to speak. He was evangelical in his performance. He concluded his talk with the postscript to all of us to, "never take anything off the island."

This stern warning caused about twenty heads of family members, including my sons, to simultaneously turn back to me in row six. Jesus, I thought, what are they doing? Thirty minutes earlier I had quietly placed the moose antler haphazardly into my sleeping bag and secured the treasure below my seat, thinking how happy I was to have a souvenir from our trip to Isle Royale for my children.

I quickly responded to my family's turning heads by also turning around and looking to the people behind me. I lucked out, as the entire group of seated visitors followed suit and everybody began looking at the row behind them. It was like a wave in a football stadium. I remained undetected and dodged the proverbial bullet. I had also wondered if he had the authority to issue a ticket for my expired license tabs. He sure as hell looked like he did.

◁ ◁ ◁ ◁ ◁

Frankly, I'm only a little ashamed. I wonder if the moose is still alive? I still have the antler in safekeeping.

CHAPTER 19
GRIEVING FOR DAD

MOM'S SADNESS, BUT ALWAYS A BRIGHT SPOT

MOM'S GRIEF-COUNSELING SESSIONS were scheduled to begin at the United Methodist Church in Birmingham almost nine months after Dad died. It was 2007, and she was deeply distraught over the loss of the love of her life, her wonderful husband and my remarkable father. We kids discussed seeking professional help for her, but we mostly prayed that time would bring relief from her melancholy.

She would never go to a psychologist; it just wasn't in her universe of acceptable professions. The lady in Mom would have likely remarked, "No, thank you," and meant it, even if her children suggested such avenues for her to explore to minimize her grief. Additionally, this was a woman still fully in charge of her faculties. She was the mother and we were her children, and I needed to remember that fact. Sometimes I didn't, and was reminded by her of her seniority in decision-making.

There was good news. On her own, she cut out a newspaper article that announced a new support group forming for those experiencing grief after a catastrophic loss. She reasoned that the loss of Dad fit that classification. We children thought this was a positive sign and were much relieved. The workshop was organized by three female ministers from Birmingham's network of churches. It promised to not be overly religious in its approach, and that fact alone was likely the tipping point for Mom. The workshop format met with wholehearted approval from her children.

The ministers had organized this gathering to help seniors deal with their grief. The group was to meet for six sessions weekly, beginning in the early spring of 2007. She enrolled over the phone and pledged one hundred dollars to the church's general fund. Mom simply declared the day she signed up for the class, "I'm going to give it a try." Then she burst into tears.

The loss of Dad created such a void in her life. It was an extremely tough time, not only for Mom, but for all of us. We found that when Mom cried all of us children would join her with our own tears and feel the deep emotions. We were a bit uncomfortable expressing these feelings in her presence, reasoning that our own tears weren't helping her with her coping skills. Mom wasn't at all embarrassed, and she just let her tears flow. Trust me, this was not her demeanor when we were young.

The general consensus was that we children certainly all missed Dad, no question; but we were devastated by the sadness that gripped our dear mother. I am tearful as I write this passage, remembering this particular period. We all wanted this daily pain to reduce its grip on her, and looked at the ministers' workshop as such welcome news. Such a constructive step forward, we all hoped.

The irony is that Mom had already shown very positive signs of successfully moving on in her life without Dad. The signs we observed were numerous. They included her dressing promptly and nicely every day. No housedress and slippers for this gal, not Mom. Staying in bed in the grips of depression was never part of her life. She wore very little make up, and was still a physically beautiful for a woman in her mid-eighties. She rode her exercise bike six days a week; it was still housed down in the damp basement in her Bloomfield Village home. All her children checked on her regularly, and she would frequently engage her grandchildren with some factoid or witticism, as a lifeline to her greater family.

She also had a network of girlfriends that she chatted with and saw regularly for bridge, or dinner—all sorts of outings. She looked forward almost nightly to a tall whiskey and diet 7-Up on ice, her drink of choice, at five o'clock. She now drank it with a straw, as her teeth had become sensitive, a side effect of her heart medication. The straw was the only hint she was a bit fragile.

Her adventurous soul and humor came through at times, especially as I was with her in what became the last months of her life. In the spring of 2007, she wanted a new car as her Buick had become a bit stale in styling, and though it had only 14,000 miles, it was her wish to get a newly engineered Cadillac STS. Oldest brother Fred and I conferred, and concluded, that while a little quirky for Mom, she could definitely afford a new car, and we would pay the balance out of her trust account. I helped that day with the transaction, taking the old car in, securing the new car, and getting her home with her new baby safely in her garage.

On our way to the house she dropped a bombshell on me. She was discussing her thoughts and a realization she'd recently had. It was basically that she would never marry again, because she wanted to be with Dad in heaven. Mom explained that this position could help her meet the next chapters of her life. She explained to me that she could see herself having a relationship with a nice man, but true to her earlier statement, never get married. I encouraged her to express her inner thoughts, as stoicism defined Mom and inner thoughts were usually kept private. We chatted about her future plans and desires, and it seemed almost therapeutic for both of us.

I reassured her that a companion who could join her to play golf or bridge and dine out would be very nice for her. I told her I fully hoped this would become the case in her future. As I was driving her new car home, I was encouraged with our line of discussion. Looking straight ahead as we drove west on Quarton Road, she revealed exactly what she was thinking and stated to me, "You are missing the boat just a bit, honey. I'm talking sexually."

Oh my God.

"Ding, ding, ding, hello?"

I about threw up with this unexpected piece of information and reacted very childishly for a man nearing his sixtieth birthday.

"You can't tell me stuff like that, Mom. You need to tell that to some therapist, or a minister, or a girlfriend." I faltered and thought I ended my near-rant, emphasizing that this new tidbit was, "not meant for me." I tried reasoning with her that she shouldn't be thinking such thoughts. "I'm your son, and the youngest one to boot," I reminded her.

My dismay continued. I was totally embarrassed and wondered how my mother thought like this. Why is an eighty-five-year-old discussing an interest in sex? It was unnerving to me. It caught me totally off guard and for a person noted for thinking on his feet, I was befuddled and extremely flat footed.

I imagined disclosing this conversation to my older brothers. They wouldn't believe me. I'm the youngest brother and their mother (as differentiated from my mother), would never say such a thing. This is the honest truth. I was confused and lost in thought. I concluded that Fred would not comprehend this desire and therefore it would not exist. That was his coping mechanism. Dick would make one quick grunt, buy some time, then respond with some off-color comment about our family lineage and somehow indict me in the mix.

Insight might have been useful here, needing to put two and two together. Mom had been reading several steamy novels lately, and my wife was always kidding me that Mom had this side to her that was very licentious. I thought this was a bit of a projection on my wife's part. I never quite understood her position, nor did I probe on either count. It was not the realm of a husband, or a son. I often am the last to know. Far better to be shocked than neurotic, was my reasoning behind this lack of insight.

Mom had indeed been reading nonstop, and would polish off a couple books a week. It kept her mind away from the sadness of Dad; that was the justification I used for her lusty interest in these novels. I searched Mom's storage garage to confirm my suspicions, and sure enough, *Always* by Lynsay Sands, and several paperbacks by Judith Krantz were unearthed. A quick review disclosed that these novels were full of passion and sex. Yep, Mom was fully into the steamiest popular novels one can purchase at a grocery store, and she was likely immersed into their lust and drama. These were facts and feelings and I could not pretend they weren't in her life. I wanted the white-picket fence illusion of my parents being together into eternity. Instead, I had a horny octogenarian widowed mother, and I questioned which of us needed counseling.

◁ ◁ ◁ ◁ ◁

The grief-counseling workshop couldn't have come at a better time. My belief was these sessions would be helpful for her to explain offshoot behaviors of the trauma she was experiencing. She would gain insights into her sadness and learn new coping mechanisms.

I also had repressed any further introspection into her sexuality.

I called to see how the initial session went and inquired into the highlights of the meeting. She said, with very little affect, "It was okay."

She went on and volunteered, "The minister is very nice and positive."

She continued, "I really liked her."

I asked further, "Do you feel it helped you?"

"Oh, maybe a little," she remarked.

She said it was helpful to know that other people were also having emotional struggles. She stated that she didn't feel alone in all her tears. This sounded pretty good to me and I pressed on, asking another question, thinking I knew the answer.

"Are you going back?"

"No," she responded.

"What?" I asked in disbelief. I was shocked, but not at all surprised.

"Well, honey, there was only one other person there who had lost a spouse."

I interrupted, reminding her she had said earlier said that there were nine people in the session, sitting in a semi-circle of chairs around the attending minister.

"Yes, that is correct, but seven had lost either a cat or dog."

I had to catch myself from snickering as I visualized a room full of grieving pet owners sitting with my mother. I tried to keep the light of the session still positive and engaged so she would change her mind about attending the following week. With my background in sales, and knowing the critical skills it often took to shift attention to the positive, I changed focus to the other person who had lost their spouse to help move the conversation in the proper direction.

"Did the other person have similar concerns that you could relate to?"

"No," Mom quickly responded, almost with her own chuckle about my efforts to keep the conversation positively engaged to salvage the therapy sessions. "The lady was in her early seventies and she was angry that her husband had died and abandoned her. She missed clucking at him."

I was tongue-tied, and before I could ask another question Mom said, "Honey, the gal sitting two over from me had a collie that reminded me of our Missy, and I could really relate to her pain. Do you remember Missy?"

"Of course I do," I stammered.

"Bob, I'm glad I went, and I know it will be good for those people, but it isn't for me."

This ended our discussion and her formal attempt at grief counseling. She was a very resolute person. She was not going back.

The irony of this is she took what was dealt and didn't complain or begrudge the forum, or whine about the intent and purpose of the workshop. It was not in her makeup to complain. She understood the level of grief that these people were experiencing with the loss of their pets. She probably would have liked something like that when she was in her forties with her own loss of one-year-old Missy. This church-sanctioned grief counseling was not going to help her with the loss of Dad.

She tried.

◁ ◁ ◁ ◁ ◁

We all missed Dad, and eighteen months after his death Mom joined him. It was her wish to be with him for eternity. Those eighteen months were living hell for her.

CHAPTER 20
BIFF

BEST FRIENDS

BIFF STAPLES AND I BECAME BEST FRIENDS as we navigated through grade school and junior high. He was my best man in my first wedding in 1972. Sadly, he is a recent widower after losing his wife Sandee to an unfortunate illness in 2012. They had been married for almost forty years. I had the distinction of introducing them when he was starting his business life after a two-year stint in the U.S. Army. It was a simple blind date that sparked their interest and subsequent courtship. I was reminded of this as I peered from the balcony at the church during the memorial service as the minister eulogized Sandee's life. I was fifteen minutes late because of Chicago's awful traffic. This was very much a payback to my buddy Biff, for his earlier bouts with tardiness.

In third grade, Biff's family moved to my neighborhood in Birmingham from Summit, New Jersey, after his dad was promoted to a sales manager to handle Detroit automotive sales for a specialty steel company. In high school, Biff was always taller and stronger than me, opting for team sports over golf. He always made fun of me, noting my sport was for wimps. Now golf is his life in retirement, and I am writing and still working, so go figure. We could laugh at the dumbest things. That is what best friends do.

My first recollection of Biff was his huge head sticking above all others in the hallways of Bloomfield Village School. This was the grade school in our neighborhood subdivision. No buses here, we walked to school from our houses. Biff's real name was William, but through all of life's changes, including college, the army, and corporate life, the name remained steadfastly Biff. One of my earliest memories was a class report that Biff did in fourth grade about Miles Standish and John Alden. They were leaders of the 1620 landing of the Mayflower on Plymouth Rock, Massachusetts. You know, the Pilgrims. Biff called them the Mayflower Boys. His elaborate story was that he was related to John Alden, and somehow the last name of Staples became the offshoot of these original founders. It totally impressed me that his roots were from our original founding families, and he had all these graphs and charts about his ancestors that clearly depicted the Staples' connection using "tree branches." It was clear only to Biff.

His report introduced me to genealogy. It contrasted with my own family roots, which was best be described later as "spontaneous combustion," in Ohio. My parents had this expressed belief that the United States was a melting pot, so there was never any great need to go back too far in the family's history. Today, with the ease of the Internet and accessibility, I may try to find the deep secrets of my ancestry, but not this week. After my parents died, I found pictures of a great grandfather, a minister, with many Indians in the towns along the Great Lakes in the late 1800s. Curiously, every fourth child in my family resembled some of the tribe's offspring, with very dark eyes and matching complexions. Oh, what a surprise. In fact, my youngest sister, Holly, must be most representative of this part of the mixture. Her rather full hair needs a headband to this day. Perhaps my parents' parents and beyond had deep dark secrets? Of course they did.

◁ ◁ ◁ ◁ ◁

The summer we graduated from high school delivered a memory that Biff and I bring up each time we meet, reminding us both of our forever bond. We took a summer remedial English class in Dearborn, Michigan. My reason was to meet and resolve my probationary status to enter Albion College in the fall of 1967, and Biff's, because his mother made him go. When she learned that I had enrolled, it became a necessity for Biff to join me. His parents thought it would be good for him, as he was entering Western Michigan University to play football, party, and attend class, in that order. He learned early on that he could only do two of the three. He often reminds me that I was like Eddie Haskell of Leave it to Beaver fame, often expressing in jest to his mom, "You look lovely today, Mrs. Staples."

Mrs. Staples always was charmed by me, thinking I was a good influence to her little boy, Biff (all six-foot-four of him). Oh boy, that was a stretch on several fronts. He still wants to kill me for insisting to his parents that I would love to have Biff join me for the summer refresher class. Refresher was a misnomer. There were many topics we both had never known.

Certain events made this summer-school attendance extremely memorable; as our eighteenth birthdays neared, Biff and I began to experience a world outside our cloistered environment in Birmingham, where we had grown and begun to mature. Still, we were mostly green, and I do not mean the color.

The refresher English class was to begin in late June and met two nights a week. It was scheduled to extend to the second week in August. The opening-night class was one such early lesson on learning to read and comprehend important details. These were skills needed if we were going to make it on the outside. Ironically, two different instructors reminded us within twenty minutes that we needed help. The two had quite different mannerisms.

Biff and I both had our registration letters that clearly showed we were to attend our English Review course in Room 201, beginning at six thirty on June 20 at the University of Michigan, Dearborn campus. After an early dinner, we drove to Dearborn down the Southfield, exiting on Ford Road, and we drove around grass berms and cement circles, paying little attention to signs and landmarks. GPS did not exist. We parked the car. We were even a bit early and headed through the back entrance of the school. It soon became obvious we were in a school environment with very typical linoleum floors and lockers. The smell of sweeping compound infused the air as we stepped over a janitor's four-foot push dust mop. He was just like Birmingham janitors; there was no stopping, or interfering with his routine. Straight, methodical, lines were mandatory as if he was mowing a green.

Going up the stairs to the second floor, we found a long corridor that we boldly entered. We peered through some wire-reinforced windows halfway down the hall and looked up. Sure enough, over the entrance was a small plaque with the room number, 201.

We entered the strange room that curiously had several disassembled automobile engines on heavy carts scattered about the perimeter. It was like a shop class from junior high, only much larger. It smelled of grease and oil like our Standard gas station on the corner of Cranbrook and Maple, a place we stopped at often on our way to school. At the station we were surrounded by the whirring sounds of pneumatic lug-nut drills, so distinct in their pitch; and then the station bells, their "ding, ding," the result of sets of passing tires compressing the small rubber hose as the cars slowly progressed through the station and around the gas pumps.

Biff and I looked at each other, puzzled. This room was more than a bit odd. Biff immediately went down the path that he was going to kill me for getting him into this unwanted situation. He also announced that he wanted a dollar for sharing the gas expense to get to our summer English class. He was very agitated. I think he was also nervous. The only thing I ever knew he feared was heights. I recall leaving him stranded in a near-catatonic state by pulling down the ladder several times on the roof of my house we had painted the previous summer. It made me laugh.

Young men meandered into the classroom; we quickly figured that they must be interested in better writing and grammar skills. They had appearances that were foreign to me: tattoos, t-shirts, pointed shoes, and cigarette packs rolled in their sleeves. Biff and I had on our white Levis, penny loafers, and brightly colored Banlon knitted shirts—pretty standard garb during the summer in Birmingham.

Ten minutes passed and the classroom was full of these very odd characters. Not one student acknowledged our presence. This strange feeling was further compounded when the teacher suddenly exploded onto the scene, his eyes fixed on us. From his point of view, we were clearly two irritations sitting in his classroom, on benches at a high-top table in the back of the room. I smiled at him, but this only brought deeper examination by the instructor. Something wasn't quite adding up.

The first words from the instructor came loudly, almost demanding an explanation, "And who are our guests tonight?"

With this grand welcome came fifty eyeballs searching and inspecting the two Martians from Birmingham.

I quickly and respectfully responded, "We're here for the refresher English class."

"Wrong room, this is an engine rebuilding class."

I turned to Biff. He was flexing his biceps as he often did when he was challenged by threats of this nature.

Under my breath I whispered to Biff, "Let's get out of here."

I moved forward to the front of the classroom with Biff just a step behind, very cognizant of the door to the classroom as our potential escape route. I looked to the instructor, trying to engage his eyes, seeking some compassion. It was nonexistent. At the front of the room I showed the instructor my paper with our notification of the time and room number that I had thankfully placed in my spiral notebook.

The good news was we had a lot right. Like right room number, right day of the week, and right time of the day, just the wrong college. He told us we were at Henry Ford Community College, a trade school, and we were supposed to be at University of Michigan's Dearborn campus. The U of M campus was to the west of this location.

Another "oh shit" in my life.

We quietly slipped out of the room, acknowledging our appreciation for the instructor when he wished us well in our class, and remarked that he hoped that reading and comprehension was in our refresher English class. He was a prick. He had fun at our expense. I suspected he thought we were from Birmingham or Grosse Pointe.

Jumping into Biff's car, we roared out of the lot and looped up and around Ford Road. The car was spewing clouds of smoke from the exhaust pipe and I thought how apropos for what we had just been through. Biff's hand-me-down car from his mom, then sisters, needed piston rings badly. Perhaps destiny was knocking at our door, based on our experience that night at Henry Ford?

Biff was ready to bail, already devising a plan to tell his mother that he was attending class with me as he partied at our other friends' houses. I pleaded with Biff to relax and explained that I had to attend the class. In my case, there was no way out. We arrived on campus and quickly stepped into the large main building. It was institutional, but much nicer than the community college building. We scurried down hallways and came to the closed door of 201. Our class was already in session. We had finally arrived.

Our new female instructor welcomed us after I briefly explained our earlier miscalculation and misfortune, and we apologized using our acquired Birmingham manners. It worked. She nicely introduced us to the class of fifteen. We fit better here, though we were certainly immersed in a broad mix of nationalities and ages. The fact that we were on a similar page and had attained some skill level made us feel more comfortable after the first abbreviated evening class.

I recall nothing about the course work whatsoever, but I do recall a large black female classmate, twenty-five years our senior, repeating her revelation of discovery at least five times every night we were there. She had a way about her that was not offensive and I'm sure made the instructor feel fulfilled in her life's work. The wonderful and assuring statement of note was uttered each time the instructor carefully exposed a rule of grammar that we should have all mastered years earlier. Our classmate would exclaim, "Mmm hmmm, I remember now." The "now" always floating, swirling and elongated, as she recalled rules of grammar coming from the depths of her memory to her own amazement. Our classmate was so urban and so appreciative for the insight the teacher would bring with her list of long-forgotten rules. The light bulb was glowing brightly for our classmate, much more than for Biff and me.

Biff and I would drive back after class to Birmingham repeatedly mimicking the phrase that our classmate immortalized. We literally buckled over in laughter and tears every time we repeated it. It makes me laugh right here, as I use these descriptive words to capture the voice that was so familiar forty-five years ago. I can hear it now. I wish I had a recording to play anytime I am sad. It would be the best elixir on the planet.

We did not quite make it for the entire eight-week session in our summer term, as we had many goodbye evenings planned with friends that were much higher on our commitment ladder. An interim report from U of M made this diversion possible. The report was sent to Albion in mid-July that I had been progressing satisfactorily in the course. Thankfully there had been no tests. I quickly received notice from Albion that I had been accepted into the graduating class of 1971. I had the signed letter to prove it. My parents were quite relieved. Albion had a very positive outlook, implied in their acceptance notification, that I would be done in four years and congratulated me for my success in my summer course. This is when I learned that checking boxes was what most of the world does.

I went back to class once more, basically to reinforce that I was really accepted to college in the fall of 1967. Biff was done, and had devised an elaborate way to receive the "fail" notification in the mail chute at his house. His parents would never know. I knew my parents would never open my mail, so I was covered. We took these previously scheduled nights and saw all of our friends for last hurrahs prior to going off to college.

◄ ◄ ◄ ◄ ◄

As I began this chapter I had several notes about memories with Biff. I now realize I could write a novel just on these events. I will leave that for later and only mention the plots here. Like his spirited vocalizations one morning heard by four female members of Meadowbrook Country Club as they were teeing off the fifteenth hole, during the summer I got him a golf-course maintenance job in Northville. He didn't realize that your voice, when talking while your mower was running, could carry for hundreds of yards. I pleaded with Andy Bertoni not to fire Biff. It worked. Then there was trip to New York's Niagara Falls. Biff locked me out of the motel room and I slept in the backseat of Rick Talbott's Ford Fairlane 500. Finally on this list was the time we were fishing on Lake Mitchell in Cadillac. Biff's brother-in-law threw the untethered minnow bucket off the pontoon boat in thirty feet of water as we prepared to bait our hooks while fishing with Mr. Staples. The list goes on and on. All topics to explore in greater detail at another time.

One more night continues my Biff memories at this juncture and brings a more recent memory, many years after all of our high school escapades. We were in our mid-forties and I was invited to fill in for a late cancellation in Biff's fall golf outing at Boyne Highlands in Northern Michigan with a group of Chrysler engineers and suppliers. There were sixteen guys and I was available at the last minute to devote three days to playing golf in the greater Petoskey area. Golf's popularity had exploded and the economy was supporting vast expenses around such recreation and entertainment.

Biff's group consisted of all good guys, not a bad apple in the lot. It's just that sixteen guys, while not nearly as problematic as two women together, all had different ideas of what constituted a golfing getaway in beautiful Northern Michigan. Biff and I had not spent time together for years; working and raising small children was mostly our charge in our thirties and forties. So we saw this as an opportunity to catch up and let our hair down.

We had grilled a spectacular steak dinner on two grills that had been supplied by the resort, and most of us had enjoyed wine—the beverage of choice for these executives. Cards seemed to be the evening game of choice, which was not my interest. Some read and others were on their new cell phones. Biff and I were two of the consumers of spirits, and as the evening progressed we began reminiscing and laughing. Many of our compatriots were beginning to retire to their rooms after a long day of driving and playing a late afternoon game of golf, not Biff and Bob. We had a second wind and were ready to venture into Harbor Springs, some ten miles from our encampment to check out the downtown scene and have a nightcap, or two. We invited several in our group to join us, but everyone was tired.

Biff and I drove to Harbor Springs. It was a very swanky and elite little town that was frequented by many wealthy individuals from all over the U.S. It was like a Michigan version of Carmel, California. We may well have taken a "traveler," since we had a plethora of cup holders in Biff's Chrysler.

We arrived downtown and stumbled upon the New York, a restaurant and bar one block from the marina. We entered the establishment with smiles pasted on our well-lit faces. To our delight and fascination, there was a very mature lady playing piano. She was all decked out in a cream-colored lace dress with a black button-type sweater. She wore heavy powder makeup, looking as though she may have been related to Mae West, perhaps a younger sister. She may have had a mole on her cheek.

Biff and I went to the bar and began a tab, opting for single-malt scotches. This seemed fitting, given the establishment. We would pass into the late evening with a more sophisticated beverage. They were charging eight dollars a glass for scotch. We didn't even blink. Biff went over to the piano player and charmingly requested certain show tunes from his vast recollection of piano adaptations. This gal was most accommodating, and mixed playing with singing and did a very admirable job. Biff thought she was absolutely the greatest act on earth.

He stuffed a ten-dollar bill in her glass on the top of the restored piano. This, however, was her glass of water. She was so surprised that this yahoo had stuffed money in her drinking glass. Mistaking it for a tip jar, Biff hadn't even noticed. I winked at her, hoping she would remain calm. She did. Thank God for her age. She let Biff stay next to her while he snapped his fingers and whistled to the tunes, totally enjoying his addition to the evening of entertainment. They made a great duet.

I went back to the bar and asked the bartender for a drink of the piano player's choice. It was indeed just water. No games were evident here. I quietly came back to her other side and slipped her a new fresh glass of water that she placed over to the left of the piano, safely out of the reach of Biff. She knew not to bite the hand that fed her. Biff was having a ball and it was great to see. Biff never noticed my moves and he placed a second ten dollars in the glass. The optics caused by the water magnified the bills, creating a very fat and puffy Alexander Hamilton and a large numerical ten. I can still see the glass with the wet bills resting on a doily above the keys on the piano. Mae West's sister just smiled.

We enjoyed a few drinks and got out of the New York for under a hundred dollars and drove back to our waiting beds. It was a great night to catch up on our lives and we certainly did. Neither of us played well the next day, blaming our errant shots on something other than scotch.

◁ ◁ ◁ ◁ ◁

Biff and I are still the best of friends and hopefully will experience additional chapters in our lives as we move into our newer senior phase. Thanks buddy for the great memories.

Bob

CHAPTER 21

MY BUSINESS LIFE

WEAR A DARK SUIT AND NEVER GIVE UP

GENERAL MOTORS WAS GOING THROUGH MANY ORGANIZATIONAL CHANGES in the mid-1980s. It took a Houdini to figure out who and where your buyers and engineers were located. This bode well for me financially. I was in a class of sales that they called an independent manufacturer's agent. Small manufacturing companies really had so little clue on how to do day-to-day business with GM, or for that matter, any of the then-Big Three (GM, Ford and Chrysler). They often elected representation by an agent versus hiring their own salesperson.

Many agents represented these businesses, and it was their job to know where the corporate bodies were hidden. It was the automotive buyer who needed a savvy relationship with a company, often because of an efficient and forthright agent who knew how to handle the nuances in the transactions to get the job done. Getting through uncertainty and keeping positive was the strength one needed. I had the resolve and fortitude to prosper in that environment. It was worth the rewards of a lucrative commission income.

The thousands of components used in vehicles created a marketplace in automotive parts that was quite remarkable for its amazing size. Original equipment manufacturers (OEM), often referred to as the Big Three, made fewer of their own parts and this trend continued through the nearly three decades I was in the automotive supply business. I do recall a buyer confiding with me about the risks inherent in sourcing small-dollar parts. While so little in the scheme of dollars for GM, if a small part didn't show up, or was defective, it could shut a line down, costing GM millions of dollars per hour in a line stoppage. There was pressure in the game we played, even for penny parts. I use to refer to myself as a "ground feeder," liking to stay below the radar, working best singularly, so I could get my job done.

The nature of commerce in Detroit was a symbiotic relationship where one procured and one supplied. This was about relationships, and this scenario worked well to make a very handsome sum of money acting as an independent agent—the famous middleman of industry. The best policy was where you represented both sides of the transaction to support a lasting relationship. There was much hand-holding and late-afternoon counseling with the principals you represented. My psychology major did come into use in this business scenario. My patience, after twenty-five years, however, began to wear thin.

I learned much about the game of representing these small family businesses. When I began in the mid-1970s, we represented firms that sold about $10 million of goods. Through changes such as adding assemblies, and in orchestrating a changing deck of principals, I built the business that represented over $100 million by 2000. It was a fun time, but with an unhappy junior partner, and my desire to exit, the stimulus to try something new was in the air.

◁ ◁ ◁ ◁ ◁

I need to be careful in my disclosures and identities, as much of our business life was about confidentiality and protecting the valued business relationship; always much to gain and to lose. I have changed names here to protect their privacy.

◁ ◁ ◁ ◁ ◁

Early on, I represented a local, metal rolled wire and tubular manufacturer that made the drivetrain assemblies for both transmission and engine-oil measuring, known as "dipsticks" to the world. I was amazed that I was given this responsibility so shortly after I joined the agency. Little did I know the relationship was nearly terminal, with a few gasping breaths left in the relationship. Be careful when a senior partner hands you a gold mine, it usually is booby-trapped. Especially when, after your second day on the job, he takes off to a safari in Africa for three weeks and leaves you minding the shop without quite telling you his plans, or the salient issues. Somehow I helped make it more stable and we prospered for two years longer. I met a lot of great people, and began in earnest to earn my spurs in the game of representing manufacturers. My indoctrination to handling the GM business came from Mr. Cameron, with his advice on where to park my car when calling on the divisions. After that, I was on my own.

Bob Cameron had no interest in how parts worked, or in their engineering. His life was about getting inquires and winning contracts with low prices, then matching numbers up to secured contracts and studying the commissions each month that were assigned to paper invoices. He had a very simple approach and never would stress about anything. Maybe he had learned this through his unfortunate experience in contracting polio as a young man. He survived the attack, and though he had subsequent leg paralysis, he likely made a contract with himself if he survived that he would never worry. He was described by one of our principals as a "water spider" in his approach to business. He had two remarkable traits: he was always on time and dressed to a T. That was Bob Cameron. He wore designer clothes and expensive footwear. Most buyers liked his display of affluence.

It was the late 1970s and I was on my Wednesday rounds at Chevrolet Central in Warren, Michigan, home to the famous Tech Center for General Motors, the largest industrial corporation in the world. GM always displayed their newest vehicles in their marbled lobbies. I was forever waiting in the lobbies of General Motors offices, calling on the plastic, rubber, and stampings buyers to make sure there were no issues on current parts, or to update the buyer so there were no surprises as we tooled new parts that they had contracted from our companies. The first three years was about jumping off the cliff and growing wings.

Gloria was the receptionist in the vast lobby of Chevrolet Central. She was efficient and had a memory of some repute. It took about a year, but she began to call me by my first name, always a good sign. I was there on that early November day to see Truman Biteman, my dipstick assembly buyer. He and I had begun to develop a decent relationship and I was in for an across-the-board price increase on the twelve parts I had on his "buying deck." I had studied the steel increase that the mills had forced on my principal and made sure I understood the math and calculations behind the requested price increases.

I was nervous this day as my principal was in for about a twelve-percent price increase, representing about $100,000 in needed annual recovery. There was another sizable player in this business area, and we split the business for dipsticks. My company needed relief, but privately the owner took the position that if I could get about half of the request he would be happy. These were my marching orders.

That morning I had arrived early in my office and consumed four cups of coffee, readying myself for the presentation to make the compelling argument of why we needed the price relief. This was a game of high stakes as several of these products were double-sourced, depending on what final assembly plant used them. Inflation was gripping our nation and price relief from contracts was essential to the suppliers, as we were called. I was reminded the day earlier that this increase was needed to keep the doors open of our business.

I registered that morning, waiting in line with my briefcase and topcoat. It was quite busy, with over thirty salespeople scattered around the lobby. I acknowledged a few of my compatriots with a simple smile and nod. After I was on the docket for Mr. Biteman, I headed over to the coat rack to hang up my coat. Mr. Cameron was insistent that I wear three-piece suits, so in my first two years I used any extra income to upgrade my wardrobe every few months. That morning I wore my new medium-weight, light gray three-piece suit, purchased from Redwood and Ross. I had just picked up the suit from Zack, the onsite tailor. He was such a gentleman, I believe an immigrant from Lebanon. He had quite a twinkle in his eyes. I can see his smile and the measuring tape draped around his neck to this day. His tailored suit was soon to take on a new shade.

The earlier coffee had my attention now and my rush had dissipated into a more relaxed state. Nature was calling. I headed through the heavy wood door that led to the small men's bathroom. With me was my manila folder that had all my information to help justify the price increases we were asking for on my dipsticks. The urinal was occupied, so I went into a stall, quickly deciding that my best attack was to sit down, do my duty and study my lists.

To my surprise the toilet had a new seat that was quite high. I guessed that it was to accommodate newer handicap access regulations that were on the news every night. Undeterred, I unzipped and let my pants fall down; my briefs joined them, settling around my ankles. I proceeded to sit on the new seat, smiling that it seemed indeed like I was literally sitting on a throne. It seemed funny to be so high off the ground.

As I was waiting for my muscles to relax, I opened my folder and began reviewing the changes in steel prices with the accompanied mill invoices that would help justify my company's need for relief. I began the process of letting my bladder go and was happy that I relaxed enough to begin the job at hand.

The seat was oddly shaped. I felt like a little kid so high off the ground. Then a realization came over me as I was sitting quite forward on this new seat and had been peeing for nearly half a minute. I realized that there was no noise or rippling of the water in the toilet. My attention quickly switched from my notes to the issue that had now become obvious: I had peed through the opening of the new seat and its large rubber bumpers, all over the back of my pants. They were sopped. My light-gray slacks had turned a new shade of charcoal gray. I was thirty years old and had had an accident.

There was one escape route and that was to put my pants back on and cover up my accident with my topcoat, which was hanging about five feet outside the men's bathroom. With the solution at hand, I re-entered the lobby, taking an immediate right and securing my topcoat from the rack, and as if I had the grace of a matador, the coat swung around me, covering the evidence of my unintentional mishap. I grabbed with one hand the wall phone we used for outside calls. I looked to Gloria and even interrupted her, generally unacceptable in lobby etiquette. She handled my interruption quite well after she saw the panic on my face. Very perceptive, I thought.

"Please tell Mr. Biteman I have an emergency at home." I had the phone near my ear as if I had just made a call.

She nodded in full comprehension, her brightly colored orange nail pointing to the sky. The meeting had been cancelled.

In a flash, I was out the revolving door, heading to my car for safe refuge.

Two days after my incident I made it back to Chevrolet Central, now with my much handled and tattered manila folder. I looked like a seasoned salesman in a very dark suit this time, as precaution. Truman received me warmly in his glass-surrounded office and had no problem with my midweek cancellation. I simply let him know that it was a family emergency. This qualified me for his forgiveness.

I immediately disclosed to Truman that I had the unfortunate task of requesting mid-year relief on our contracted parts. He interrupted my well-thought-out sales pitch and said, "Bob, how bad?"

"It isn't good, about a twelve percent increase across the board," I stated with apprehension.

A long pause now came between us. His head tilted down and he was studying a list on his desk pad. I knew not to interrupt.

"Bob, if I move you from 50% to 100% on the 233 and 378 assemblies, can you give me a two percent discount on those two?"

I quickly realized these were some nice runners for our company and we had fifty-percent contracts currently; this meant another $300,000 in new business for my firm. But I was panicked, as this was the wrong direction for my pricing negotiation.

"Truman, I need price relief."

"No, you dumb shit, I can grant you your twelve-percent increases, that's fine. I just want to teach our Milwaukee neighbor a little lesson. You've got to give me something, so I can get it through my boss."

I about barfed, as I had been authorized to settle for a six-percent increase. He was going to give me twelve percent on all my parts and also move our volumes up to one-hundred percent of their use on my two best runners with just a symbolic two-percent give back. It was a no brainer. I knew I could get this all approved by my principal.

Staying calm, I responded, "Truman, I think I can get that done."

He then said, "Good thing you were delayed this week, Bob. My other supplier was in yesterday with the wrong tone and wrong news."

The luck of the delay played itself out, and on that particular Friday he was buying and I knew this was a good deal for me and my company. He, too, likely had worse news the day before and this was a way to leverage his suppliers. The cards were played, and he had the knowledge of my competitor's pricing position. It was competition at its finest. I was also very lucky.

◁ ◁ ◁ ◁ ◁

One of the great lessons taught to me early on was to never give up. This wisdom was generally imparted to me by my dad, who often used this on the golf course to his great benefit in friendly golf matches. He always believed he could come from behind. and that belief seemed to go his way most of the time. This implanted philosophy played out in a sales call that I made with Bob Cameron in Adrian, Michigan. It involved a terrible first meeting at a GM facility with their newly assigned general purchasing agent. The plant had been sourced by GM Truck & Bus to be one of the first, just-in-time, Japanese-inspired module assembly facilities where the entire instrument panel and interior door trim were to be fully assembled, and then shipped to four North American truck assembly divisions. The sourcing of all the small plastics perks, like speaker grilles, bezels, trim-plates and air-conditioning louvers—all parts that my company was good at supplying—would be handled by this GM plant. This was a new way of doing business for GM, and this change in procedure found many potential suppliers missing the opportunity.

I filled Bob in on the business strategy, and he knew we had an opening based on the senior buyer from GM Truck that had given me this small bit of information. It was passed on as a "head's-up" opportunity. Bob wanted to attend the introductory meeting. I introduced myself on the phone to Don Rice, the purchasing agent in Adrian, and set up an introductory meeting. We arrived in Bob's big Toronado ten minutes early. This was a very old plant and was not at all like any of the GM facilities I had visited. The lobby floor looked like it had been laid in the 1930s, consisting of green and brown tiles. I read on the walls as we signed in that this had been an aluminum plant during World War II. One of many Michigan facilities that helped in the war effort, making parts for military planes that Michigan was so famous for, retooling from their peacetime charge of producing automobiles.

We were escorted to an office that looked like it had not been used in years. The entire plant was being readied with new enormous presses that needed thirty-foot ceilings. They were in the midst of a major upgrade. This older buyer smiled briefly and welcomed us to Chevrolet Adrian.

"At least I have two chairs to accommodate our meeting for you." It was kind of cute, and he also softly admitted to us that he was aware of the very-unlike-GM appearance that the facility exhibited.

I was going to be gracious and let it go, but Bob Cameron said, "What did you do to deserve this assignment?"

These words simply were ill chosen. Bob was trying to be funny. A silence hung like cold syrup and I almost stopped breathing. My stomach is still responding to these words and the scene more than thirty years later. How insensitive, I thought, and he's my business partner? How can a man who has experienced such sadness in his life with polio not have any propriety to this man's own issues?

Don bolted from his desk chair and came forward on top of his desk, scattering paperwork. Even with him looming over us, with his pointed finger at Bob, I realized he was a small-statured man dressed nicely with an expensive silk tie. In a fit of rage, Don let Bob know that he would not have any person insult him in his own office, and did not care to learn about our principal and "all their fucking expertise."

The meeting was doomed and about to end. I tried to salvage the encounter by shaking Don's hand, embarrassed myself, softly admitting, "Not one of our better first meetings," trying to ease the tension with humor.

Emotions were spent and out of control, and we left his office unescorted. Bob's expensive leather shoes clomped down the linoleum floor as his effects from polio etched a further notch in his mobility. He placed his fingers around the window frames to steady his shuffling exit down the hallways of GM Adrian. It was a momentous day for me; I had grown into a seasoned businessman and it was time for me to take charge.

I gave it the weekend, trying to reexamine the ridiculous and insensitive way Bob embarrassed this man in his own office, and tried to understand why Don was so reactive. Both men were wrong in their behaviors that morning.

The following Monday I had mustered enough courage to call Don. I wanted a follow-up meeting without Bob.

"Don, this is Bob Adams, might I have ten minutes of your time this week?"

This was my very sober sales approach.

"That will work. Pick me up tomorrow out front at 11:30 sharp."

This follow-up was slated as an apology platform for me to try to explain my partner's remarks. I wasn't sure what Don's motivation was, and we had only shared but a couple of words in a few very brief conversations. I did not know what to expect and was still nervous, but knew that I had to try to salvage the relationship and the potential business for my firm.

I was fifteen minutes early, a rarity for me. Don came out in his crisp beige topcoat and sat next to me in my car. With a handshake he said, "Welcome back."

I was speechless and simply astounded at these words.

He quipped, "I am impressed that you called me."

I told him, "I want to prove to you why we should have your business."

Don said, "Bob Adams, I checked you out. You're respected in Detroit."

We had two drinks and lunch at the Brass Lantern, Don was a twenty-five-year veteran and tough as nails. Three months later, after several quotes and meetings with my engineers and his people, Don awarded me all the injection molded plastic business for the new truck platform module he was responsible for sourcing. He greeted me that day at his office with these words: "I trust you will not let me down." He shook my hand.

◁ ◁ ◁ ◁ ◁

The lesson for me was many-fold. I had won a contract worth between $6 and $8 million a year in business, but more importantly, it gave me the courage and power to complete the buyout of a fading business partner. I assigned a full-time employee to this account. Don was a great friend in the end. Though there were bumps along the way, it was a great lesson in never giving up.

Rob at Frankfurt beach

CHAPTER 22

THE POWER OF FLOWERS AND PLANTS

THE LITTLE THINGS IN LIFE CAN MAKE A BIG DIFFERENCE

IN 1999 I TOOK A TWELVE-WEEK CLASS to become a certified master gardener in the state of Michigan. I was preparing to sell my automotive sales and engineering firm, and beginning preparations for my next business life. Flower, vegetable, and landscape interests had been an early undertaking of mine. I even did a stint with a seed company after graduate school for three years. With more schooling, I began to use terms like horticulture and agronomy; ever more sophisticated terminology to unearth the miracle that plants brought to our universe. They certainly do: ask any botanist. Nature and the vegetative plants that make up my surroundings are at the core of my spiritual connection, and I am thankful of their presence and contribution to my well-being. Like Native Indians and their spiritual constitution, it is in the woods and meadows and lakes where I find the blessings and connections to the universe, and right in my own backyard.

Each week I find and share a colorful bouquet or potted plant, enjoying them in my home environment. Flowers from the grocery store or a plant placed on my patio are a big part of my life, and certainly help in my daily happiness. My dear friend, Linda, finds greenery at small garage sales and shares her finds with me. Dr. Andrew Weil also encourages the purchase of weekly bouquets of colorful flowers to help lift one's spirits in his strategies for long-term happiness. Flowers are near the top of his list in his book, *Spontaneous Happiness*. It makes all the sense in the world; give it a try. Buy a bouquet or plant flowers to enjoy the year round.

◁ ◁ ◁ ◁ ◁

I was twenty-years old and home on college summer break. I was working in ground maintenance at the famous Oakland Hills Country Club in Birmingham, Michigan, for Ted Woehrle, the golf-course superintendent. In high school I had worked for four years for Andy Bertoni at Meadowbrook in Northville, Michigan. Here I learned to operate virtually every piece of equipment used in golf-course maintenance. Both country clubs had been wonderful summer jobs that got me up early and allowed me to finish the day early so that I could pursue golf and girls. Life was pretty simple, as it should be.

Actually, these summer maintenance jobs evolved from my oldest brother Fred's lead after our first jobs as *Detroit Free Press* paperboys. We were up very early to "do our routes," as we use to say. We had the greatest companion dog, Lady, a Springer spaniel, who in those innocent days could run free, i.e., without a leash. She selected one of us three boys to join on our daily paper routes. She also was our emergency morning alarm should we have chosen sleep over responsibility. Her nose, cold and wet, would bury in our sleeping faces should we have strayed from our wake-up routine. This experience began my habit of rising early and helped me when the golf course jobs came calling. I suspect my brothers feel the same. It has lasted a lifetime.

Through college, graduate school, and marriages, "Early to bed and early to rise" was my steadfast rule. Even over the last few years as a single senior, I have stuck mostly to this schedule. My great friend Steve Wentworth kept telling me that I would never meet anyone if I didn't stay out past 7:30 at bars and restaurants in Traverse City.

He was once again wrong.

I was getting to know my dear Linda at Minerva's, my favorite watering hole in Traverse City, Michigan. Early in our meeting one another, I announced that I was heading home to my dinner already in the oven, to watch the late news, in my case ABC's seven o'clock broadcast, and read my magazines. I told her, "I'll be in bed by eight thirty, asleep by eight thirty-five." How beautifully boring is that?

Linda bit, and emailed me. My goodness, there was interest even with my disclosure. She now admits it was principally because of my silver hair and bedtime routine. It has been the near perfect fit. Perhaps a bit exaggerated here, but we are both steadfastly in bed before nine most nights, with or without each other!

Rumor has it from my other night-owl friends that women come out of the woodwork after nine, and I have missed a whole flock. My retort to them is simple: "Any woman that would be out that late is not for me!" They apparently had no early morning jobs and obligations.

My duties at Oakland Hills varied. My golfing skills and past experience placed me as a valued assistant to my boss, Ted Woerhle. I was primarily the cup changer and go-to guy for the daily special projects. We summertime employees joined the regulars who were characters of all shapes and demeanors. There definitely was an unwritten pecking order that took time to recognize.

Ray, whom we called "Heavy Duty," syringed the greens in the afternoons to prevent wilt; he knew where every hose was located on the course, and nobody touched them or he would get in your face with life-threatening taunts. Then there were the Rizzuto twins; both may have labored much too long in the birth canal exiting their poor mother. They would have easily won the longest-cigarette-break contest, feeling their jobs were mostly to watch the female members play golf. They enjoyed viewing the grounds we maintained after a halfhearted morning push when their energy level was at peak performance. Stress was not in their life plans. Ernie, the union steward whose eyes pointed outward from his nose, told me that his Teamsters would "grind me up to never be fucking found." This display of temper was the first time I had ever seen his eyes straighten. His response came when I challenged him as to why I had to pay twenty-six dollars to be a Teamster union member for a summer job. A couple years later, Jimmy Hoffa disappeared about one mile from my work place. Wouldn't that be something if Ernie knew something about that murder? The regulars tolerated the summer help, but just barely, and vice versa.

The job of changing cups was about selecting new pin positions daily; it took some knowledge of the game of golf, combined with sound turf management. In effect, we were moving the players around the greens to avoid excessive wear and compaction—the curse of most greens. One of the additional high-profile jobs given me was cleaning the two toilets out on the golf course. The two bathrooms were in need of great attention. I had taken this as a challenge, as the toilets were surrounded by cinderblock and plywood and were very shabby in their appearance. They had been a low priority to the maintenance department until I arrived. Ted gave me the green light because he had been scolded by a female grounds-committee member about their horrible condition. I talked to Ted and suggested that if I put some effort into refurbishing them I could get them in much better shape. I got the boss's nod to proceed, and I did.

Two weeks of intense work followed the green light. Learning along the way, I spearheaded the renovation of these toilets and sinks. Paint, trim, sealants, caulking, and scrubbing were all part of my upgrades. I had a plumber come in and replace valves, floats, and rubber flappers. I even added a cloth valance window treatment to help in the look. Voila, after two weeks I had two very acceptable bathrooms, no longer just toilets. I would even sit on the commodes, no longer fearful of repercussions. They were so improved and near spotless in their presentation.

Something was still missing. It occurred to me that we had a couple of flower gardens up by the clubhouse. So, like a man with a mission, I headed in my Cushman Truckster to the gardens. Armed with scissors and makeshift vases, I cut two bouquets of various summer flowers. Various shades of blue, yellow, pink and white all were represented in the developing bouquet. After creating these two visual masterpieces, I drove out on the course and placed the arrangements on top of the porcelain tanks on each toilet. Perhaps not quite subject material for a Manet, but still pretty darn nice.

I had a great sense of accomplishment in the bathroom upgrades. I also created job security, as I would freshen up the bathrooms every couple days with new water and add new flowers in the ever-changing bounty found in the gardens as the summer progressed. I also discovered Glade aerosol that had several acceptable fragrances to help make the bathrooms even fresher.

I was surprised when Ted called me into his office on an early afternoon shortly after the new bathroom upgrades and the cleaning protocol was in place.

"Bob, get in here."

I walked in with my typical smile and said something like, "What's up?"

"Jesus, I've been here for seven years and we spend hundreds of thousands on the goddamn golf course and all I heard today at the women's summer luncheon was about the bathrooms and cut flowers." He went on, "This was not at all what my talk was going to be about."

He wasn't really pissed, just amazed, perhaps baffled. He said he took the compliments with bewilderment, not fully understanding where the ladies were coming from. The women golfers were finally happy about something was his bottom-line and was the takeaway message.

"I pass their compliment onto you." It made me smile because I knew it is often the small gestures that matter most.

Ted was not going to look a gift horse in the mouth and we both knew we had benefitted from the power of flowers.

◁ ◁ ◁ ◁ ◁

I realize that flowers have played a central role in my life, and that my horticultural background and master gardener certification really is a long-term and very unifying thread in my life. The interest has run through my veins with full intention and has spanned many decades. My writing has heightened this discovery and understanding.

It was my parents' own interest in gardening that got me started on vegetables and flowers. At our second childhood home in Bloomfield Village, we had almost an acre of land, and there was a very ample garden for all to enjoy. My parents worked very hard at its creation. We were introduced to the joy of planting seeds. We also had to learn about the responsibility of tending to a garden. This involved the necessary chores of weeding, watering, fertilization, and pest control. With their watchful eyes, we all selected seed packets that were of interest to us. Mom and Dad helped prepare the tilled ground in spring, and Mom would take the back of a wooden-handled rake and mark the plot that we could utilize to create "mini-gardens" of our own selections. How fun.

Flowers like zinnias and marigolds were planted from seeds, but we still mostly chose vegetables. Early favorites were radishes, peas, beans, carrots, yellow squashes, and cucumbers. We children got to select one tomato plant that was instantly staked, and this introduced us to potted plants from a local greenhouse. Tomato plants had such an earthy smell when you touched them, and their scent meant only tomato, nothing at all like the scent from the eventual fruit. If you closed your eyes and bruised a stem or leaf, you would experience the defining aroma of a tomato plant.

We hated weeding. It was a chore that Mom took very seriously, and though she allowed a bit of normal protesting from all of us children, she would gently remind us of the chore and task we had signed up for in the spring. Even with her perfectionistic nature, she never butted in to do it herself to complete the task. I'm sure she bit her lip many times for the good of our training. However, she was a taskmaster and it would not go unattended for more than a day or two. The weeding was to be done and we children knew it. It was where I was introduced to the term "nonnegotiable."

This was a great lesson and I often try to figure out her style, which was unique and the furthest thing from nagging, but she would look you squarely in the eye and you were miraculously made accountable for your chores from earlier agreements. She used logic and reason, not a quality that I found over the years in most of the women I ended up with. Yes, that's it, accountability. How refreshing.

Waxed (yellow) beans with their two cotyledons supporting the emerging leaves were one of my favorite vegetables; watching the first signs of their growth from the ground with their stems and curled leaves popping through the ground. It was thrilling to behold. We would also get a sense of how straight one's rows were made from the earlier planting of the seeds; not perfect, but most acceptable. Watching the waxed beans mature during their couple of months of growth was an incredible experience. I hope there are enough of us gardeners left to show our children that the world is bigger than handheld electronics.

The bean's first leaves led to many more, all absorbing sunlight to perform photosynthesis. This allowed the small flowers with pinkish faces to begin their mission to create more of their kind through pollination and subsequent fertilization. Within days, small minute first pods began showing. After several more days, the pods would elongate and it seemed like overnight would expand to five inches. First they were green, then turning yellow to attract our harvesting ways. This miracle all takes place in a mere seventy-five days from the drop of a seed.

I would take the shiny metal bowl Mom reserved for the waxed bean bounty out to the plot and straddle the two rows of bush beans. I remember bending over and picking the ripe pods, leaving behind the immature pods for another few days to elongate and mature. I learned that deep roots would help the plants anchor themselves from my aggressive harvesting hands.

Within an hour of harvest I would watch the trimmed and cut beans be immersed in boiling water on Mom's stovetop. Soon butter and salt topped the steaming beans, and they accompanied Mom's meatloaf and baked potatoes on our dinner plates. This orchestration of beans within a meal just could not get any better. Here I learned, and now recall, childhood memories and sensations from the garden and their destiny into Mom's kitchen.

Growing your own food, how good is that! Try it.

I was always good about picking up flowers for my third wife, at least for the first ten years. Part of the moving out of our marriage was she now had allergies to my flowers and had lost total interest in their life-giving properties. It was always a puzzle to me? Perhaps the flowers symbolized both the joy and the demise in our marriage. She once had interest in many of the horticultural and gardening endeavors at the farm and at our home, but over the years that joy turned to a burden, culminating in a total loss of interest. It was sad for both of us, and as I look back I realize that this behavior was illustrative of our lives together as a couple. I would return home to see dead blooms from my cuttings in tabletop vases and dead geraniums and brown alyssum in their pots from a lack of care on the upper patios. That is an environment I will never share again because it was not healthy, not for me or for the plants.

◄ ◄ ◄ ◄ ◄

One of my up-North acquaintances began a basic garden in my small postage-stamp-sized yard surrounding my wonderful loft in my new digs in Beulah. My loft is three stories and overlooks beautiful Crystal Lake in Benzie County, Michigan. It is late winter and already I am planning the charge next month to add outdoor plants, blending annuals with the established perennials and putting some basic structure to the haphazardly conceived side garden. It has an undersized rock that cost a fortune and was the doings of my landlord's former girlfriend. You instantly know it was placed there by a well-intended human, but is totally out of place and symbolizes so much.

My personal downsizing brings with it a much more simplistic approach to my relationship with the plant world. I have budgeted one hundred dollars and have a three-prong approach to its creation. My plan is to divide a friend's perennials and intersperse certain shade-loving plants into the existing garden. Having just moved in September, I need to watch a season of display before I can assess the garden's full needs. Perhaps I'll add a couple of annual showy colors that can take shade and dry conditions. It will be beautiful, guaranteed.

I do have the wonderful opportunity to break virgin ground on the only sunny spot behind the loft, off my little patio steps. It is mostly sand, piled by the work when they did the basement and deck footings. It needs soil amendments and fertility, but it will be transformed into a four-by-eight-foot vegetable garden. This year I will mostly plant multiple tomato and pepper varieties. The patio will have all types of potted creations with the blessings of my girlfriend, who loves antique pots and planters. She creates these wonderments from her dollar investments at garage sales. I am so excited; a gift this spring of creating gardens to fully enjoy.

The last plant this year that I will purchase is a gift to me that I will leave here for as long as it can survive, hopefully past me. It was introduced to me at the side driveway at my parents' house in the 1950s, when they first planted a fragrant spring woody bush that will take years to fully mature into an eight-foot specimen. It is a *Viburnum burkwoodi*, or Korean spice plant. It is of average appearance in its leaf stage, but the fragrance coming from its three-inch pink-and-white flowers is something no plant or bush has ever matched. It is hard to have both attributes in a plant. Like cinnamon in a baked roll fresh from the oven, it has an evening scent that wafts through the air and curls your toes. It is awesome. It is popular and prevalent, so somewhere most readers will have been mesmerized by its nighttime fragrance.

CHAPTER 23
UNCONDITIONAL LOVE

PETS IN MY LIFE

MY FIRST INTRODUCTION TO PETS was in our small, cramped Washington Boulevard house in the early 1950s. We had a beautiful black-and-white Springer spaniel named Flush. Joining her were two cats named Salt and Pepper. Apparently with such fancy names, my parents were already trying to keep their lives simple and would need little effort to remember their names. Their first three sons were named Fred, Dick, and Bob, so there was little pretension from my parents on naming anything, even children.

Pepper may have succumbed to my folly when she delivered a litter of kittens after the ride we gave her in our Frigidaire clothes dryer. Roger Handren, my next-door neighbor, and I got into mischief while playing with this female cat. At the age of four we had mastered the ability to climb on top of the white porcelain dryer and turn the large dial, getting the beast to rotate. We combined this skill with grabbing the cat by the nap of her neck and placing her through the door into the dryer. This gave the cat the ride of her life. It didn't last long with the racket, but we got the attention of the sitter and all hell broke loose at 1885 Washington. Not one of my better moves. The cat was soaked from being out in the rain and we put two and two together to arrive at such a clearly obvious solution. We hadn't even had our arithmetic tables at this age. We all survived that calamity and moved on to another day, likely a little wiser.

Mom was a perfectionist, but loved a house full of pets. We children think it was her reaction to her upbringing in New York with her father, a strict, no-nonsense, corporate attorney, and her lack of pets growing up. She was going to fill the house with children and pets. That was her charge and calling, and of course, playing golf for therapy from this calling.

We had in our two childhood homes a plethora of pets that included fish, birds, rabbits, hamsters, gerbils and, of course, cats and dogs. Mom was not into exotics, though I realize today there is a fine line. The only real recollection I have of parakeets was that one of them turned up in the toilet bowl in my sisters' bathroom, quite dead. We were taking care of our regular sitter Martha Moody's prized bird, and I was cleaning the cage and also adding new water and seed. God, could that bird shit. It seemed brilliant to place him in the pink bathroom while I attended to his cage. Martha was on vacation and was returning the next day to fetch her baby. He was a biter too, but a beautiful yellow parakeet.

Using a firm grasp, I captured the bird, and then released him into the upstairs bathroom. He landed on the valance of the bathroom curtains quite pissed at me, squawking away. That was the last I saw him alive. Apparently birds are not strong swimmers. After fifteen minutes of cleaning, I focused enough to go retrieve the bird. As I looked throughout the bathroom it was a rather late discovery that found him floating in the toilet bowl. Martha handled it well and we replaced him with one of Dick's nine birds. A different color, though, and another childhood trauma was diffused with an acceptable solution.

◄ ◄ ◄ ◄ ◄

Twinkle, our tabby female, was acquired just as we moved to our Bloomfield Village home in 1954. She was constantly pregnant and often delivered her litters in the clothes chute right on top of our dirty clothes. The clothes would be sent down the twelve-inch square chute that was upstairs in the larger pink-and-gray bathroom, and collect in a two-by-three-foot bin that was a built-in to Mom's bedroom closet. This was the same route Twinkle would use in her hour before delivery.

I remember the builder and painter developing this little clothes chute to the delight of my mother. Sally, my sister, used it as an echo chamber to listen to the parents' cavorting. I thought that smacked of invasion of their privacy. Plus, I didn't ever want to hear that anyway. Books were better.

Dad hated cats, but the fact that Mom felt that cats were part of the family experience, and were what her children wanted, caused a tempered reaction from his very strong position. He would give Mom his famous endearing look

Lucy

Tigger asleep

and then shut up. It would have been a nice quality to inherit, but sadly, my mouth often moved before my brain was allowed to screen its utterances.

My siblings and I observed Twinkle giving birth to kittens a couple times a year for several years. The cat would eat the placenta, lick the amniotic sac from the babies, and soon begin nursing the precious kittens. The afterbirth would necessarily ruin some clothes, but generally Mom always figured out how to get rid of the telltale signs of Twinkle's labor and delivery; she may well have tossed many of the clothes. Mom would allow the cat her week in the clothes bin, and make us put our discards in an old temporary hamper; taking masking tape she would crisscross the pink door to keep it shut for the week-long moratorium. All this to get the little kittens launched. She would eventually move the new feline family into a very nice, waxed cardboard container that had printed the word "eggs" on all four sides. This was the preferred home and nursing station for the baby kittens. I recall several times taking kittens in our red wagon and selling them for twenty-five cents to neighborhood children. Several were returned, as we always had a money-back guarantee if they could find us.

This affinity for pets was evidenced with a much deeper bond when it came to the many dogs we had throughout our childhood. After the loss of one of our Springer spaniels, I recall for the first time my mother outwardly sobbing over the dog's sudden death. Missy (aka Mistle), the young Springer spaniel we had for less than a year, was hit and killed on one of the residential streets in our neighborhood. She was a bundle of energy and I'm sure today she would have been classified as a recognized ADHD pet. Mom adopted the puppy when she became an empty nester, when my youngest sister Holly, the last of her children, left for college. The bond was very strong. Missy's unbridled enthusiasm got her in trouble and was the root problem that fateful day.

I had called that Sunday from Traverse City, where I was living, to hear Mom sobbing, announcing the news of Missy's death. She was having a difficult time dealing with this loss. The news brought tears to my eyes; at twenty-one, I had a difficult time dealing with this in my own limited emotional makeup. The death of the dog was an issue, but the tears from my mother, who rarely showed emotion, were even harder to process.

Dogs were a big part of our lives, and as I look back I realize that these companion animals created a thread through my life that I have richly benefitted from, with their unconditional love that they so easily exhibit, at least most of them.

◄ ◄ ◄ ◄ ◄

Lucy was a rescue dog from the Cherryland Humane Society of Traverse City, Michigan. She came in my life for about ten years. She was what the shelter called a BBD, standing for a run-of-the-mill Big Black Dog. Apparently these were harder to find homes for as rescues. It was conjectured by many that Lucy was a product of Rottweiler, Retriever, and a little German shepherd. She arrived one sunny day on my farm after Jessica and Carol went to Traverse City to "just look." I find that happens a lot with women. Though the first few months proved that Lucy had some issues with skittishness, especially around humans with hats, she gradually became an absolute delight, and our family's love helped her exhibit her gentle ways.

She was massive, especially her barreled chest. When I came home after days of being absent she would go bonkers, so excited to see me. She thought she was still a little puppy, never realizing it took all my strength to calm her down and deal with her mass. Throughout her entire life, her excitement in seeing me was always apparent, not matched by other females under my roof, I might add. I often described with my humor to my kids that she likely had "been caught in the birth canal."

This comment, meant in a loving way, attested to behavior that could be characterized as a bit slow. Give her a stick and she would demonstrate no interest in chewing it, whatsoever. The simplest of tasks was beyond her capabilities. She was a beautiful dog, especially her face. I am so happy that I took a picture of her on top of the sand dunes in Leelanau County just a few years ago, when I was first using my new iPhone. She looked so intimidating and this always brought comfort to Carol to have this watch-dog-like appearance. She'd let out two barks and that was it. She was indeed a gentle giant, in all ways.

Lucy died this past winter and this news saddened me, bringing back all the pet losses in my life. Carol had moved out of our previous home into her own condo, and this necessitated Lucy moving to Carol's nephew's home that had lots of acreage. The end came quickly and I hope it was not from a broken heart, as it could well have been. It was a rough time for all.

Lucy also was a low-ranking female in the animal kingdom hierarchy, and her brief period with a miniature terrier named Bear created months of anguish in our attempt to manage two dogs. Jessica somehow convinced her mother to get this specific breed, with the story line that poor Lucy needed a companion. Bear entered our family as a rescue, having had two owners in less than six months. This should have been the warning cloud, so massive and dark, clearly an indicator of problems on the horizon. We overlooked every sign during the adoption, because he was so cute.

The major issue that lost my support for Bear wasn't his biting of several service people or a couple of uncles. It was his wandering ways at our farm, leading poor Lucy astray. Their roaming and exploring the woods, and ultimately arriving into dens of porcupines—this is what spelled his doom with me. Three events in less than seven days led to three veterinary visits and treatments totaling $2,500. The bottomline, not one quill in Bear's mouth or paws, but hundreds penetrated Lucy's face and mouth. She would follow that little shit around in his escapades and he led her into every porcupine battle while I'm sure she was protecting him from harm. After a heart-to-heart family meeting, son David and stepdaughter Jessica took Bear to the Humane Society and filled out the paperwork. Bear was reentered into the world of the homeless. I do have some empathy for him, but very little.

◄ ◄ ◄ ◄ ◄

Abbey was a yellow lab that lived the first five years under our various roofs in Bloomfield and Leelanau. She lived an astounding seventeen years; the last twelve she lived with Dave and Rob and their biological mother. I had lived through all her chewing the first few years, when she ruined about everything. The trainer claimed it was the result of her separation anxiety when Carol and I would leave for work. This same trainer, who made house calls, after lots of money and frustration, quit. I deduced that she had met her match in Abbey.

I finally lost it one day after Abbey ate my brand-new plastic sprinkler when I was attempting to water the yard and gardens. It was snapped off and chewed into smithereens, the hose flooding the spot in the lawn where it had been set. My stress level was a bit high that summer; she moved out of my house that afternoon under the protective custody of my son David.

I knew Dave would enter the world of sales after he got Abbey to be domiciled in his mother's house rather than mine. He took the approach that Abbey needed one week for Dad to cool down and his mother accepted. Somehow the right chemistry existed in this household and Abbey endeared herself for twelve years. I was proud of Dave for orchestrating this resettlement; never in a million years did I imagine that it would work.

I remember Dave driving back from Chicago a couple of years ago to be with his mother, joining Abbey in her last days. His skills at handling crossroads such as these are wonderful, and I am amazed at his strength of heart! It was certainly not one of my particular strengths. I had just watched a Saturday college football game at Traverse City's Blue Tractor and was walking to my car parked near the Boardman River weir. On my way up Union Street, Dave called, his sobbing quite evident. He had been with Abbey as the veterinarian injected the barbiturate to end her suffering. Age was her final curtain, after overcoming about every calamity dealt to her over her seventeen years. She had been run over by my tractor and hit by a car. I was overcome with emotion and my tears started.

Forty years earlier Mom had called me to inform me of our Missy's death after being hit by a car. Both calls took place in Traverse City. This juxtaposition brought forth emotions that shook my foundation. I felt so much relief, which is the beauty of tears. I was proud of my son and thankful for my own mother. The power of tears and the realization of how our companion animals mesh into the fabric of our lives became so clear on that cool day in October.

◀ ◀ ◀ ◀ ◀

Ironically, dogs and cats entered my business life in 2003 after a serendipitous comment brought to life a product we developed called cherry Hip Bones. Carol and I, during an evening of partying, learned that Michigan State University had several patents for their scientific discoveries that tart cherries had anthocyanins, which were natural Cox 2 inhibitors and touted to offer relief from the pain associated with arthritis and gout. Major drug companies had discovered this same anti-inflammatory and they were in the process of selling billions of dollars of their Cox 2-inhibiting drugs to humans. In our brilliance that night, we decided to make a cherry dog bone that we would market in the U.S. It just made sense that dogs were getting bigger and older and they suffered from arthritis just as humans and at unprecedented levels. A daily treat could be given to a dog to help deliver relief to their hips and joints at a tenth of the cost of drugs, or so we theorized, and bet the proverbial farm on it, and I'm not kidding.

There was a movement afoot to once again "let food be thy medicine." A quote ascribed to Hippocrates, both a physician and philosopher, from 430 BC. We simply thought that this was just a great idea, and a great direction that the health industry and government would encourage.

Nope. We had apparently had not met the FDA and the U.S drug companies that were in each other's hip pockets. A food product cannot make such a claim. To make matters worse, they regulated claims more heavily for companion animals, which meant dogs and cats, than humans. So much for freedoms in the U.S. Gosh, there seems to be a pattern I keep unearthing in my life.

I had been getting to know the licensing agents at Michigan State University on an entirely different project, which had made more sense with my background in automotive components. This engagement involved using cellulose fiber and orienting this natural fiber into laminates that could be developed into structural panels for automotive applications. This was the beginning, actually a continuation, of using nature's bounty in the form of plants to make industrial materials. Henry Ford, the founder of Ford Motor Company, was also an avid inventor and visionary. He saw great uses in the soybean, which was just gaining popularity in U.S. agriculture in the 1920s. Ford's early work just prior to World War II also included cellulosic fibers, including hemp and flax meshed in a resin from soybeans. Now this made sense to me, and I was on an evangelical pursuit to help my graduate alma mater, Michigan State University, find homes for its "intellectual property."

It didn't prosper. The automotive companies were in dire straits, barely hanging on for dear life, and new technologies would have to wait for another day.

In a natural extension of getting to know the operatives in the patent office at MSU, I pursued licensing for my claims in dog bones with a phone call to one of the agents I knew. The licenses for the Cox 2 cherry discovery first went to a billion-dollar player in human health. However, I was informed they had not locked up rights to companion animals. So, after a year of wrangling, we did. It was a package of licenses, salvaged by Carol, when I lost patience with the due diligence procedures that took forever with the university.

Finally, after two years and many roadblocks, we began producing our Hip Bones—The Original Cherry Dog Treat. After five more years we sold the brand and the patent rights to a California-based supplements company that markets the product formulations supported by their national distribution.

I am no longer affiliated with the brand, but still very proud of the product and the care we put into the recipe to deliver the healing power of cherries, flax, added calcium, and antioxidants. It was an interesting ride during a difficult time.

◄ ◄ ◄ ◄ ◄

I started this chapter with the story of Pepper, the family cat, the one I placed in Mom's clothes dryer to the astonishment of one of my sitters. It was not a good move. I end with a tribute to another cat, Tigger. I introduced Tigger in the beginning of my memoirs as a valued companion to me, hanging with me in my darker hours. He was a lifeline to me. Tigger, surprisingly, is a bit of a complainer, and this last year, as he nears his fifteenth birthday, he has become less fun. This may be a bit anthropomorphic. We are a team together, even if we are both a bit grumpy.

I recalled about ten years earlier when we had taken Tigger back to our new Bloomfield home after an unsuccessful year living full-time at the farm. That was one long winter. I had females who missed their friends and felt isolated in the hills of Leelanau County, needing to get back to civilization. Son David was also having some teenage issues with his mother, so I decided it was time to reboot back to Bloomfield for the good of the clan, and we did.

Tigger was a very ruthless hunter in those days, particularly fond of bunnies, voles, and songbirds. He learned much on the farm as a young rescue, and brought these skills to Bloomfield. I saw him one winter day try unsuccessfully to tackle a squirrel off the back porch. He had not been around squirrels at the farm. Tigger had this ruthless predatory nature, but in contrast absolutely loved humans and was obsessed with visiting everyone in the new neighborhood. Food and being petted were his priorities.

He also exhibited one of the oddest behaviors I have ever seen in a cat. It started with taking Lucy on a walk in our hilly neighborhood. Tigger would appear, coming out of the bushes at the foundation of the house and through the neighbor's lawns, and begin to follow us. All the strict commands that dogs might understand to stop them in their tracks, a cat doesn't at all comprehend, or care about. Tigger would safely, a hundred feet behind us, follow the leashed Lucy and me for the thirty-minute walk. I did this just about every day, and Tigger, if in the yard and not sleeping in the house, would follow us for the duration. Neighbors would smile in total disbelief, such a sight this was, always a hundred feet behind us, walking in the center of the street.

Carol had identification tags made for Tigger that said, "I am a pest" with our phone number. On the opposite side it said, "Just let me go." Our neighbors never read these tags. Phone call after phone call was the weekly norm the first year we moved back. All callers assuming Tigger was lost and we must be missing him so much because he was such a good cat. Nope, that was the furthest thing from the truth. He did not favor any particular neighbor and was letting his own curiosity and his sense of adventure dictate his visits. We tried to make him an indoor cat, but it just didn't work. I recall the veterinarian asking whether Tigger was an indoor or an outdoor cat.

I said, "I don't know; he's whatever is the cheapest."

I liked Tigger, but he was simply a cat.

◄ ◄ ◄ ◄ ◄

Years later I received a letter from the condo association that governed where Tigger and I were living. Tigger, apparently, had befriended the "wrong types" and this resulted in a letter admonishing me as a negligent resident for not adhering to the strict code about leash requirements for pets. The next day, I tried a leash, thinking Tigger might actually like it. It did not fly. I dragged him for fifty feet down the cement driveway into the circular roadway at the complex. He was clearly not going to be part of this nonsense, come hell or high water. It was a scenario meant for the much-stricter laws of the Humane Society and county animal control officials.

Bob and Dennis

CHAPTER 24
POLICE STORIES

MY FANTASY WAS REALIZED

I HAVE CHOSEN A FEW STORIES INVOLVING POLICE that are worthy of a new chapter. After all, these memoirs are stories of insights gathered from my life's experiences and my inventory of police encounters are amazingly plentiful.

Most all are funny with nice outcomes; however, in Chapter Two, I described the aftermath of my duplicitousness in stealing a car in eighth grade. The fear that was exposed by my criminality knocked some good sense into my head after my mischievous behavior with junior high friends. Thankfully, a local cop taught me a lifelong lesson that scared the bejesus right out of me.

Even today one of my bar buddies is a retired Detroit cop. We relive funny stories as if I'm in his police fraternity, bonded by sharing war stories on both sides of the ledger. I even worked as an undercover "cop" in the 1970s, so these police stories with their continuing connective threads have woven many warmhearted memories into my life.

Police are all quite human; they simply have to perform roles for the perceived good of society. We hire them to protect us, enforcing ever-changing laws, and use our tax dollars to pay them. I always respected their uniform and recall chatting with them even during protests I attended to end the Vietnam War. However, the law and police's role have changed in my sixty-plus years. The stereotype of the friendly cop seems to be a lost, or perhaps a dwindling attribute in today's men in blue. The enforcement model seems to focus on speeding and alcohol in my up-North world, and a wary eye on both sides now seems to be the bridge between the citizens and the local cops. Also, I ask, why do we chase marijuana users? Okay, enough of that. I'm simply going to tell a few stories I experienced in police enforcement that I found very funny.

The first real recollection of a police incident actually arose out of a family story told by Dad that was embellished over the years. I did not experience the actual event. The scene, however, took place right below my bedroom window at our first little house on Washington Boulevard. It was retold by my father, as he shared wonderful stories of his life over the years with his friends and family. This particular recollection was about the night a police officer thought he helped Dad home after an evening of celebration at the bars in Royal Oak. Birmingham allowed no alcohol by the glass, hence had no bars. This forthright cop helped a very inebriated Doc Adams get home to his very understanding wife. The truth, now revealed, is that it was a case of mistaken identity, and remains that to eternity.

One long-time friend of Dad's was Bob Seiler. Mr. Seiler had three daughters and they lived several houses up Washington Boulevard. The Seilers and Adams were best of friends, going back to their Ann Arbor days at U of M, and this friendship allowed this mistaken identity to progress to its conclusion that night. The evening might have tarnished Dad's reputation, but not likely; he had enough goodwill to balance any minor personality flaws. Bob Seiler was in industrial sales, and likely had a side to him that was fun loving and wild, exhibited here when he was away from his family role. This is how I knew him, as a father and husband, and I never saw him inebriated at any of our neighborhood functions.

Mr. Seiler had a strapping and handsome look to him, as did Dad, and people would occasionally mistake them for one another. A Birmingham police officer fell for this same identity issue after pulling over an overly cautious vehicle creeping down Lincoln Avenue. He discovered behind the wheel an individual he thought was Doc Adams.

It was the early 1950s and he felt it best for all to get the good doctor home where he belonged. The car had been pulled over on Lincoln, which was 14½ Mile Road, just down from Woodward Avenue, for you that understand how greater Detroit's streets are laid out. He placed a very compliant Mr. Seiler in the front of his patrol car and immediately turned off the red blinking lights. In his gesture of compassion, the officer drove his secured drunk driver safely into the driveway of 1885 Washington, where he was going to deliver an inebriated Dr. Adams to his wife.

It was nearing eleven and the doorbell rang; Mom answered the door in her robe, very puzzled. She noticed a uniformed police officer tipping his hat and almost apologizing for the intrusion.

"Mrs. Adams, how are you tonight?"

"Fine," was her slow and drawn-out response to the officer, as she tried to figure out what Bob Seiler was doing propped up by the officer at her front door. Dad was apparently fast asleep in their pullout bed in the back study that served as their bedroom in our small bungalow.

"Doc Adams was with his buddies and may have had one too many in Royal Oak tonight." The officer went on to explain that they had moved the car and it was now parked over on Pierce and the doors were locked. He handed the unfamiliar keys to my mom.

"Well, thank you." I'm sure she was trying to figure out the joke that was seemingly playing itself out on her front porch.

The officer went on, "My wife loves your husband, and I remembered where you lived because we brought one of the kids over last year to see him on the weekend." The officer then added, "Good night, ma'am."

`"Good night." Mom was still very puzzled.

`The door closed, and Bob Seiler opened his eyes very slowly and said, "Hi Lou, where's Fritz?"

OFFICER'S DISCRETION

Dad and I were in his green Plymouth when we were pulled over for speeding. We were heading down Lincoln Avenue to go to our new house in Bloomfield Village to meet with the builder to review some hardware choices for the cabinets in Mom and Dad's bedroom. It was a late fall afternoon and the elm and maple trees that lined Lincoln were stunning in their glorious yellow and orange hues. I was in the back seat, fully untethered, as was the way in the 1950s. Recall that the interiors of automobiles had at least fifty assorted knobs with chrome and metal surfaces that could cause serious damage to one's face and head during an accident, let alone simply a fast stop. The entire instrument panel was a brightly painted metal stamping.

Those were the good old days!

I was placed in the back of the car to be safe and not distract Dad's driving. Mom had a different strategy: she would put me right next to her in her Ford station wagon, I assume to be near me so she could use her extended right arm to protect me. They both had differing views on child safety. It was not on either of their built-in radar.

There was a strap in Dad's car, I think called an assist grip, that hung down from the upper sidewall pillar trim that I would hang onto and swing from in the back seat when we were "motoring," a common term that meant traveling in a vehicle. It was fun to grab onto this strap with both hands and swing, bouncing into Dad's seat back and then into the cushions of the rear seats. It had many other functions I eventually learned, as knowledge came to me through the ages.

That day when Dad got pulled over by the Birmingham police, the cord was my security ring to hang onto. The officer pulled over our car just off Lincoln onto a side street past the aging Rouge River Bridge. Ironically, I had said not a minute earlier to my dad that I thought he was going too fast, but he was late for his builder's appointment.

As a five-year old, seeing flashing lights and hearing police sirens directed at our car introduced me to my first adrenaline rush. It was awesome and exhilarating. It also was an event that introduced me to the word "shit," An expression that I was not to repeat; I got that, too.

Mom also liked the word and used it a few years later in my life as I came to play golf with her. Here it was reserved for missing a short putt on the golf course among our family only. Again, this word was for adults, and I knew and accepted this and was restrained in its use until I was older. Now, in fact, it is one of my favorite expressions, always in a selected audience.

I recall Dad immediately reaching into his hip pocket to retrieve his wallet that contained his driver's license. This action was in anticipation of the cop's quite recognized behavior approaching the car, and Dad squinted at the officer in his side view chrome mirror. It was almost like Dad had done this several times before.

The officer stuck his head into the front window, looking about the interior and quickly came to his point as he viewed and reviewed Dad's Michigan driver's license.

"Mr. Adams, I had you going over 40 in this residential area. Do you know what the speed limit is?"

From the back seat, hanging onto the assist grip, I interrupted and announced that, "My Dad is a doctor," anxiously adding, "I told him he was speeding."

I saw the hair on Dad's neck stand up that afternoon in October. I had breached confidentiality and needed to learn a lesson for the future. A large smile engulfed the officer and he interrupted me, looked at Dad and said, "Well, Dr. Adams, you sure have a smart kid there. You need to listen to him."

It became a story that Dad embellished over the years, and the consequences may have been much different for my young hide had the officer not nicely handed the license back with only a verbal warning. I suspect that the officer was making sure this scene wasn't going to move into a case of child abuse.

Police had the authority back then to use discretion.

Things have changed.

FOLLOW ME

I had moved to a small town in northern Illinois after my post-graduate degree. It was my first real job at a major seed and chemical company. My first wife, Cindy, had landed a school teaching job and we were fast-tracking her graduate work in school counseling at Northern Illinois University. We had arranged to accompany friends for a Saturday night in Chicago to see their new apartment in the city where they were attending Northwestern for graduate degrees in education. The plan was for us all to drive our own automobiles into the city from Rochelle, Illinois, where we resided. This would allow me to leave Sunday, on business for a week on the road in Indiana and Michigan; Cindy would drive back to Rochelle. It was all so logical.

We began the adventure by trying the new east-west tollway that had been constructed and just opened to Rt. 51, not more than three miles from our rental home in Rochelle. It was such an anticipated thoroughfare, as the only other real route to Chicago was the old Highway 30, which went through many towns and was as slow as molasses.

I told Cindy to follow me closely so we would not get separated on our journey into greater Chicago where we would hook up with our friends, the McMillans. I was in my Ford and Cindy was in her Chevrolet Chevelle. She was dutiful back then, and true to her word, she followed me right into a speed trap by the Illinois Highway Patrol after only a few miles on the tollway. There was nobody on the highway except for cops, and I had used the new stretch of beautiful pavement to catch up, making up on our tardiness in meeting our friends.

We pulled over in unison and all three vehicles were aligned nicely on the side of the road, with the patrol car in the lead. I exited the vehicle with a smile and looked at Cindy, a bit embarrassed, and decided to take the lead on the explanation. I was sure the officer would show pity on us young adults and our predicament. A lesson was about to be revealed: the proactive approach does not work well with a trained highway patrolman.

Our personalities mixed like oil and water.

Placing his hand on his holster, he barked back to me as I exhibited my bouncy jovial self. "You get back in your vehicle."

I announced to the officer, "This is my wife," pointing to Cindy in her car behind me, and simply concluded that he would see how nice we were. My actions alarmed him and tipped the scale in the wrong direction.

The officer, relaxing just a bit, offered, "This is going to be a shitty day for you, son."

It was, indeed. Two speeding tickets issued by the unrelenting Illinois Highway Patrol officer. He had heard it all, and was not in the mood for discussions with my exuberant personality trying to explain to him that I led her into his speed trap.

It was a very expensive start to our weekend in Chicago. He also didn't care that I had worked in undercover in Michigan trying to break up a prostitution ring in Traverse City.

All my charm could not save the two tickets from being issued.

UNDERCOVER BOB

My summer in Traverse City was progressing quite well. I had been married about a year, and Cindy and I decided to take a summer off from my graduate classes and her waitressing. We wanted one last fling at college-age fun before we moved on in our careers. It was the summer of 1973.

One of our dear friends from Albion, worked as an assistant buyer at Milliken's in Traverse City. She was dating a detective with the Traverse City Police Department named Sam Blue. Can you believe his name—nearly perfect, especially for his role and particular occupation?

My undercover assignment that midsummer from Sam was the result of our getting to know one another from the many evenings of partying on the sandy beaches of Grand Traverse Bay and enjoying the aqua-blue waters of Lake Michigan. It was a near-perfect summer, including many evening activities that consumed most of the meager wages earned during our day jobs.

Sam was listening to me describe my fantasy from childhood about having a holster and six-shooter, and having a fair maiden take me to bed, where the only image I can recall was unbuckling my holster and placing it on the spindle on the headboard. Just that move alone, of placing my holster set on the bedpost, was my fantasy, nothing more. The sexual exploits were very muddled and not really in my moves or universe at the time. Clint Eastwood had arrived on the big screen in the early 1970s and his moxie just fueled my fantasy. He was a man's man in law enforcement in many of his early movie roles. I suspect he was my fantasy role model.

Getting such a kick out of my antics, Sam announced one night that he and Dennis Finch, another detective, had an assignment for me that they thought I would be perfect for, especially if I owned a sport coat. The great news was, I did. It was my trusty dark-blue blazer that got me through weddings and funerals. I had it in my closet at George Carr's house, where Cindy and I were living in on top of Radio Hill overlooking all of Traverse City (visible in the winter only, I might add). George forgot to mention this small detail when we were negotiating the rent from my phone in East Lansing. It was a dump, musty from all the trees surrounding it. The kitchen was full of spent and stacked pizza boxes, a clogged sink, and one smelly refrigerator. The three of us made it our home for two months during that summer of 1973.

My assignment was to infiltrate the Holiday Inn on West Bay and establish that the hostess was soliciting bar patrons to attend her brothel of two females that she was housing at her downtown home. That was it; it was a no brainer. I was there to establish that this solicitation actually took place. They were then going to perform a raid with real policemen to break up this prostitution ring. This was vice at its finest, and my role was critical to prepping for the raid and building their case. I was into this title role.

Ironically, my summer group, including Sam, had attended several dances at the Holiday Inn, as it was a hot spot for the twenty-something bar crowd. I knew the environment quite well. Sam and Dennis had negotiated a twenty-dollar wage for my services, rendered per evening on assignment. I was dressed in my blue blazer, accompanied by my rep tie. I was to take on the role that I was a traveling salesman looking for a good time. I even took off my wedding band to add to the suspense of the role I was playing. I did not have a holster or a gun on this particular assignment, but it was still getting so close to my fantasy realized.

Cindy dropped me off at the police station and told me I was an idiot, in very nice terms. I filled out release forms and vouchers at the police station, and they gave me a roll of ten-dollar bills to use for the evening of drinking and flirtation with their mark. My prescribed assignment was to stay in the bar first, then have dinner, then return to the bar and make sure I let the bartender know I was in for a convention for the week, looking for a good time, as the police suspected he was an accomplice in the hostess's scheme of soliciting for prostitution.

The unmarked police car, which everyone in town knew was a police car, left the station on Cass with the three of us in it. Sam and Dennis were in the front and I was in the back. They were both giggling as they saw my jovial side take a turn to that of being on assignment. It was a surreal experience as we headed out Front Street to the Holiday Inn. I was quite nervous and had butterflies in my stomach. It was an odd feeling, and both detectives knew this and thought it was just funnier than hell. I used my humor, but began asking questions as to how to get in touch with them if I got in trouble, or should something go wrong. This just brought more howls from the front seat.

We pulled into the driveway at the front entrance of the Holiday Inn and Sam said that I had lots of money and to basically go get a stiff drink to calm me down. He quipped, "This is exactly what we wanted you to do Bob, drink and have fun."

"Remember, you are here to get propositioned because you are a high-roller looking for a good time," remarked Dennis.

I left the back seat of the car emboldened and now fully charged with courage after both detectives gave me their pep talks.

But, I began wondering, what in the hell was I doing? I had been in the lobby several times earlier in the summer to have fun, but this time it was different. Christ, I was an undercover cop, and here at the Holiday Inn of all places. I had trouble reconciling this, and thought back to the days when I could have my powder-blue security blanket to get me through a rush of insecurity.

I immediately bee-lined to the bar just off the lobby and sat by myself at the bar, where a thirtyish bartender, who did not resemble an accomplice at all, greeted me. He asked me what I wanted for my "poison," and I immediately took on my new role of a traveling salesman and ordered a Manhattan. Realize I had never had a Manhattan before; seven-and-sevens and mostly beer, but never all alcohol. It tasted like very strong cough medicine, I thought. In a matter of a few minutes my apprehension had disappeared and I was finally quite relaxed.

This kick was what I needed, and I surprised myself when I ordered another drink so quickly. I was always on a budget and would slowly play with intoxication, but the wad in my coat pocket could support any imaginable expense that I would need for my evening of being on the prowl, and being paid too. How good was that?

Within minutes the subject of our sting came into my universe. I had learned the language quickly in my ten-minute indoctrination by detectives Blue and Finch. The hostess was decked out in a glittery dress and was at her station greeting dinner guests and seating them throughout the restaurant. She was attractive, perhaps in her mid-thirties, with pulled back hair. I wondered where she had gone wrong. Then I was reminded that she lived in one of the nicest homes in town and was double dipping, so to speak, in salaries and fees—a true entrepreneur before the term became common.

In her duties she came to the bar area several times. I had practiced in the mirror earlier that day the look I would use to entice her to approach me. I thanked God I didn't have to take this engagement further, as I was married and was way too nervous in such a conflicting role. I sipped the next drink much more slowly and seemed to take on an air of confidence that was sorely missing twenty minutes earlier—the magic of alcohol.

I was beginning to get a bit annoyed that I couldn't even get her to talk with me. The only rise out of her was an acknowledgement that I was going to have dinner after a few drinks, and she had a table reserved for me. Like that was some big deal? There were about thirty tables in the dining room and only about five were being used. I actually began to feel some pressure to perform. After all, I had been given cash and payment for my services. I ordered another Manhattan, now starting to like their flavor and any hint at cough medicine was now gone. I started chatting it up with the bartender, remembering that he may be complicit in this ring of iniquity.

He wanted to know what brought me to Traverse City and I told him I was here for a bed-and-bathroom convention and that I sold toilets and accessories. It was what we had rehearsed on the way over with my detectives, and I did a very convincing job defining this noble occupation. I had a very hot line and was lucky to land this job at my age, was what I spun at the bar. I was tipping him dollars at every turn, revealing my wad of money and flushness.

I asked him where in town I could meet some "experienced females." This was supposed to indicate a pay-for-hire strategy. He simply said that the Holiday Inn was a great place to meet women, and the band started at eight, nothing more. I stood up and went to the hostess's station, waiting for the lady to greet me, one on one. She now had a solicitous look to her, and I was finally relieved that she was paying attention to me as she walked toward me.

"Are you ready?" With a little chirp I detected.

"Oh, I am."

She grabbed the menu and I followed her like a spring duckling following its mother, back to a table where she efficiently seated me and that was it. She quickly walked back to her station and exited into the dark hallway. I would have done better with a librarian, I thought.

The waitress was wonderful, and I began to have fun kidding with her. She recommended the two Maine lobster tails on special for $5.95. I had never had a lobster tail because I was an Adams, and this was unbelievable that the police were paying for this. How lucky could I be? The waitress tied a big white and red plastic bib on me and I ordered another Manhattan. I was beginning to laugh and chat aloud to myself about the lack of response I was getting from the hostess. My concern was now evolving as to whether Blue and Finch would be pissed. Wine was not on the menu in the early 1970s, so I had one more Manhattan as the dinner was served.

Three events the rest of the evening during dinner stick out in my mind today. First, the waitress couldn't believe that I ordered a Manhattan, plus a glass of milk with my dinner. She indicated that no one had ever done that before. To this day, I see nothing wrong with those two beverages at the same meal.

Second, I kept dropping the buttered lobster morsels on my bib. Butter stains were everywhere, but I was enjoying those that did not fall to the ground; they were exceptional.

Finally, Mr. Wares, a local contractor and the father of a college friend, was dining with customers a few tables over, and kept yelling over at me, asking how I could afford lobster when I was gardening for Mrs. Bolling?

He blew my cover, I thought.

It dawned on me that I was not going to be solicited that night. I was now quite drunk to boot. I kept trying to blow out the heated butter dish's flame. Apparently, I had to slide a metal disc over it.

I paid one more stumbling visit to the hostess stand and found from the bartender that she had already headed home as it had been a slow night. I headed to the lobby of the Holiday Inn and used the pay phone to call my detectives. Fortunately I found the slip of paper they had written their direct number on. They arrived in five minutes, exactly where they had dropped me off some three hours earlier. I entered the back of the unmarked car and exploded in laughter.

"I couldn't get her to even talk to me," was my pronouncement as I tried to catch my breath.

We sat in the car and all laughed for fifteen minutes in total hysteria, the right kind of tears were everywhere. Thank goodness they had air conditioning and the windows were closed, or a rookie cop would have arrested us for disturbing the peace.

◄ ◄ ◄ ◄ ◄

The aftermath was not much better. I never could get the hostess to acknowledge me, even on my second attempt. It was a hoot, but I did it! I found out later that one of her tenants had been in a dispute with her over rent and she started the rumor of her madam services at a local bar? Sgt. Dennis Finch first survived Vietnam, but I learned in the mid-nineties that he was shot and killed in his line of duty as a Traverse City police officer. Hell, he now has a building named after him. My brief encounter with Blue and Finch in the summer of 1973 brought back such fond memories. Thank you. Here's to your duty as soldiers and policemen. You both were good guys.

CHAPTER 25

GOLFING

NO BETTER PLACE TO BE

THE GAME OF GOLF WAS MY DELIVERANCE. When all my buddies were playing team sports in grade school, I was learning to play golf. It was a game that involved acquiring both physical and competitive skills, it was played outdoors, and it allowed me to be with my family, especially Mom and Dad and oldest brother, Fred. We all had the bug, as Mom use to describe its mesmerizing allure and attraction. I just didn't know how difficult it could be. It can deliver the greatest highs, but it also can greet you with lows often delivered from the "golfing gods," a term we used to describe mystical influences when we missed a putt, or skulled a sand shot, catching the lip of a trap. It is indeed a reflection of life's follies played right out in front of you in only a few hours and mostly on manicured grass.

Our country club had a great junior program that was headed by the seasoned club pro. It was high on the assigned list of his job description and responsibilities. I felt sorry for him. Joining him were the many volunteer mothers charged with teaching us juniors the etiquette of the game, which included the appropriate behaviors that were quite defined as well as very subtle. I just wish the ladies would have remembered to be quiet themselves.

I recall my early present of a beginner's set of Spalding clubs. They were carried and displayed in divided compartments in a small off-white canvas golf bag. They were awesome and so appreciated. I've always wanted to watch a golf club being manufactured in a fabricating plant. I guess an early inkling to my eventual manufacturer's agent career.

During junior golf day I was allowed to get one edible treat and a soda at the halfway house (the name stood for the refreshment shack halfway between the front and back nines). For fifty cents you could get the best-tasting, infra-red-heated hamburgers, or ham and cheese sandwiches. After the bell rang on the gray metal cooking machine, Pauline, the server, would cautiously remove the sandwiches and tear away the burnt plastic wrap. Steam and unusual gas-tronomic fragrances would escape into the air upon opening the wrapper. It was a smell not easily defined, but so familiar back then. This is also where I developed a special affinity for yellow mustard. I used lots to salvage the sand-wich's flavor. I suspect the food scientists developed these sandwiches after studying preservative science. I do not want to know if there may be lasting health issues associated with their consumption, perhaps like asbestos or lead-ed paint. The sandwiches were nearly heaven. I exhibited, early on, the Adams' appetite.

Besides eating at the golf course, I remember the early exhilaration and im-mediate feedback you received when hitting a great golf shot, even if only once or twice on the practice range or during a mini-round. The game itself was the challenge of staying calm and being instantly rewarded for one's correct series of actions, best described as the golf swing. It represented a challenge of discipline and concentration. I tried all kinds of sports, especially baseball and hockey, but was not a fan of being yelled at by coaches or depending on teammates, and both were essential to these group sports. I was a loner, or small-crowd type of athlete. I fell in love with all aspects of the game of golf.

From my youth on the golf course I remember the smell of cut grass, es-pecially during the morning hours. The grass clippings would combine with sunlight and create a special scent as I walked the lush fairways at Orchard Lake Country Club. It was, and is, an olfactory sensation that most have expe-rienced even if on a home lawn or in a city park. The greenery enlivens one's space, and so nicely softens the hard structures around the home or in the city. Grass loves to be mowed. The green lawns enhance urban life, and golf courses are such welcomed additions to be revered in our expanding world of urbanization. Here's to grass and green lawns.

My experience today is that golf courses in my northern Michigan area are appreciated for their mixed offerings of grass, woods, and water. They can be ground zero when a reflective and thankful retreat is needed. I use an eve-ning round of nine holes to remember and recall my happiest of times. Being seasoned and worn, I remember how thankful I am to still be able to play the game; played on more modest venues now with my awareness and acceptance of my lower skill level and my finances.

Still the great game of golf lures me in: the feats of holes-in-one, birdies, and club competition are now softly imprinted and placed in my past. Today is about living in the present, the here and now, which makes me think I wouldn't trade this moment for any other place or time. I thank the past, but it really is the current moment that is pretty darn special to me. I am most thankful for my ability to still get up and play the game and smell the cut grass and try to knock that dumb white ball into the stupid little hole.

◄ ◄ ◄ ◄ ◄

I've chosen to highlight a few of my times and memories of North Carolina. It is such a beautiful state, and my family seemed to be attracted to it—not surprisingly for the game of golf. I spent many vacations enjoying rounds, first with Dad and brother Fred in our teens and twenties, then later on with my own sons. In between, the pleasure of golf in North Carolina included many friends and associates. The state's slogan, "A better place to be," is truthful and seems more definitive than my own state's slogan, "Pure Michigan." The budgets for attracting tourists and golfers are expanding as we move out of our toughest recession since the 1930s; both states know well the attraction golf has in helping in their state's economic and psychological recovery.

Dad was introduced to Pinehurst, North Carolina, in the late 1940s and early 1950s when he competed in the North and South Amateur Championship. The competition was played on the famed number-two course that had hosted the Ryder Cup and a couple of U.S. Opens. He, and his great college friend Ben Smith, would head to the Carolinas in May and see if their winter-recessed golf games could withstand the test against the great Southern amateur golfers and many soon-to-be PGA touring pros.

The North and South, as it was called, was first played in 1901 on the several golf courses of Pinehurst. It was billed as an invitational, conceived to bring in players from around the country hoping to use the event to showcase the resort and, per its archives, "to develop a rapport and mend our regional souls." Donald Ross, famed world golf architect and early professional, designed four of the courses.

Dad qualified for match play once, and made it to a field of thirty-two, not bad for a doctor who had a family, too. Ben, who had been captain of the University of Michigan golf team, fared better and made it to the final eight a couple of years. Ben also was the Michigan Amateur in 1950. He was a great player and we enjoyed years of friendly and competitive matches with "Uncle Ben" and his sons.

For several springs in the 1960s and 1970s, Dad, oldest brother Fred, and I would join Dr. Al Larsen, a surgeon from Bloomfield, in our "father-son" outings in the town of Pinehurst. We would fly into Charlotte, rent a car, and head the 100 miles east to the Pinehurst area. In the mid-1960s we stayed at the recently constructed Country Club of North Carolina, designed by Ellis Maples. We would rent a home on the course and would play four days of golf. It was my brother's and my treat, paid for by my dad. I hope I thanked him enough for such thoughtfulness. I do here, again. The course and experience was unmatched in beauty and sheer enjoyment.

Dr. Al Larsen was a gentle and very competent surgeon, and one of Dad's favorite and closest friends. My lasting memory of Al was his love of the game and the comradeship it brought to him. He was an introvert of some measure. Surgeons are quite different people, is mostly my take today. He saved my bacon my senior year in college when he loaned me one-hundred dollars with the promise that I never tell my father. My rationale was that Dad had four of us in college and pediatricians were not highly paid as physicians; my take was Dad had enough burdens on him, let alone supporting my beer money requirements. Dr. Larsen had no children and was well heeled. He saved me my senior year in college and, as agreed, I paid him back the following summer, with interest.

A few years earlier from this senior year rescue, on the Dogwood's front nine at CCNC, Dr. Larsen said one of the oddest things I can ever remember. It was not meant to be insensitive, but it flustered me. Frankly I played poorly for several holes, trying to recover from his attempt at a very appreciative remark.

We had all hit very respectable drives up the winding par-five third hole. The morning sun had begun to warm us, with the actual sun partially hidden behind the tall longleaf Carolina pines. The reverence was remarkable, and only the footsteps and grunts from us eight could be heard. Four of us were the players, dressed in our nicest new golf attire, sporting Footjoys and Sans-abelts. The other four were our older Negro caddies who carried our clubs for their livelihood. They were poor, and their clothes were hand-me-downs, for sure. They were lucky to have shoes that even matched. We two foursomes, players and caddies, were joined at the proverbial hip. Caddies were mandatory at the highbrow clubs we frequented. Power carts were not yet acceptable, except on rare occasion.

Dr. Larsen, after we all had teed off not more than seventy-five yards out, was swinging his arms in delight, and as we all walked spritely toward our drives announced his appreciation that all could hear in our group, "I wonder what the poor people are doing."

He was speaking only in total gratitude for the gorgeous day and company he was keeping, and was letting the universe know he was so thankful. Nevertheless, I just about shit. My eyes widened and my shoulders crunched at what I had just heard. Maybe I'm remembering this in my new altered state of recovery, but I recall that everyone responded, "Yes" and "Yes, sir." These affirmations came from the voices all around in our group. I was unraveled and wondered why there were no repercussions at all to his remark? Everybody just went on with their business of walking to their drives, no worse for wear.

Was this total denial?

Was this where the term pregnant pause originated?

The caddies were as poor a lot as there could be, and here some wealthy doctor from the North utters these words. How could he make such a remark? It was unnerving for me. I was flustered and embarrassed. Maybe I had been tarnished by the news of our day. It was, after all, the mid-1960s. I think I was the only one who thought anything of Dr. Larsen's casual and passing remark. I hit five approach shots and three-putted for a nine. Not my usual game.

◄ ◄ ◄ ◄ ◄

I just now walked down to my beach in my tattered clothes and old tennis shoes in my unshaven state and thanked the universe for such a glorious morning here on Memorial Day on Crystal Lake in Benzie County. At the same time I thought of the phrase, "There but for the grace of God, goes I,"… still happy and poor. Maybe I finally got the Pinehurst remark? It is for all of us to enjoy. Poor might be just a state of mind.

◄ ◄ ◄ ◄ ◄

Son David was a very lucky person. This was an observation made both by his older brother Rob and me. He just seemed to have a way about him, always landing on his feet quite upright, in games, mishaps, and sports.

Years after my introduction to North Carolina, the three of us visited the same golf courses that I played in my youth. We had planned a couple days with just the three of us, and then Grandma and Grandpa Adams would fly into Southern Pines and we would enjoy their company for a couple more days. The boys were fifteen and seventeen and learning to play the game quite well.

Brother Fred had become quite successful in banking, and with his finances in order he purchased a beautiful home on the grounds of the Country Club of North Carolina, where he had become a member. He was so nice about letting his family members use his home and be guests at the club. He did rent the home out, and in this arrangement maintained an "owner's closet" in the home that was under lock and key. The beauty is we also had a key. This was most useful to access liquor, crackers and nuts, and his bank-logo golf balls. Fred reminded me that the balls were for customers and the booze was for our mom and dad when they were joining us. I smiled at his remarks, and knew that he was more than half serious in his message. It was of no problem to me, as I had brought my favorite vodka and was in no need of golf balls. The nuts and crackers were another story.

Rob, Dave, and I had planned menus for our days at Fred's home, and our finale was to prepare steak and lobster on the balcony grill when Mom and Dad arrived later in the week.

I introduced the boys to the clubhouse and pro shop, and they were in awe of the grounds, just as I was as a young teenager some thirty years earlier when the club was just launching. So little had changed: more homes for sure, but the wispy pines and flowering shrubs were still reminiscent of Augusta National in their character. The joy the boys experienced was playing itself out nearly at every moment after we drove in the gated front entrance, learning that they were expecting our arrival.

"Yes, Mr. Adams, welcome back to CCNC."

This spot was for the very well heeled, and had a feel of absolute permanence that is very rare in golf course developments throughout the South. It was not possible to fake the aura of class. We fit in just fine, and then some.

On the morning of the day of my parents' arrival, we had arranged with the pro shop to play nine holes in the morning and then come back for our second nine in the afternoon, after we had retrieved Grandma and Grandpa from the airport. We would get them settled into Fred's home, and they would enjoy a very happy afternoon nap. It was their prerequisite, now well into their seventies.

We teed off on the Dogwood Course and had placed our three golf bags on one cart. Here I reminisced to the boys about the time when we had to use caddies, and while they understood the previous custom, they loved the new carts, taking their turn driving them. We were getting into the round and the familiarity of the holes, which, while so clear to me because of my years of play, were just starting to become part of the boy's recall. We started our round out with no remarkable shots, just taking in the morning air and the bright blue Carolina sky that greeted us on this fabulous golf course. It was warming quickly.

After finishing the second hole we drove to the third hole and prepared for our shots. It was a par-three island green, and while short at 134 yards that day, it was extremely difficult and full of peril, especially the surrounding water feature. My goal was to hit but one ball and have it land anywhere on the green. Yes, that was true before, then and now. Both Rob and I had hit our shots and somehow landed on the upper tier, some fifty to sixty feet away from the lower pin position. We were quite pleased our balls were safe. It was now Dave's turn, and he addressed his teed ball. He waddled and fidgeted, trying to get set over the difficult shot that he was trying to envision. I'm sure he was attempting to relax and visualize his forthcoming shot. All of us have different mannerisms as we prepare to hit a ball. In fact, I can see Rob and me watching Dave go through his somewhat comical routine in his preparations. It is especially keen here as I relive the shot of the century, as we have come to call it.

Dave took a mighty swing with a nine iron and lifted his head early, and as usually happens with such postural mistakes, badly topped the ball. It screamed down the front of the tee in what we Adams affectionately call a "worm burner." It then hit the water at a low angle, splashing water in all directions, and skipped. Next a large "thump" could be heard as it hit the island green's sloping landmass that was grassed. There was still an enormous amount of energy in that little ball, and it popped straight up in the air some thirty feet and landed just on the front portion of the green. Oh, it was not done. It was like slow motion, all these actions right in front of us boys, and I think we even glanced at each other as the ball was going through its unfathomable routine. As it landed on the surface of the green, it paused for a millisecond, and gathering steam again, spun up the green's slope and traveled fifteen feet, hit the flagstick and disappeared into the hole. It was as if a vacuum had sucked it in to the hole. A hole-in-one, right in front of our bedazzled eyes.

Our faces met one another in expressions of total disbelief, and our mental abilities could not comprehend what had just taken place, at least in the very beginning. Rob was disgusted, not yet ready to surrender to his little brother's good fortune. I began laughing hysterically, and was joined by both boys hooting; then all three of us were rolling on the tee, grabbing our stomachs trying to gather in needed oxygen. It was by far the oddest hole-in-one I have ever witnessed, but as we all know, it was indeed a hole-in-one. Congrats to my little Dave Bear.

◁ ◁ ◁ ◁ ◁

As I write about these golfing memories, I do admit that part of my recovery plan is to again join my sons in the future to play golf as a family. Oh, I almost forgot, Dave's plaque has the ball that he used to make the infamous shot. Embarrassingly, it had Uncle Fred's bank's logo on it. Sorry Fred, I couldn't keep my eye on the boys all the time.

CHAPTER 26

RICHARD TUDHOPE

A SIMPLE LITTLE MISTAKE

I HAD JUST MOVED BACK TO BIRMINGHAM, having lived in and been routed through East Lansing; Minneapolis; Rochelle, Illinois; and Grand Rapids, Michigan. My mid-twenties were a series of starts and stops, and at twenty-eight years of age, I was hopeful that I had found a career spot where I could use my schooling and work experience and make a nice living. It was a move back to my home area, and I was a bit embarrassed as I had three years earlier announced to Dad, "Why would anybody live in greater Detroit?" I did eat some crow, as they say, but I did so quite happily.

I was back on my home turf, very glad and relieved. I missed my family and many of my friends. It took living too far away in the greater Midwest to get that fact straight in my head. It was a growth experience in helping define my life steps.

I had interviewed earlier in 1976 with Asgrow, a division of Upjohn, a proud Kalamazoo pharmaceutical company, and they wanted me in San Antonio, Texas, of all places. Northrup King had wanted me to head to California, but a vacation in 1974 did not result in the greatest impression of life in California. Patty Hearst and the SLA had the city of San Francisco under lockdown, and I was in the downtown when dear Patty robbed the Hibernia bank. I have never heard that many sirens echoing in downtown canyons in my life. These career options were not of interest, and the past and future were tugging at my gut. It was a very tough time and I was seeking my own *terra firma*. It was elusive. I was still glad I had not pursued the Nicklaus opportunity to build golf courses in Laos and Vietnam. Christ, I'd be in some foreign land, wearing steel-toed boots, riding a tractor. I simply wanted to wear a tie and become a successful businessman. Yikes!

So I was back in Birmingham in 1977, living briefly for the summer in the home of in old friends of my parents, with Cindy, my wife of five years. The Beiers so nicely offered their home to us for our transition. They lived on Walloon Lake in the summers, and Mr. Beier quietly stayed in his room when he was occasionally in town. We eventually took up residency in an apartment complex in the fall, in fast-growing Farmington Hills, just off of Twelve Mile. It was great to be home, and I recall being invited over for Sunday dinner at my parents' house that first week back. It just felt right. I could again talk to Dad face to face at his grill by the back step.

Cindy was not in the same camp, and her sadness was evidenced in many of her behaviors. The marriage was in trouble, and it was soon to be doomed in actions, and then by decree. My first matrimonial bonds were sadly coming to an end. When I hear her voice now, I cringe at its nasal inflections. What was I thinking?

"When the bloom is off the rose" now made sense to me.

I had started my new job as a manufacturer's agent in the spring of 1977, and had much to learn about the job and the nuances of this newer business undertaking. One of my associates, Fred Alcorn, an older gentleman who handled samples for the firm and called on smaller accounts, had suggested a local agent for me so I could update my car insurance to State Farm.

Fred was not much with words, a very quiet and sad man, I observed in our first weeks together at the firm. My boss, the day after I started, headed to Africa for three weeks of vacation and I was left basically arranging my desk and getting things in order, having little knowledge or confidence in what I was supposed to be doing. Fred nicely suggested an insurance agent he had used, and gave me a slip of paper with a local 548 phone number and the name Tud Hope. I was happy to have him be this accommodating, as he was not pleased about my entering the firm and displayed an air of coolness by usually ignoring me.

Back in my office I dialed the number, and a nice voice answered the phone, "State Farm, how may I help you?"

I responded by saying to the receptionist, "Good morning, may I speak to Mr. Hope, please."

"Is this Jimmy?"

"No, it is Bob Adams." She obviously mistook my voice for a friend of Tud's, and I felt for her embarrassment as she stuttered and nicely recovered with an apology. Explaining that Jimmy was always playing jokes on Mr. Tud Hope.

I was absolutely fine with this, and even recall that this gal must be working in such a nice office and was feeling warm about buying my insurance from this firm.

"I will connect you now."

Another friendly voice came over the line, this time a male, "Hello, how can I help you?"

"Tud, this is Bob Adams, and you have been recommended by an associate of mine as a capable agent to handle my insurance needs."

"Why thank you, but it is Tud Hope."

"Yes, I know," and I again said, "This is Bob Adams."

"No, it is Richard Tud Hope."

This struck me as a bit odd, wondering why the guy is using his full name while talking with me. So, when in Rome, I thought, and responded by saying, "Okay, this is Robert Bruce Adams. Mr. Hope, your office is delightful, but it's too early to keep playing jokes. I mean, come on."

"Mr. Adams, my last name is Tudhope, not Hope."

"Oh, you're shitting me?" How embarrassing. My associate didn't fill in the blanks. It was sabotage. No, it was my stupidity, perhaps a little of both.

◄ ◄ ◄ ◄ ◄

I did indeed get the insurance and every year we would chat, laughing about our initial conversation and I, of course, called him Tud.

CHAPTER 27

WRITTEN LISTS

A GUIDING LIGHT

I'M EXTOLLING VIRTUES THAT HAVE HELPED ME GET THROUGH TOUGH TIMES and inspire those of you who can benefit and apply the wisdom in your own situation. My strong recommendation embodied in this chapter is for you to develop and maintain lists.

Yep, it is that simple.

I am a fan and advocate of lists. I think they are a key element to success, and can help build the foundation for one's happiness. Lists guide you, remind you, and monitor your actions. Seems so simple, but I know many people who do not care for lists. It may be that they would rather float and procrastinate, perhaps for fear of accountability. Lists prevent me from being aimless and keep me on track.

They are centering in their magic and act as a scorecard.

Honestly, I have lost some confidence, so I feel a bit queasy in making life-long suggestions or pontifications about the importance of lists, but by the same token, I have gained some humility and new strengths out of my life's struggles.

I am indeed a changing soul, but I look back to attributes that helped me become reified and happy. A few lists pop into my awareness as of this writing. They changed my life and helped me feel solid and well grounded. Isn't finding a firm foundation a goal for most? I think it is.

My older brother Dick reminded me that our mother was the "Queen of Lists." She could well have invented Post-Its, but selected scotch tape as her fastening system, nicely choosing discarded paper remnants and affixing them to her kitchen cabinets and refrigerator door. Short pencils were her markers of choice, likely because the pencils for golf scorecards were free at the country club, and darn if they didn't have erasers. She, too, could have been the author-ess of a business strategy called "management by objective." These lists were not just suggestions. They had no room for "perhaps" or "wishes"—they were concrete reminders. She had not even a glimmer of dementia in her last years. Lists were not to ward off forgetfulness; they were her gospel.

Yes, simple accountability. She was the master of lists and, even in her soft ways, you did what you signed up for and it was recorded somewhere in her system, dotting the cupboards in her kitchen command center.

I had a consultant for several years in my business in the person of Mr. Mike Kerr. He was an insightful man, and his forty years of business experience was quietly shared with me as I took helm of my own business in my late thirties. I needed a shoulder, and a quick boot, on occasion. He served that purpose for me. A lasting impression I have of him was his contemplative style, which included this admission after we shared two martinis one evening when we were meeting and updating one another.

"I really believe that I have accumulated some valuable knowledge, and have years left to still offer help to people in business, but I can't find anybody who'll listen, except you." For us baby boomers this was, and is, a foreshadowing of a certain reality that is coming more into focus for us as the inevitable "shift" takes place.

I also remember Mike's pearls that were always floating around me, though I had to slow down a bit and take a deep breath to take them in.

One such Kerr quote offered, "It is better to pull a rope than push it." I think he butchered a saying or two, or my recollection suffers, but the point was about futility of effort.

Thankyou Mr. Kerr. Your little pearls were greatly appreciated, and I have recorded a list of them for my continued reference. I miss you.

Remember too, I began these memoirs from a list, after reading Dr. Weil's *Spontaneous Happiness* book. I started a daily list in 2011 of things that made me happy and for which I was thankful. They were just one-line bullets, but nevertheless they were a list of thoughts that documented my appreciation for my life. I needed to be reminded as I was spinning and reeling from change and loss. I do not like floating, and I needed my feet firmly back on the ground. I am indeed getting there.

◁ ◁ ◁ ◁ ◁

Another list changed my life in my late twenties. Remember, I slaved at an MBA in my early to mid-twenties, just squeaking through the academic rigors of a "Big Ten" two-year program. I found myself on a flight in California a couple years after graduation, facing a typical business layover. I was in the airport's newspaper stand and just happened to find a little paperback by some obscure author from a local university. It had a list of "Ten Commandments for Building a Growth Company." I remember after purchasing the soft-cover book, compliantly sitting in a molded plastic chair that had such flex and give to it. In two hours I combined both reading and skimming of my new acquisition, and finally understood what I had been hoping my education would have brought me during my two-year struggle: a simple list to help guide me. Both influences were on far differing wavelengths, but darn, this little booklet at $3.95 was a list of ten absolutes to build your new business. It was so simple, and yet profound. I typed the list and had several carbon copies in my home and office for ready reference.

TEN COMMANDMENTS FOR BUILDING A GROWTH COMPANY
by Steven C. Brandt

1. *Limit the number of primary participants to people who can consciously agree upon and contribute directly to that which the enterprise is to accomplish, for whom, and by when.*

2. *Define the business of the enterprise in terms of what is to be bought, precisely by whom, and why.*

3. *Concentrate all available resources on accomplishing two or three specific operational objectives within a given time period.*

4. *Prepare and work from a written plan that delineates who in the total organization is to do what, by when.*

5. *Employ key people with proven records of success at doing what needs to be done in a manner consistent with the desired value system of the enterprise.*

6. *Reward individual performance that exceeds agreed upon standards.*

7. *Expand methodically from a profitable base toward a balanced business.*

8. *Project, monitor, and conserve cash and credit capability.*

9. *Maintain a detached point of view.*

10. *Anticipate incessant change by periodically testing adopted business plans for their consistency with the realities of the world marketplace.*

It was first useful to me as a product manager for my first employer, but it really came into use when I took the reigns of my sales and engineering firm from the previous owner. It was simply a concise list, and each year of actual experience seemed to further reinforce the author's practical list of concerns and advice for building my main business. As I reflect about launching my dog biscuit business in 2003, I violated a few principles on this list and was dealt the surly blow that business can easily deliver. Hell, I thought I knew most everything in my late fifties. Nope. I will move forward in my new ventures with this old list of Ten Commandments right next to me. It will be reviewed frequently.

◀ ◀ ◀ ◀ ◀

TARGET TEN

As I began expanding my automotive components business, I realized that my own individual lists that I used to guide and direct my actions were not at all universally accepted by my staff. I wanted everyone in my little firm to document and list in each business quarter their ten most pressing issues and the improvements they wanted to enact in their immediate sphere of influence. Yes, they were short-term goals, if you will. I would review them, and we would together clarify, amend, and then add our signatures to form an agreed-upon roadmap. Our written list and document was the formal aspect to a process leading to rewarding outcomes.

Because we were a sales-generating company, our main documented score-card was realized in developing purchase orders. The support staff's mission was to assist salespeople and perform roles to aid in their sales goals. Sounds so simple, but it wasn't, and isn't. It was what managing was all about, and documenting goals shifted the burden from what I wanted for me, to an agreed-upon 90-day window that the sales and engineering associates want-ed, of course, with my approval. That was the theory and it worked. They were never far off.

It was a solid way to run a business. I will use it into my eighties. So, here's to documenting objectives with a list. Yes, it even allowed for surprises, which constituted at least one-third of the purchase orders back then. I called this effort "reinforced achievements" because our buyers often rewarded us for our displayed intentions, and were always in need of our products even if they pretended not to be interested. Life should have nice surprises, too.

If half of the goals were met from our mapped plans, we figured there was wealth in those hills. I think it is time for an encore.

So, here's to Target Ten. I will again document them on my quarterly list.

◁ ◁ ◁ ◁ ◁

TEN GOLDEN RULES TO LIVE BY

The following list of Ten Golden Rules to Live By were obtained simply from a web search, but this ease of locating them should not cast aspersions on their value. I have read the list hundreds of times these last couple of years, and the rules are well versed. I propose here that I would not change, or add anything, to this list. Okay, maybe a little more on humor's restorative value and less on white lies. Take a look; it represents values and rules that many of our parents likely imparted to us as we grew.

1 – Do unto others, as you want others to do to you. Maybe you believe in karma and maybe you don't. It's my experience that you reap what you sow or what goes around comes around. Treat others with kindness and respect to get the same in return, but treat others like garbage and you can be pretty sure it'll come back to you (although maybe only much later and not the same people you did it to).

2 – Treasure your body for it is the vessel that guides you through your life. You may think that money or success is important, but nothing is as important as your own body. Without it you can't live. Make it a habit to eat a healthy and natural diet, be sure to exercise regularly and above all get plenty of sleep. Also try to keep your life as stress-free as possible, stress makes you age faster and can make you old before your time.

3 – Be honest and always tell the truth. Honesty is the best policy and it will do you far more good than harm. Be honest in your relationships, with your business ethics and personal morals. Although honesty is usually the better option, there will be times when a white lie is necessary to prevent hurting people's feelings.

4 – Success requires hard work, persistence and a little creativity. The best advice I can give you if you want to be successful is to not hope for a quick fix but to be prepared for the long haul. Real success with anything usually takes months and even years to achieve. Believe in yourself and believe in your dreams, keep learning and never give up. Try to find yourself a mentor to speed the learning process up. Sooner or later you'll achieve your goals.

5 – Make a difference to a least one other person's life. I believe that we're all on this planet together. Life isn't meant to be completely selfish; we're here to give to and help each other. Right now there are countless people who could use a helping hand. so why not give back a little? You don't necessarily have to give money. You can give some of your time or experience to help someone else with something you've already overcome. Helping someone else is one of the most rewarding things you can do.

6 – *Admit when you're wrong and apologize. Nobody is perfect and everyone makes mistakes from time to time. It's perfectly okay, even if you screw up and waste money, or time or hurt people's feelings. But only if you admit you were wrong and apologize. You'll be amazed how understanding people are when you're humble and modest enough to admit that you made a mistake.*

7 – *You can learn something from everyone. Don't think you're too good at something to listen to someone else. Don't think that you're better than someone else. Just as you can learn something from the successful CEO or entrepreneur, you can learn something from a homeless person. Everyone has something that they're good at, so don't be too quick to dismiss someone as having no value.*

8 – *Don't be scared. Go through life as fearlessly as possible. Fear is an emotion designed to keep us alive. In our primitive days it kept us aware of our surroundings, suspicious of harmful situations and wary of unknown territory. Fear also holds us back from following our dreams, telling people how we really feel about them, and can force us to stay inside our comfort zone for way too long. Ask yourself, "Would I rather play it safe to not risk failure or would I rather risk failure to really live and do what my heart tells me that I should do?"*

9 – *Smile and laugh every single day. A simple smile from a stranger can light up your entire day. Laughing makes your worries disappear. Make it a habit to laugh and smile as much as you can, because life is just so much better when you do. Positivity is contagious, and you'll find that people will like you a whole lot more if you're always happy compared to being grouchy and cynical.*

10 – *Count your blessings and be thankful for all the good things in your life. The past is history, the future is a mystery and right now is a gift; that's why they call it the "present." You have no idea what tomorrow will bring, so be thankful for every single moment that you're alive. Be grateful for your family, friends and freedom. Be grateful for the food you eat, for the fact that you have a warm, dry place to sleep with a roof over your head. Soak up every single drop of life you can, because all you'll ever have is this moment, right now.*

CHAPTER 28

COMPLEXITY OF FEMALES

LIFELONG LESSONS FROM WOMEN

IF YOU ARE SEEKING INSIGHT AND INSPIRATION I'd suggest you skip this chapter on the complexity of females and focus on the many other learned lessons. Some of my musings and insights can be downright helpful and may inspire you, or even soothe the soul. I do have confidence that the threads of knowledge in my memoirs can help you gain practical insights into dealing with life's calamities. However, when it comes to understanding women, I do not have insight or comprehension, plain and simple. This is not a complaint, as I find women so intriguing, even after twenty girlfriends and three successful marriages.

I decided that it was best to portray a few glimpses into female behavior and put together a chapter describing observations and spins on females that have impacted my life. Yes, I've even included stories about a couple of my wives and their amazing attributes.

As I said, in the introduction of these memoirs: hang on.

◄ ◄ ◄ ◄ ◄

I had what I thought were typical high school and college dating experiences, during which I learned much about females, especially that they are very unpredictable. Some of my dates were fabulous, and some were absolute catastrophes. Adventure always greeted me during my campaigns. I'm just now remembering some of these first phone calls and invitations, and it again gets me all fired up and fidgety in anticipation. You know, that feeling of butterflies in your stomach. Isn't that odd after all these years?

Coincidentally, and in contrast, I have a good friend who is just now learning dating etiquette that he so sadly missed in practice in high school. He had but one girlfriend, and also happened to knock her up. They married and she divorced him after forty-five years. Their final ten years of togetherness was committed to weekly counseling sessions. He is in his mid-sixties and was a very successful corporate attorney, but when it comes to dating, he is a nervous Nellie. I have watched him in action the last couple years, and I'll be darned, he is really improving. He has had four great months with an attractive local Benzie County lady, and their dating seems to be progressing quite well. How nice is that.

TWIN PEAKS

Near the end of my sophomore year at college I found myself on a prolonged dry spell with no female companions in my immediate life. There were sporadic dates here and there at the universities in Ann Arbor, East Lansing, and Kalamazoo, but nothing I'd call memorable or of a sexual nature. At the suggestion of one of my older fraternity brothers, I agreed to stay on campus, and with his prompting called a senior female who I vaguely knew. She was outgoing, and while stout in body shape, had a set of hooters that had intrigued me for almost the entire two years I had been on campus. She would strut from building to building in between classes with a very nice bounce accompanying her steps. She also was purported to be quite easy, which today, I honestly report, was in the forefront of my motivations.

It was the antidote I sought and was sure I needed.

I practiced the lines I would use to see if she had an interest in going out with me. I think she knew who I was, as my cousin Mike was a friend of hers. Additionally, I recall the two of us had smiled at each other while walking on campus more than once. God, I hoped she knew me. I practiced fifteen times my opening line; I'd be using the only phone in the mailroom of the fraternity house.

I was simply going to say, "Shirley, this is Bob Adams from over at the Delt House. How are you?"

That is all I thought I needed to break the ice and get her talking, just some utterance to calm us both down. By reputation she was much more experienced than I, but in those days I still had to be the pursuing party.

She answered the phone and her voice was so melodious and sweet it surprised me. It threw me for a loop. I attempted to get out my practiced line with only these minor variations: "Shirley, this is Bob of the Delt House Adams."

A pause greeted both of us, as we were individually trying to decipher the butchered sentence.

"Oh, cousin Bob. You are so funny."

She obviously knew who I was, and that I had also fumbled the opening line. Quickly, she had helped me recover by being so accommodating in her own words. I admitted that I was not skilled in opening lines for dates. We quickly got down to business and basically discussed if she would like to go to my fraternity's "Grasser" Saturday night as my date.

"That sounds delightful," were her last words.

The game was on, I thought as I hung up the phone, somehow feeling like I had masterminded a real coup.

It was spring in southern Michigan, which can be very unpredictable weather-wise, and this necessitated an early start to our party. Rain was in the forecast. An evening storm was brewing with that anticipatory electrifying feel in the air. Our party location was about ten miles south of campus, just outside of the small hamlet of Homer, on a farm with an awesome man-made pond. It was our fraternity's hideaway, necessitated by the college officials' position that strict monitoring of our living quarters would reduce alcohol consumption. Uncle Al was our farmer-landlord and we rented this spot in exchange for cases of beer each month. He had a long-neck beer in his right hand every hour of the day, and now that I reflect, so did we.

Shirley displayed herself in her filled-out, white sweater, stretched to its maximum capability. I was gloating around my fraternity brothers, those who had braved our chilly late-afternoon weather. She knew everyone in my fraternity; actually she knew more guys in my house than I did. That was of little worry to me as she was the experience I needed so desperately, not some fair maiden on this date. It was shaping up quite nicely. We were having a nice time and anticipation filled the spring air.

I was concerned that the weather would hamper our party. We knew the clouds could not hang on to their moisture much longer and downpours greeted our group that early evening. I can still remember extinguishing the fire by kicking logs apart, and then all of us hopping into our vehicles, circling almost like wild horses heading to a corral and leaving the wet fields behind. We went back to Albion and the fraternity house, a simple change in venue caused by the inclement weather. I greeted this change now as a blessing, thinking we could continue our date in my room at the fraternity. My plan was now adapting itself nicely, upgrading from a blanket to a bed.

We entered my room with gleefulness and my eager anticipation. I had my trusty cooler well stocked with Stroh's beers, the suds of choice that year. Joining the beer was a bag of Better Made pretzel rods. My roommate was gone for the weekend, a quite normal event at our small college. Shirley and I continued our drinking and talking. My suitemate's stereo had the songs from The Association playing all night. It was a near-perfect setting to implement my salacious plans.

The soft light in my room, consisting of a study lamp bent face down on my desk, accentuated the curvaceous attributes found under her white sweater. A line from Johnny Carson's *Late Night Show* came to memory, where Carson told Dolly Parton, commenting on her special endowments, "I'd give about a year's pay to peak under there." Oh, could I relate to that statement.

Sparing the hours of the detail that transpired that evening, and her consuming more beer than I could possibly imagine, the evening expanded into two distinct fronts and they were not of the nature I had hoped.

First, she began crying.

For hours she thanked me for listening to her fears and concerns about her future. I did indeed.

The second front was her slurring position that it was nice to find a man that was such a good listener and that she could call a friend. As any man knows, once you've been identified as a friend, the attempt at any sexual moves is negated and not allowed. It is like a code of honor. I may have tried briefly, but was not at all successful.

I walked Shirley back to her dorm at Twin Towers and placed a kiss on her forehead. I can still remember her huge breasts pressed into my then-flat belly. Not so bad, I thought; another memory and story in the making.

NEGOTIATING

In an earlier chapter I described the Christmas trees we had when I was a young boy in the 1950s. It seemed that most of the trees we secured would dry out and lose their needles. Somehow as kids we overlooked this shortcoming and enjoyed all the tinsel, bulbs, and bright lights that adorned our seasonal tree selections.

I can still hear Mom saying to us kids, "One strand at a time," as we placed clumps of sparkling silver tinsel on the already drying branches. Walking in the family room and just seeing our creation was such a treat for the two weeks the tree would manifest itself in our home. Truth be known, our trees were secured from neighborhood lots, and the older varieties of Balsam and Douglas firs had been harvested months earlier. They were already well on their way to their predictable needle drop from dehydration. The fact that we additionally placed it in front of the heating register in Mom's "perfect location" further added to the conditions that were not conducive to retaining needles. Yes, a combination of an early harvest and heat was not a Christmas tree's best friend. This was comprehended even when I was five years old.

Jill, the mother of my boys, was in awe of a new type of Christmas tree in the 1980s called a Fraser fir. It was raised in North Carolina, in the foothills, and adapted to the Appalachian area because it needed water and good drainage. It was however, very expensive, at least double the lot prices of the standard varieties. This caused hours of concern and worry on Jill's part as we anticipated the purchase of our annual tree. I actually felt pity for her having so much difficulty resolving this dissonance between her desire for a Fraser fir and our parting with the money for the tree.

She was quite a bargain hunter, and her entire life was devoted to rock-bottom pricing and sales. I'm guessing it still is, as this was quite an entrenched personality trait. It was simply in her constitution and when we were still co-habitating, I had to be creative to land the finest Christmas tree at our local purveyor of plants and flowers.

Lyn, the male shop owner, was an absolute tightwad, as tight as I had ever met. Jill and Lyn did not particularly care for one another. This observation is probably why I was placed on the planet for a few years to get the two of them to work in commerce together. I had a philosophy that we support the local merchants, and we bought hundreds of plants and products from him each year.

My plan to make everyone a winner in securing the Christmas tree was conceived in my office: Jill wanted a Fraser fir. I walked over from my nearby office to meet with Lyn on an early December morning and announced to him that Jill wanted a Fraser but could not resolve the price of fifty-eight dollars. Lyn immediately reacted by telling me his wholesale price and challenged me to, "Do the math."

I did not believe him, and responded, "Lyn, Lyn, I am not here to challenge your rights to charge any price you desire. That is your business. Jill and I are very good customers, as you know, and I want her to feel justified in her purchase. She so wants a Fraser."

"I'd consider a discount on the twenty-sixth."

That was his accommodating personality.

A sense of equilibrium needed to be achieved in my household, so I offered the only reasonable course of action that could possibly work in this situation.

"Lyn, may I ask a favor of you?"

"What?"

"Here is twenty dollars. Tonight, when Jill and I are in your lot, will you put your arm around her and whisper, Jill, you have been a great customer this year and I'll take twenty dollars off any Fraser you choose."

Lyn handed me back the bill and said that would be difficult for him to do that. "It just seems dishonest."

"Lyn, please," was my retort.

After a short pause, he grabbed back onto the twenty-dollar bill and said, "Okay, I'll do it."

It occurred to me briefly that he was thinking of asking me for more money to do such a deed. Seriously, that's the way he was. Hell, I was already paying full price, no matter how you skinned it.

The evening came and Jill and I drove back after work to Lyn's to secure our Christmas tree. I was actually as nervous as a pregnant nun, thinking about the high stakes I played and would pay if something went wrong. These were two tough individuals I was putting together. We had scouted the yard for nearly fifteen minutes and Jill was still concerned over the price on the Fraser firs. I was trying to convince her that we could afford such a treat for the kids and us.

"It's only once a year," was my endorsement.

I kept looking through the lot for Lyn, trying to get him to approach us, but he was busy with other customers. Jill had gone down the path that "these prices were too high" and "we should drive to Detroit the next Saturday and get a tree in the Eastern Market." I was beginning to wonder how I got myself into such a mess. Then, out of nowhere came Lyn; he actually scared me, and I jumped when he appeared. I suspect I was even more nervous than the nun I previously referenced.

He grabbed Jill's hand and the two of them marched over into the parking lot some thirty feet away from me. I was hanging onto our favorite tree. They began chatting. I have been in some serious negotiations, but this was near the top in suspense. It lasted minutes. I had no idea the outcome, or even now the topic. I was imagining the repercussions should Lyn screw up.

Jill came back unemotional, pulled me into her space, and quietly said, "We have our tree and we have a deal, but Lyn is so nervous that customers and employees would learn of the discount. He will give you twenty dollars tomorrow when you stop back." Holy shit, the two of them made this high stakes. I sat there in disbelief. We paid the fifty-eight dollars and they loaded the goddamn Fraser fir into my trunk and we left the lot in silence, as if someone might chase us down Haines Street.

When we hit Woodward Avenue seconds later I had one happy female and she went on and on about how great Lyn was, telling me the details of the art of her completed deal. She was happy and so was I; Lyn had come through. Except for one thing: I worried the whole night that I would forget to go over to the store the next day and secure my twenty bucks, or maybe Lyn would die and no one would know that he owed me the twenty. Yes, the perils of buying a Christmas tree with conditions.

This special deal occurred for a few more years, and we had Fraser firs for the kids when they were little.

We all do have our idiosyncrasies, don't we?

Jill's frugal ways that she learned from her family created quite a nest egg for the boys, so thank you, my ex-wife. I can keep trying at my own fiscal recovery.

AUNT CAROL

I came back to Leelanau County after my childhood, when the time was right, and became a resident of the county in 1996 with the purchase of a small gentlemen's farm. I will again return when my own recovery affords me this opportunity. I view my circumstances as a temporary condition, now living in a southern, contiguous county called Benzie, which also contains some of the Sleeping Bear Lakeshore National Park. I announced to friends that my physical move was meant for me so I could write these memoirs, but in reality, the rent was cheaper and I needed to reboot and recover. I've had a watchful angel in a former college mate who has taken me under his wing. Thank you, Stephen T. Wentworth. Even as a temporary nonresident, I do not want any more visitors discovering our splendid lakeshore area, just enough to keep our businesses open and prospering.

For fifteen years my Leelanau farm was a paradise for me. It was historic and splendid. I raised bamboo, ornamental grasses, and dahlias for fun, and planted hundreds of Douglas and Concolor firs to eventually be cut as fresh Christmas trees. The farm had the finest barn in all of Leelanau County. It was a testament to the handicraft during its late nineteenth-century construction, and further, to the attention and guardianship over the years of its many thoughtful caretakers, including me. I also added some features, and within the barn's walls we enjoyed dancing, and horses, and the heavenly scent that only a hundred years of various uses could create. It was divine. It was a structure to be revered. Straw and manure helped bring out its essence.

Carol, my third wife, and I purchased the Leelanau farm in the winter of 1996, and it was truly a gentlemen's farm on twenty-seven and a half acres. This spectacular property was perched on a former Lake Michigan sand dune, half the land was in trees and the other half in open fields. We dreamed of blending our children under one roof, under a unified rule.

It almost worked.

Carol had been my administrative assistant and she had been diagnosed with ovarian cancer during her employment with my firm. This condition was made more complex as it occurred while she was pregnant with Jessica, her soon-to-be second daughter. Her husband was gone, both literally and figuratively, and my wife did not like me; so it was nearly perfect for me to help Carol manage her pregnancy and help her fight the cancer. She was an incredible assistant, especially with her people skills. We just happened to fall in love in this process of going through her health challenges and healing together. After some terribly gut-wrenching times in dealing with our former lives, we decided that our own lives would be enhanced by our union through marriage. We prospered for several years, but with deep sadness. After letting each other down, our married life ended with a legal divorce in 2011. Our union became a casualty to our own foibles, plus stress caused by too much real estate, ill-timed business ventures, mountains of financing debt, and stepdaughters. This would be my post-mortem, using a single-sentence critique; in a single word, it was life.

She was a great stepmother, and I will always thank her for the prominent role she played in helping raise my sons. Rob and Dave gradually prospered beautifully, moving through the sadness and adversity caused by my exit with their biological mother. My separation from their mother finally reduced the environment of anger we all lived under. Later our lives were further balanced by Carol offering true and steadfast love and support as the boys cascaded through their formidable years; not an easy task for those of you who have firsthand knowledge of such dealings.

Carol always had the intelligence to approach Rob and Dave as if she were their favorite aunt. I applaud her for this skill, and thank her for the contribution she made unselfishly to allow a safe harbor for the boys and help contribute quite measurably to their success as teens, and then as young men. I was not equal to this task with her daughters, Sara and Jessica. It became an issue in the final five years as we both exited our marriage. Stepdaughters are difficult and my style was not acceptable to Carol.

We had many laughs along our fifteen-year union and journey. Those were very nice times, and we have four remarkable children who are prospering because of our collective contributions during our togetherness. It was simply time for us both to move on and build new sets of wings.

GOSSIPING

Authors Julia Cameron and Judith Barrington suggested that apprentice writers try visiting a coffee shop to listen to music and help unearth one's creativity, leading to effective writing. I tried their suggestions during my work hours, selected a coffee shop, and discovered a profound scenario that would serve as the foundation to finally solidify an observation that had been emerging about groups of women.

I found myself sitting in a small wicker couch in an upper room at Bay Bread in Traverse City on Randolph Street. It was a bright upstairs room, and decorated so thoughtfully. The owner, Stacey, was a pleasant gal and a hard worker. It was winter, and my mid-afternoon arrival was planned to, hopefully, find the small room void of patrons, as I was there to write and sip coffee and enjoy an afternoon cranberry scone. This desire for tranquility was selfish, as the shopkeeper was local and I wanted her to succeed in business as she offered such great value in her breads, rolls and beverages. She needed customers.

As I came up the carpeted steps, I could hear the cackle of women's voices, and it quickly became obvious that the scene and sensory noise would likely be a problem for my writing endeavors. I settled in and wrote for a bit, actually impressed that I could tune out their chatter. After some time, however, I surrendered, not capable of screening and blocking the verbal overload. I then shifted gears, writing as an observer of the ladies. Why not? It was a little surprise gift to me, and it was what I was experiencing right in front of me, as if it were an exercise in one of my tutorials. I took notes and created a diagram, catching a few of their expressive phrases.

These ladies behaviors brought back some lifetime observations and conclusions. It surfaced that afternoon simply how different most women become in group settings. The memories all came together with a very common thread, and the weave was not too flattering.

First flooding my cognitive state was comparing the similarities of my current ladies with the opening scene from my childhood movie, *Dumbo*. I recalled the scene where all the female elephants were chatting and gossiping about the size of Dumbo's ears. Walt Disney captured this dialog so perfectly in less than a minute in this brilliant animation and cherished scene. Please Google it on YouTube. It is stereotyping at its finest using female elephants.

The second group I recalled was Mom's ladies luncheon groups at the country club. She tried so hard to avoid this venue, but sometimes she couldn't, and would attend the luncheons to maintain the social bonds of her golfing compatriots. Her demeanor was so pleasant, but she had difficulty in these female group settings. She did not participate in small talk, nor did she gossip. It was not her way. She was very different, I realized then, and now.

Finally, blending scenes—I think it is called juxtaposing—there was a joke that circulated some years ago about a group of ladies out at a very swank restaurant. Apparently, the waiter would approach these luncheon ladies and interrupt them to ask, "Is anything all right?"

Those were his opening lines. It was humorous, and only he got it. He was trying to shock them into the act of efficient ordering. Such a brief break, then back to cackling. I've observed this scene so many times, even when I'm not particularly looking for it.

It seems gossip is abundant, and it is these strands I have observed in women throughout my life. The women in my bread shop could not stop gossiping. Do I need more examples? I think not. It is an observation, and it is these groups that I will try to avoid as I age and look to recovery in my life. They have a right to congregate and gossip; I have a right to avoid them. We all win.

CONCLUSION

LOOKING FORWARD

THIS ENDS MY HALF-YEAR ENDEAVOR IN WRITING MY MEMOIRS. My goal was to develop essays and vignettes, and share my life's observations and lessons with family and friends; all this coming from the wisdom that one acquires in nearly sixty-four years. I have concluded that I might be a slow learner, yet I remain optimistic, and look forward to the next real-life chapters outside this writing endeavor. They will be exciting, I am quite sure.

There are some sad stories among my inventory, but most are very happy and comical. Some are insightful, and some not. I now have a sense of accomplishment— that I took these months to record many of my life's stories and observations for my family and their offspring to read. If the memoirs get published, I hope they will reach an audience and deliver insights and enjoyment to those of you whom I do not know. I suspect most of my family will read my memoirs, then smile and place the book on a shelf for twenty years, letting their own lives progress, as they should.

I can remember when I wanted to design and build golf courses in my early twenties. Perhaps egotistical, but I wanted to leave a monument of my doings and design philosophies, something outlasting me. Maybe today, my self-published memoirs will serve this earlier goal. Or, maybe I will build a golf course in my seventies. There can be a season for many things, even cherry dog bones and wives.

This also reminds me that memories can be so different when two people are involved. I have been truthful to the best of my ability, but remind the reader that even in reality, memories are processed through filters and biases, and each person's account can be so different. When I had trouble remembering the details of an event, I did my best to create plausibility for a story's inner truth. Finally, as I've noodled scenes and situations, I have had humor as my trump card. It does work its magic in the memoirs and in life; just ask me and Steve Martin.

Writing has been my therapy. Therapeutic as a result of the process of creation and discovery, made clearer to me by Julia Cameron in her *Right to Write* tutorial. I thank her for her advice that she courageously espoused and offered.

My writings also evolved to tell the stories of my parents, who were rare leaders, quiet and obscure in the greater universe, but so powerful with their unmatched integrity and love. I always knew this, but it took these memoirs to rediscover and document their love and everlasting contributions to me and the world. This book should be dedicated to them, and I do so, right at this moment. My dad would love this for Mom. He also would love that it was quietly done and not in the headlines; that was a lesson he used repeatedly in his own life, so I quietly bury this dedication here, as he would appreciate it.

In my research I unearthed many wonderful sayings and stories that I had heard or been exposed to over my lifetime. Throughout the memoirs I noted these sayings and inspirational quotes and thoughts. They mean so much more to me today, having hit rock bottom, than they ever did.

As I conclude my heartfelt rebooting thoughts, I must thank my dear friend and love of eighteen months, Linda Heureux. All of her insights and soft humorous ways helped me see the beauty of a minimalist life. She has chosen it as a mainstay in her own existence without being a fanatic. She is such a steady companion who has joined me on adventures and discovery missions. She was born in Leelanau County, and its environmental influences show so beautifully in her core values and karma. Her soft and gentle nature brings such balance and equilibrium to my life. Thank you, my dear Linda Heureux. We are indeed both blessed.

My insistence to complete these chapters within a half a year reminds me that I always did better with a deadline. Even if there were times I violated the regimen to get there, it was advisable to not procrastinate too long. Nearly every day I wrote mornings and afternoons, and found it most enjoyable. Son Rob, after discovering my endeavor, sent over a list of inspirational quotes about writing, and I picked two that helped me open up and get the job done. In my introduction I noted that Hemingway said an author had to simply use his typewriter and "bleed" as a way to unearth great writing. Another quote amongst many was by Stephen King, who stated, "Amateurs sit and wait for inspiration; the rest of us get up and go to work." I then deduced and imagined that this would be a "bloody job," and to my surprise, never found that turmoil. I just kept my nose to the grindstone to complete the task at hand.

I remember at twenty-five I promised myself I would never write another thesis or theme paper, after the many graduate-school exercises that were enlisted to teach me something. But here I am, almost forty years later, suggesting that I am born again, and have again learned to enjoy the pen. That is discovery and recovery in one endeavor. Perhaps the introspection is that it was something in my control and it was my creation, not someone else's directive. That would be my guess.

I tried writing a few times after a drink or two, following the suggestion by many friends that it was part of the creative process that they had read about. I found this just not right for me. It moved my prose into being so esoteric, full of banter. It reminded me of elitist academicians that verbalize and pontificate, awash in their own intoxicating rhetoric. Then I realized it was their forum and pulpit, and I therefore must give them a break, so I do. Never one to reject alcohol, my solution was to focus on the rewards of looking forward to late-afternoon cocktails, and I settled into this pleasurable activity after I completed a few written pages each day.

The venues I chose to enjoy my evening cocktails during my second daily "period of enlightenment" consisted of two primary, local watering holes that I would like to acknowledge as a contributor to my happiness quotient.

First was Minerva's, in the comfortable first floor of the Park Place Hotel in Traverse City, Michigan. My midweek therapy was supported by Stacy, the bartender, who always greeted me with my favorite toddy as I hobbled in and gently positioned myself on the corner barstool. She was joined by all my patron buddies I had come to know—Dennis, Ed, Gene, Rich, Paul, Barry, and Dave— all good guys positioned in many stages of life's endeavors and predicaments. Half of them had taken a class in creative writing offered by our local college, and shared with me that the semi-retired professor ridiculed them about their written creations, causing embarrassment. Such great avatars we have today, and such nonsense. Thank you guys for sharing your classroom experiences as this saved me ninety-nine dollars and some unacceptable grief had I joined your class last fall. Thank you for your counsel and friendship.

My second spot for evening libations was only one block from my loft in downtown Beulah in Benzie County. The Corner Pub is its most appropriate name, as it is on the only real corner in the little hamlet. I could easily walk down my hill into town and enter the bar for beer and pizza. Country music boomed out of its new jukebox. It was a good old bar in Northern Michigan with high-tech digital technology blending the old with the new. Ranay is one of the Pub's bartenders, and she is quite attractive, greeting all with her delightful smile and blond curls. She handles stress and patrons very well, and these patrons ran the gamut of personalities. I watched Ranay perform over the winter when I was simply the anonymous guy who let his silver hair grow for four months. I always appreciated her competent ways and I appreciated her service. Thank you Ranay, you're a good egg.

◄ ◄ ◄ ◄ ◄

Looking into the future, I have three projects that continue to consume my business life, still needing further development. I have about one year before one of these must kick in to produce a needed $1,500 a month additional income for this old boy. Of course, this is up and above my Social Security check. I do have a few backup plans, which include mowing grass, driving the Benzie Bus, or selling horticultural plants at a local nursery should my new businesses falter. I note here that I have finally given up on the lifetime backup plan of pumping gas. Technology has dealt its changing ways and obsoleted such a position. It made it only a memory of the former rescue strategy I had imagined where I could employ my skills. Yes, it is time to move on from that archaic plan.

This is like a time capsule, as I pen and noodle these business ideas and concepts. We can see if any of them come to fruition years from now. I will be pleased, and will prosper again should one of them gain traction. You can check on me as this is my first and last book; a one-hit wonder, like songs from the 1960s.

I'm particularly fond of my newest business undertaking called, A Tourist in My Own Town—The Local's Turn. It is a web-based franchise that matches local residents with fine restaurants, and fits them into these upscale venues early in evenings, on slow nights, in off seasons. It will be piloted in Traverse City, then franchised throughout the U.S. in tourist towns that have many months of slow business. I have hooked up with a local twenty-year web design and applications firm that likes the concept, and we are vetting its launch targeted for this summer and fall. Its cash, now called "monetization," comes from a fifty-dollar yearly membership card only for qualified locals, and offers discount dining at an area's finest venues. It actually is an anti-tourist and anti-coupon play. This venture smells and tastes right. "One more coupon and we'll all go broke" is the message to both consumers and merchants alike. Our website will feature the merchant's fare, and feature locally grown foods in the farm-to-plate awakening that is sweeping the nation.

The next product and business, five years in development and still with merit in my estimation, is the development of a vehicle accessory that serves as a top-of-the-seat barrier and divider for the safety and management of traveling dogs. We have been through tens of thousands of dollars and still do not have an acceptable dog Saf-T-Barrier. We are enlisting a new designer who hopefully comprehends the assignment. Let's hope.

This broader topic of pet safety got its legs about five years ago when I engaged a college senior engineering class to develop a product other than seat belts and harnesses to protect the traveling dog. It was their last class in their senior year under their engineering curriculum; five students were assigned the pet safety project, and I attended design review meetings during the semester. I helped bring together many people from the ranks of Michigan State University, and we introduced engineers to veterinarians. My automotive interiors company associates helped sponsor these students in addressing a real-life need for managing a projectile (the dog), during a crash or a rapid deceleration event. The grand vision was discussed and bantered about, hoping to champion a coalition of stakeholders to address driver distractions and pet safety. As I express today in my website, over thirty million dogs travel regularly in personal vehicles, and our Saf-T-Barrier is, of course, the only true answer. My goal is to license our product and private label it as an automotive accessory to companies that are in, or want to be in, the pet travel business. These include Invisible Fence, Thule, Yakima, and such established retailers as Drs. Foster & Smith and Cabela's. We shall see, first things first: an acceptable prototype will be a huge step.

Finally, I have to recover from my ill-timed earlier business venture that I described in the chapter on my pets. We had a grand plan to launch a national brand of cherry dog bones to help arthritic dogs, named Hip Bones. It was about five-hundred-thousand dollars short and a year and a half overdue: so much for all my years of business experience. Business is both just and brutal. Try to explain this to a teacher or social-service sector employee. No, don't, it is a waste of time.

So, what must I do to redress and reboot this opportunity for senior and arthritic dogs and their love of sugar and cherries? The answer is to produce products that are profitable and that people purchase; it's that simple. Now that my two-year noncompete is over, I am developing a new product that will catch on like wildfire: baking mixes that can be made for both humans and dogs. It will be called Dog Gone Great Biscuits, and contain the finest natural ingredients and be low in calories. Yes, cherries will be the first ingredient. This newer product resulted from my eating hundreds of dog bones at my booth when I was helping launch Hip Bones. It should be fun.

◄ ◄ ◄ ◄ ◄

MESSAGE TO MY SONS:
DAD'S REBOOTING ON CRYSTAL AVENUE

Rob and Dave, I hope your life is as heartfelt and joyful as mine was, is, and will be. I have certainly had my ups and downs. I have watched from afar at the emptiness in souls resulting from actions not taken. Many are victims of fear and dithering, being swept aside and cast adrift in life's wake. That is not for me. It is not about a smirking smile either, but manifests itself and serves at the foundation of the poem *If*, by Rudyard Kipling. A poem I have often sought in my darkest hours and reread during reflective times when I needed this boost of inspiration and solidarity of purpose. I hope you will heed this message in your own lives, so keep it handy. It means you are living quite right. You both have exhibited brilliance in your actions in your twenties, a darn good start to manhood!

IF

by Rudyard Kipling (1865 – 1936)

If you can keep your head when all about you
Are losing theirs and blaming it on you;
If you can trust yourself when all men doubt you,
But make allowance for their doubting too:
If you can wait and not be tired by waiting,
Or, being lied about, don't deal in lies,
Or being hated don't give way to hating,
And yet don't look too good, nor talk too wise;

If you can dream---and not make dreams your master;
If you can think---and not make thoughts your aim,
If you can meet with Triumph and Disaster
And treat those two impostors just the same:
If you can bear to hear the truth you've spoken
Twisted by knaves to make a trap for fools,
Or watch the things you gave your life to, broken,
And stoop and build 'em up with worn-out tools;

If you can make one heap of all your winnings
And risk it on one turn of pitch-and-toss,
And lose, and start again at your beginnings,
And never breathe a word about your loss:
If you can force your heart and nerve and sinew
To serve your turn long after they are gone,
And so hold on when there is nothing in you
Except the Will, which says to them: "Hold on!"

If you can talk with crowds and keep your virtue,
Or walk with Kings—nor lose the common touch,
If neither foes nor loving friends can hurt you,
If all men count with you, but none too much:
If you can fill the unforgiving minute
With sixty seconds' worth of distance run,
Yours is the Earth and everything that's in it,
An—which is more—you'll be a Man, my son!

I sent this poem to my oldest son Rob years ago when he was going through his struggles of a job search in San Francisco. It is so gritty, and the entire poem is, in fact, presented from the point of view of a father giving such advice to his son. I have read it so many times and find it the near-perfect medicine in searching for the inner strength to prevail. Though I never chatted with my father about Kipling's poem, embodied in it are the core philosophies that made him such a fine man. He lived the life that he professed, and he too is completely personified in this poem.

Of course, I am not quite the perfect candidate of sage wisdom as, "Never breathe a word about your loss," but I am trying! I am in the process of recovering from life's calamities.

This is the only book I will ever write, so this scarcity should bring out the customers in throngs. Or is it thongs?

Life is an adventure, so go enjoy it, with a big smile.

RB Adams, June 24, 2013